FRED BASSET YEARBOOK 2023

Drawings by Michael Martin

An Hachette UK Company
www.hachette.co.uk

Summersdale Publishers Ltd
Part of Octopus Publishing Group Limited
Carmelite House
50 Victoria Embankment
LONDON
EC4Y 0DZ
UK

www.summersdale.com

Printed and bound in the Czech Republic

ISBN: 978-1-80007-413-2

2023

Substantial discounts on bulk quantities of Summersdale books are available to corporations, professional associations and other organisations.
For details contact general enquiries: telephone: +44 (0) 1243 771107 or email: enquiries@summersdale.com.

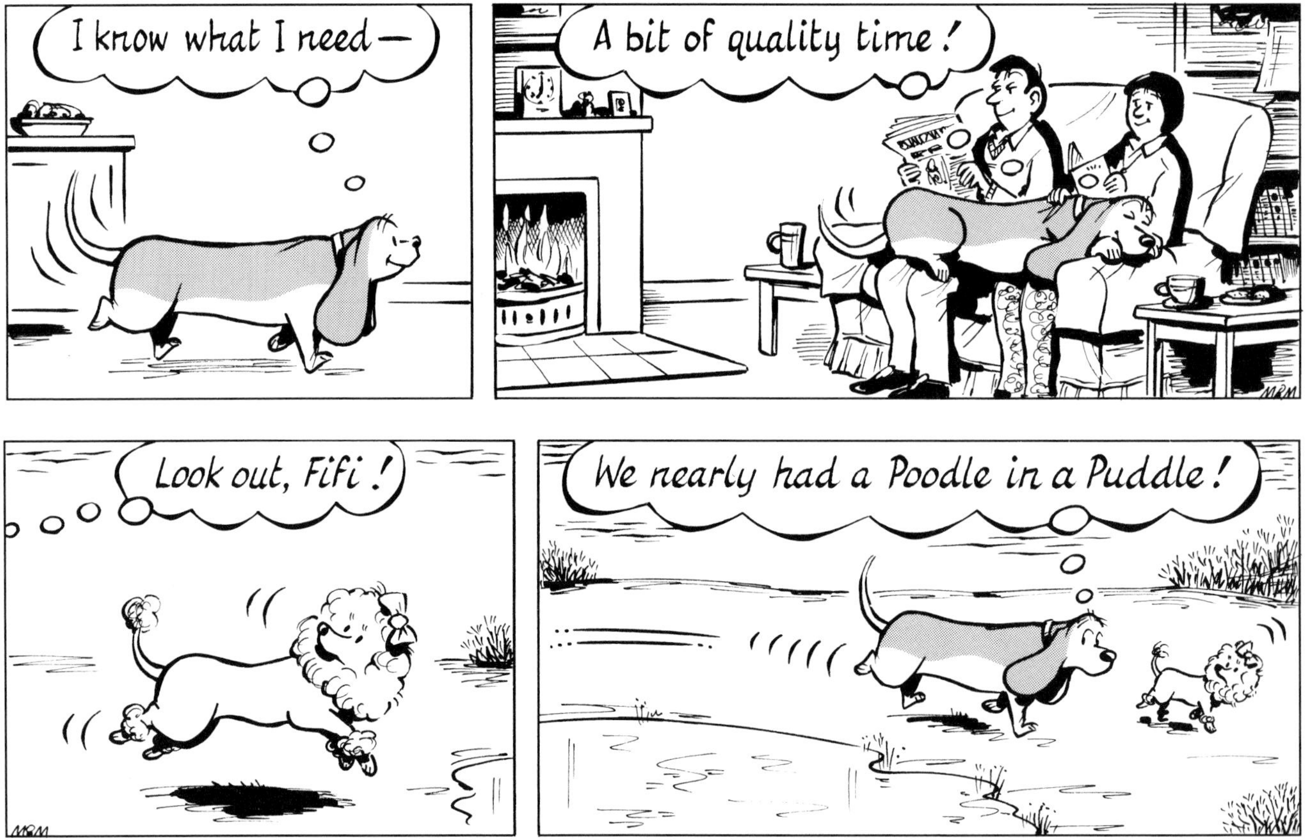
I know what I need —
A bit of quality time!
Look out, Fifi!
We nearly had a Poodle in a Puddle!

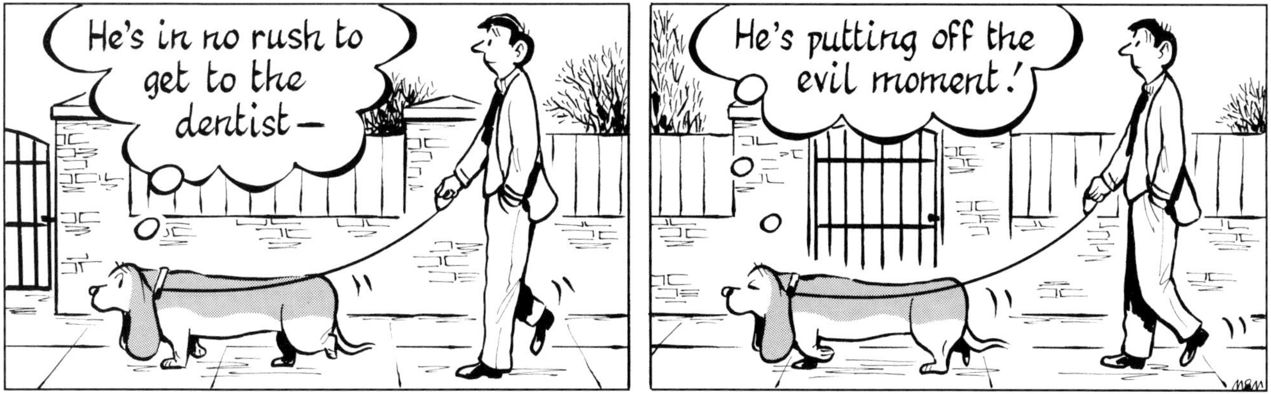
He's in no rush to get to the dentist—
He's putting off the evil moment!

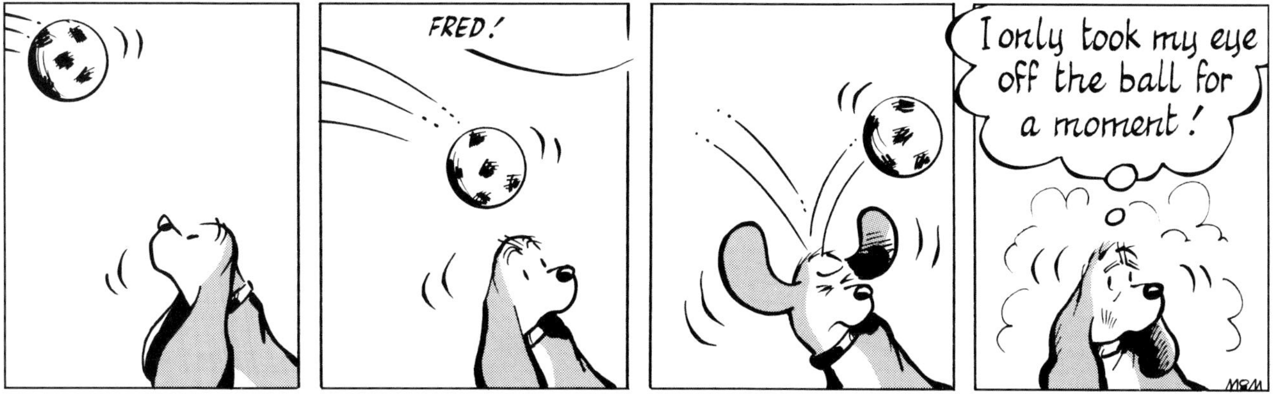
FRED!
I only took my eye off the ball for a moment!

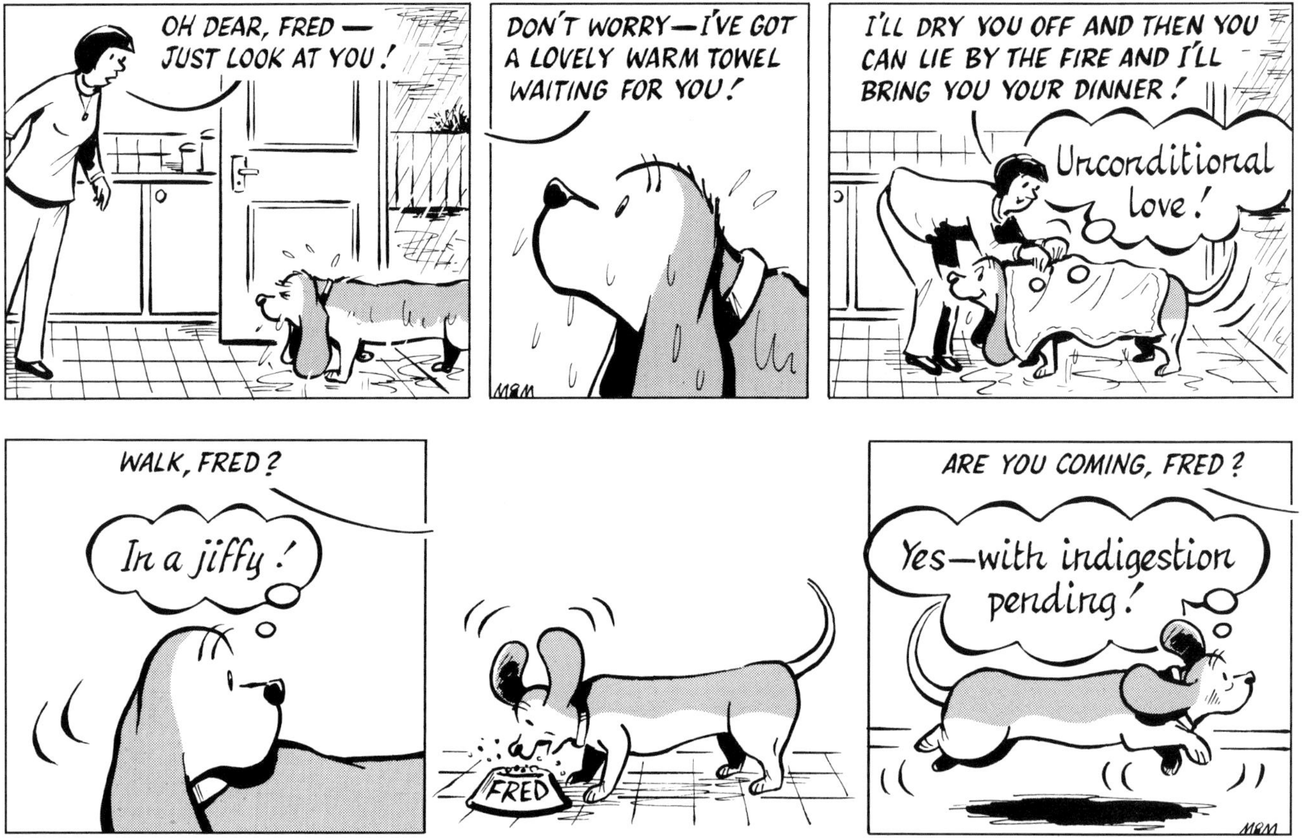
OH DEAR, FRED — JUST LOOK AT YOU!
DON'T WORRY—I'VE GOT A LOVELY WARM TOWEL WAITING FOR YOU!
M&M
I'LL DRY YOU OFF AND THEN YOU CAN LIE BY THE FIRE AND I'LL BRING YOU YOUR DINNER!
Unconditional love!
WALK, FRED?
In a jiffy!
FRED
ARE YOU COMING, FRED?
Yes—with indigestion pending!
M&M

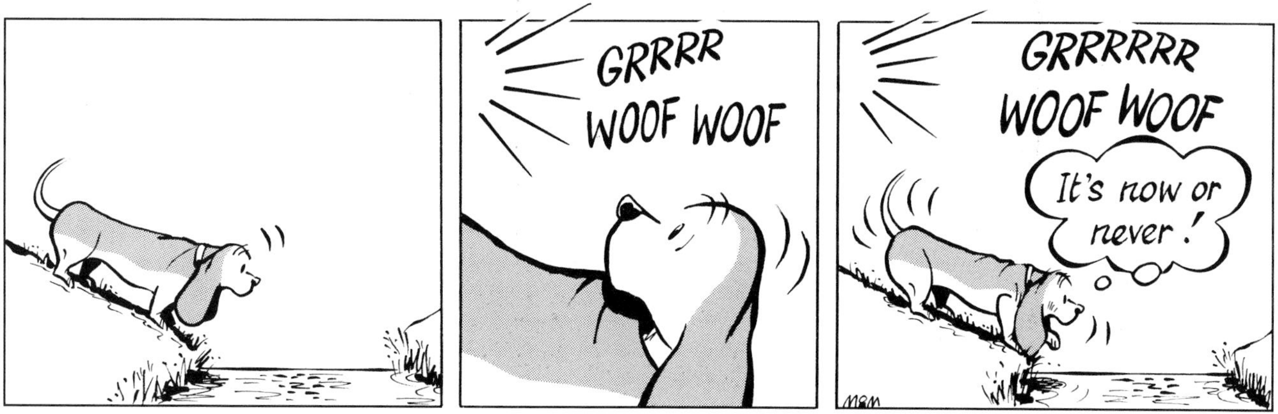
GRRRR
WOOF WOOF
GRRRRRR
WOOF WOOF
It's now or never!

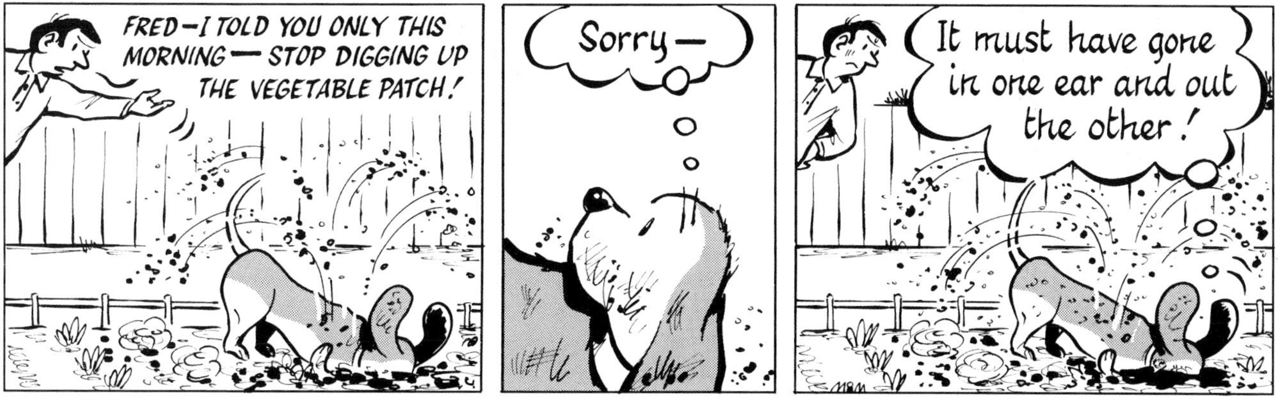
FRED—I TOLD YOU ONLY THIS MORNING—STOP DIGGING UP THE VEGETABLE PATCH!
Sorry—
It must have gone in one ear and out the other!

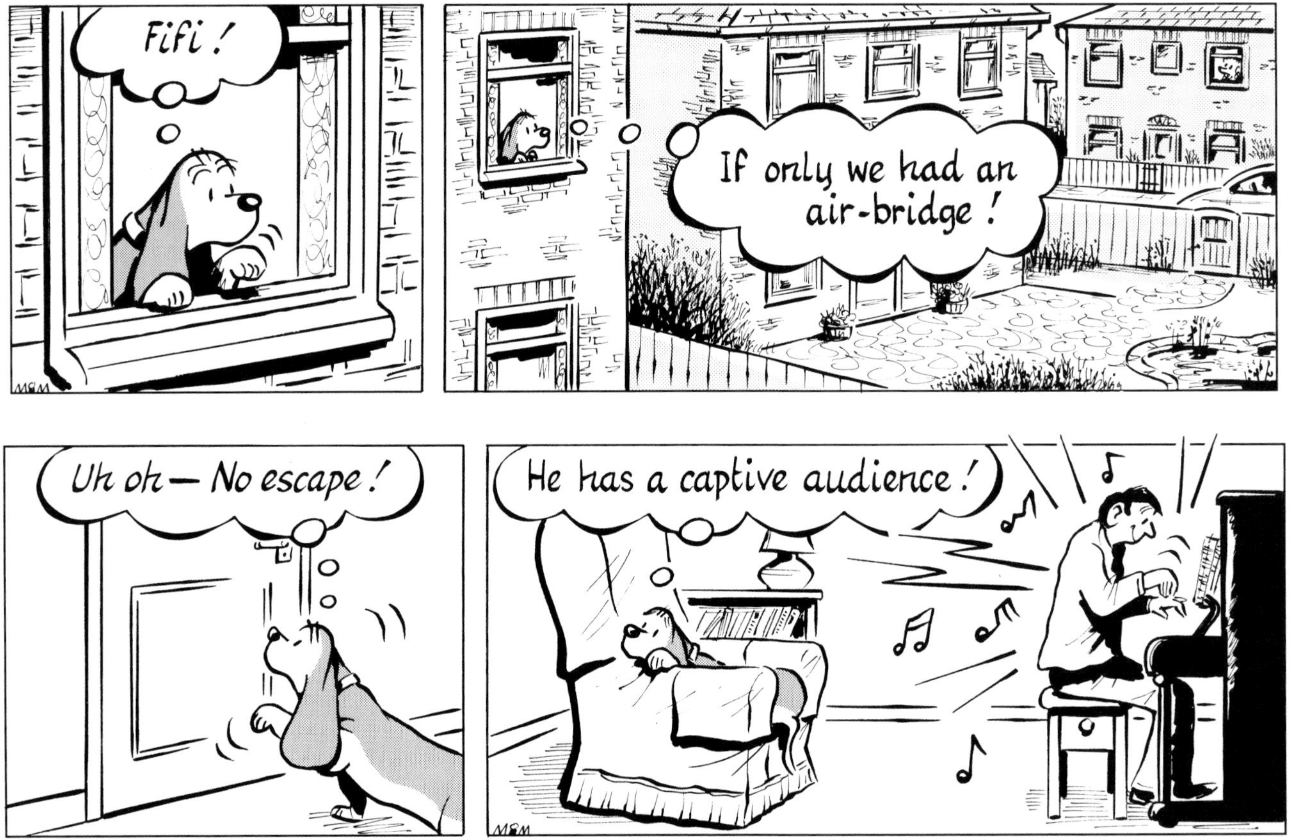

Fifi !
MSM
If only we had an air-bridge !
Uh oh — No escape !
He has a captive audience !
MSM

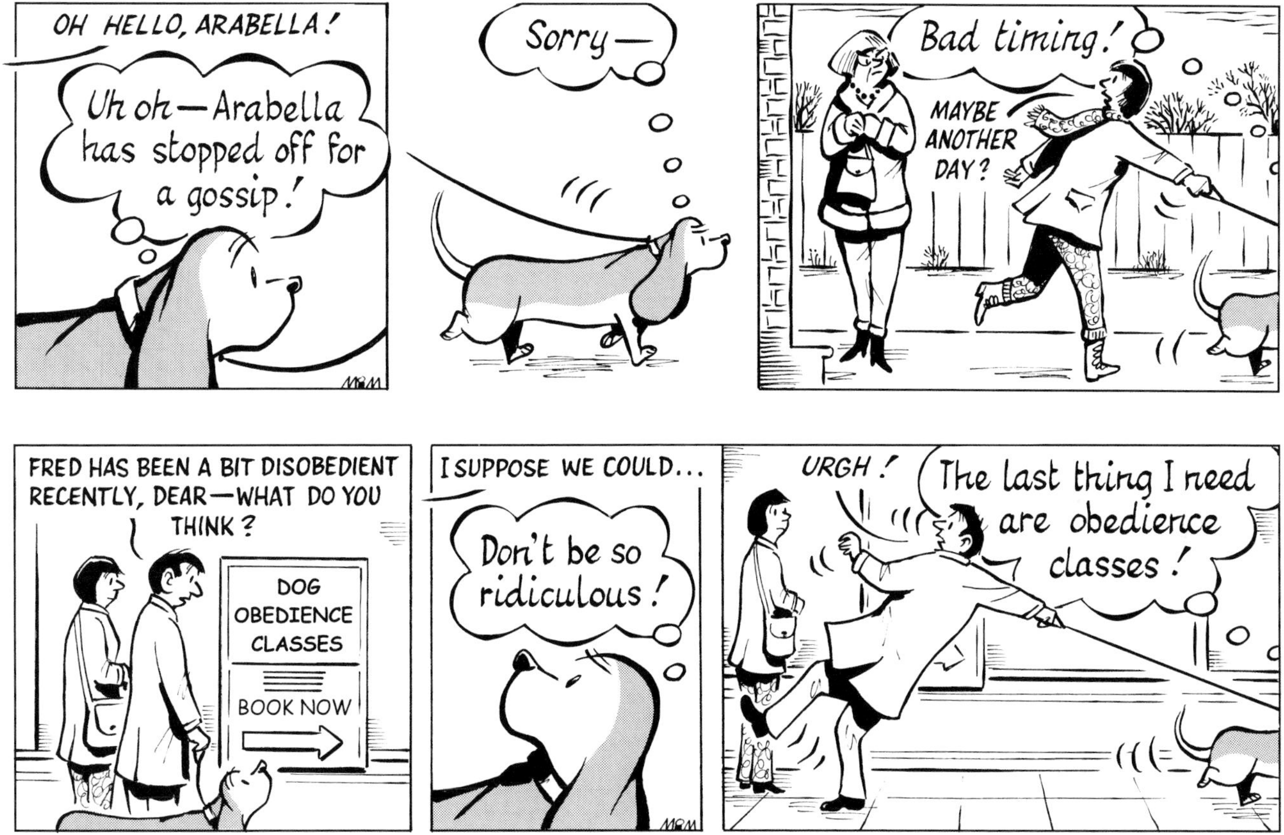
OH HELLO, ARABELLA!
Uh oh—Arabella has stopped off for a gossip!
Sorry—
Bad timing!
MAYBE ANOTHER DAY?
FRED HAS BEEN A BIT DISOBEDIENT RECENTLY, DEAR—WHAT DO YOU THINK?
DOG OBEDIENCE CLASSES
BOOK NOW
I SUPPOSE WE COULD...
Don't be so ridiculous!
URGH!
The last thing I need are obedience classes!

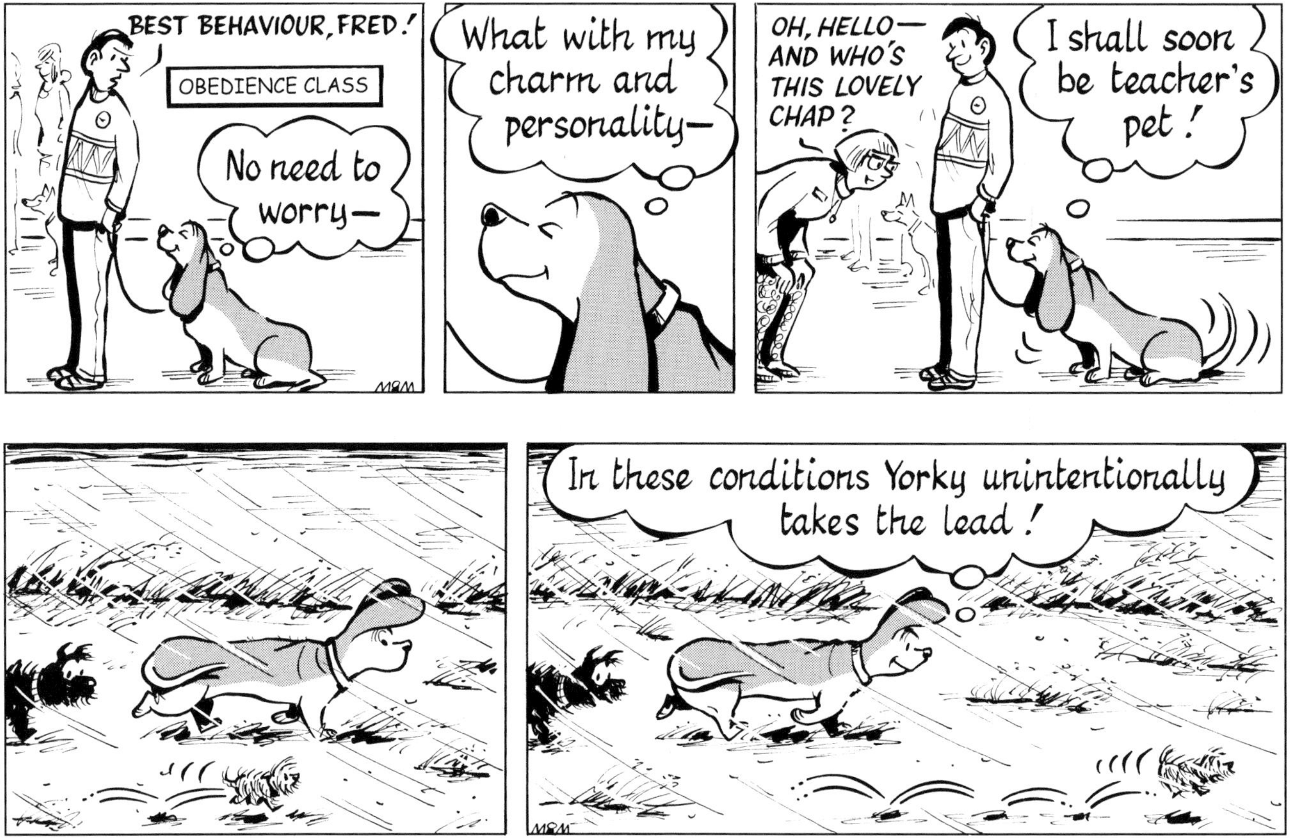
BEST BEHAVIOUR, FRED!
OBEDIENCE CLASS
No need to worry—
What with my charm and personality—
OH, HELLO— AND WHO'S THIS LOVELY CHAP?
I shall soon be teacher's pet!
In these conditions Yorky unintentionally takes the lead!

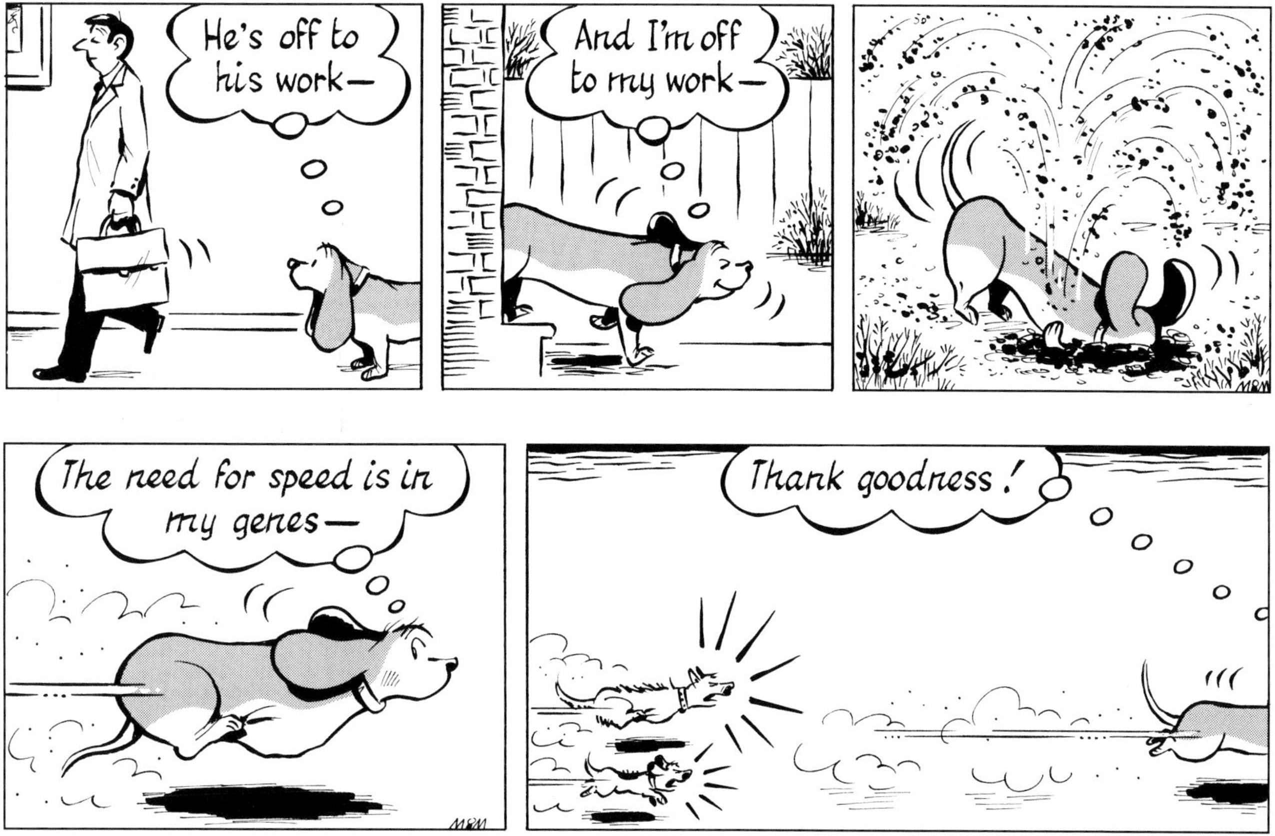
He's off to his work—
And I'm off to my work—
The need for speed is in my genes—
Thank goodness!

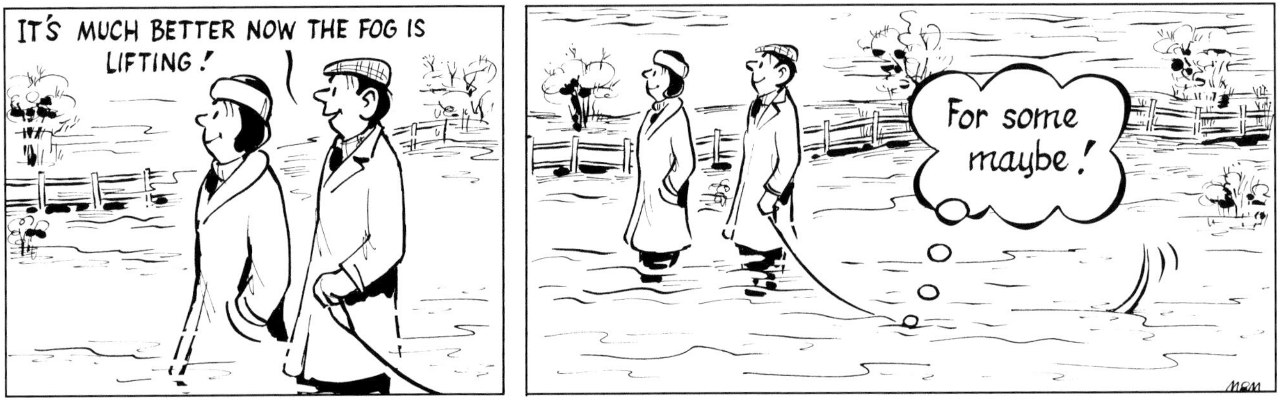
IT'S MUCH BETTER NOW THE FOG IS LIFTING!
For some maybe!

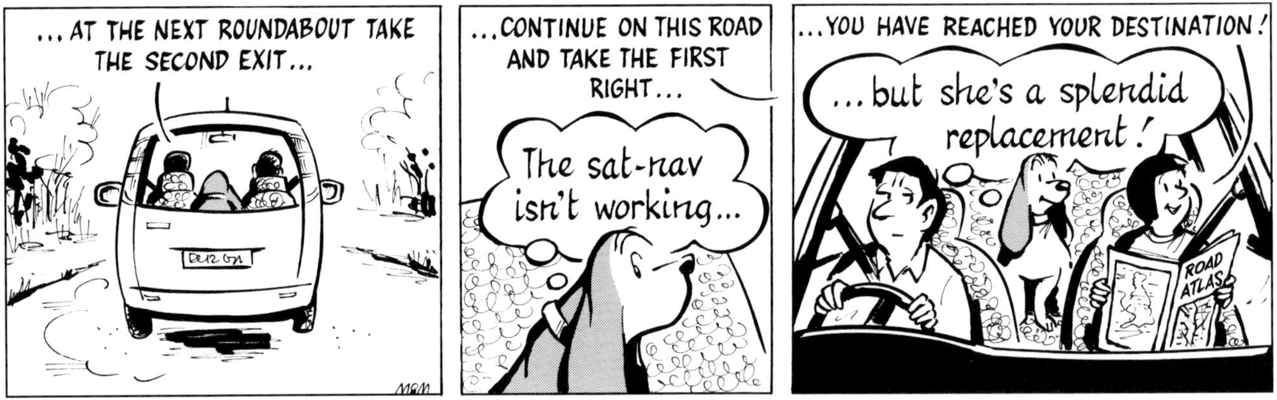
...AT THE NEXT ROUNDABOUT TAKE THE SECOND EXIT...
...CONTINUE ON THIS ROAD AND TAKE THE FIRST RIGHT...
The sat-nav isn't working...
...YOU HAVE REACHED YOUR DESTINATION!
...but she's a splendid replacement!
ROAD ATLAS

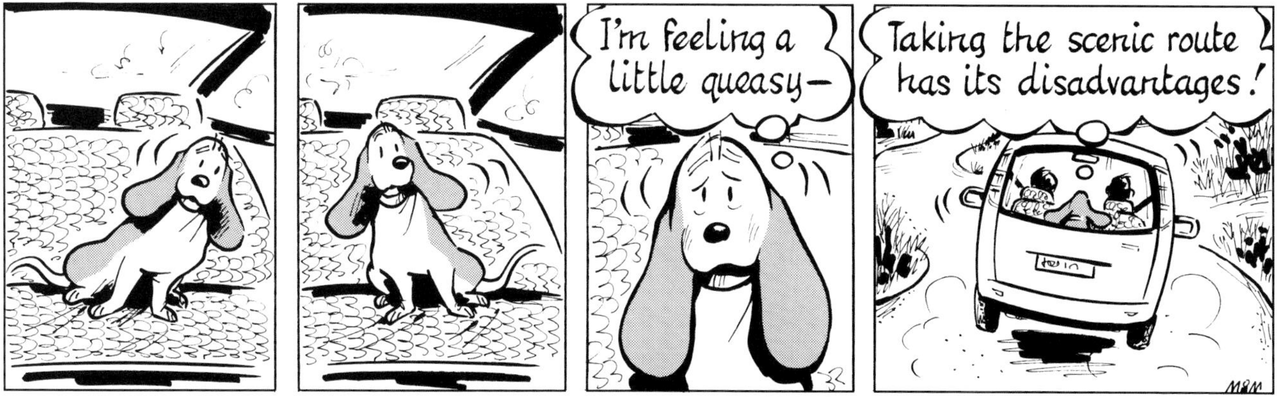
I'm feeling a little queasy–
Taking the scenic route has its disadvantages!

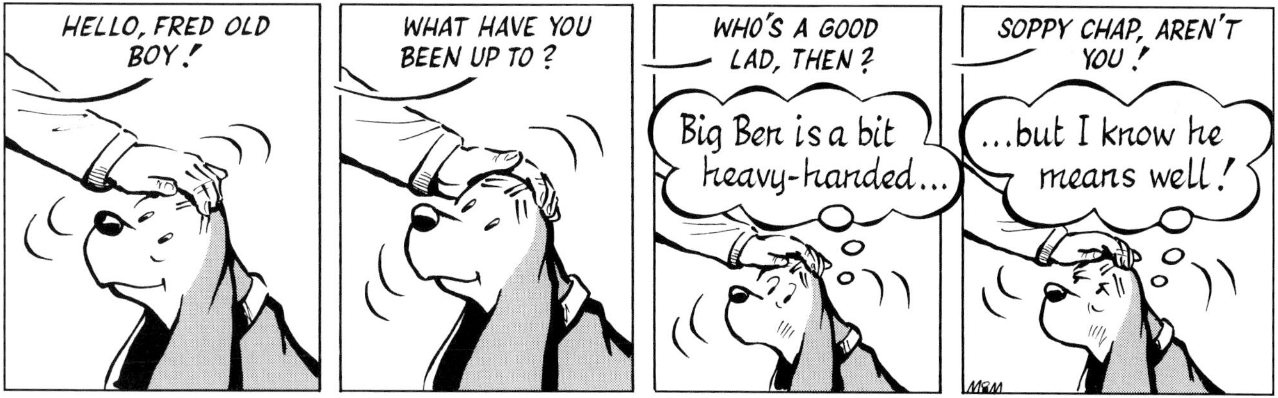
HELLO, FRED OLD BOY!
WHAT HAVE YOU BEEN UP TO?
WHO'S A GOOD LAD, THEN?
Big Ben is a bit heavy-handed...
SOPPY CHAP, AREN'T YOU!
...but I know he means well!

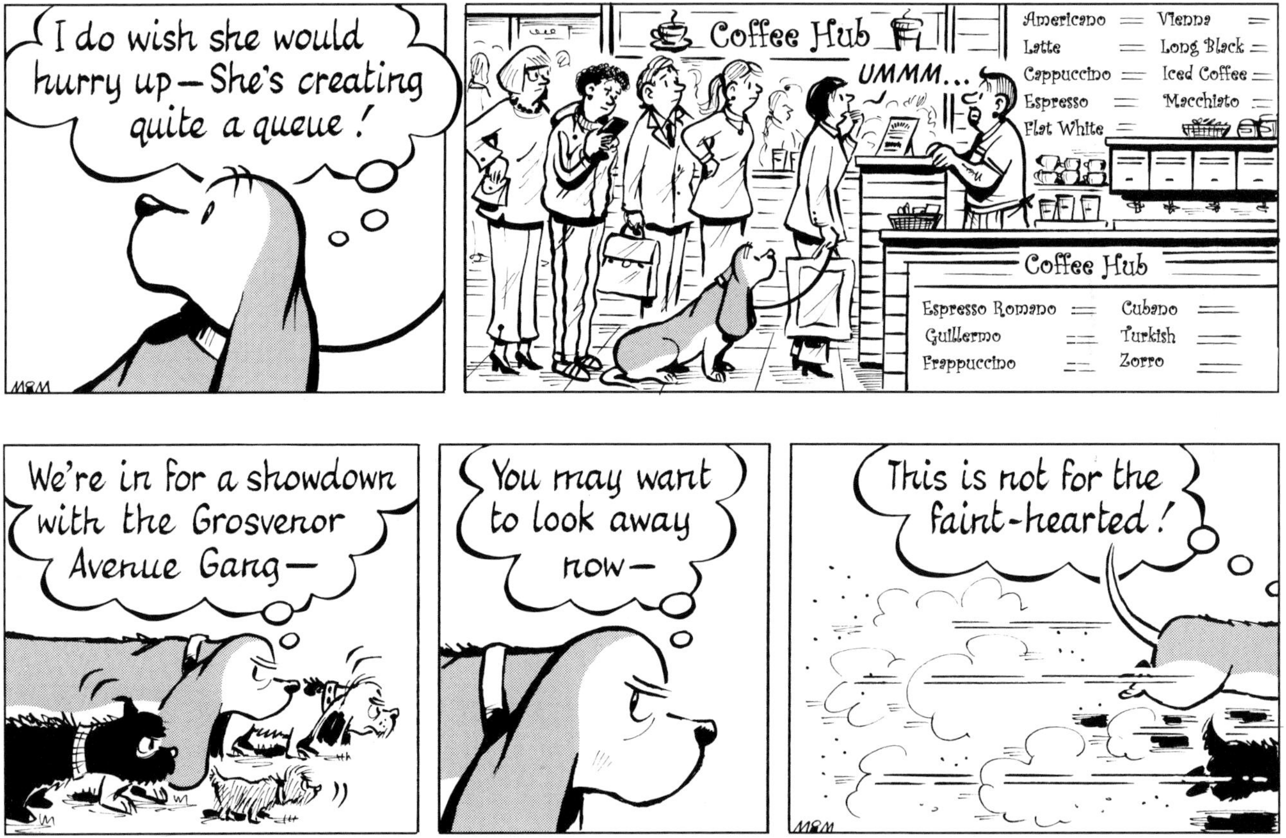
I do wish she would hurry up—She's creating quite a queue!
Coffee Hub
UMMM...
Americano
Latte
Cappuccino
Espresso
Flat White
Vienna
Long Black
Iced Coffee
Macchiato
Coffee Hub
Espresso Romano
Guillermo
Frappuccino
Cubano
Turkish
Zorro
We're in for a showdown with the Grosvenor Avenue Gang—
You may want to look away now—
This is not for the faint-hearted!

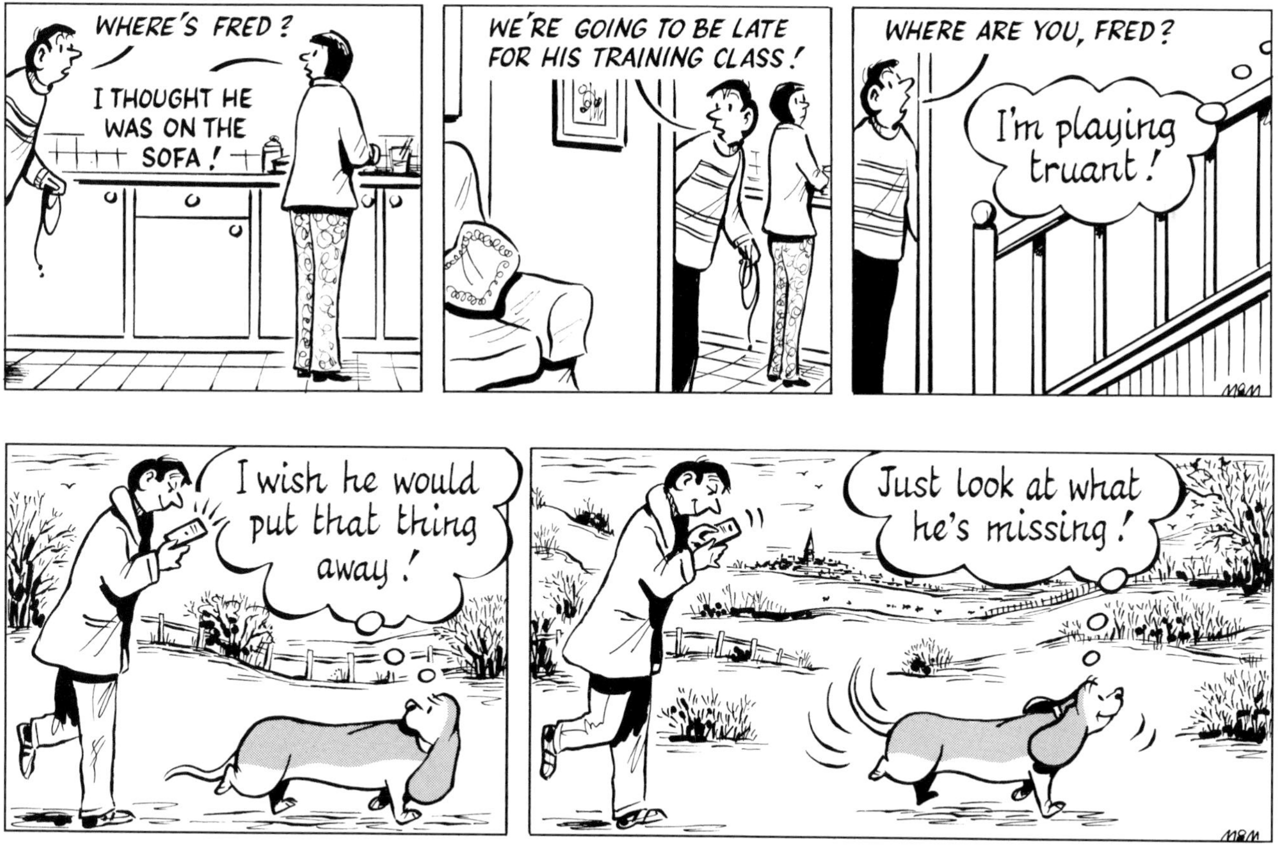
WHERE'S FRED?
I THOUGHT HE WAS ON THE SOFA!
WE'RE GOING TO BE LATE FOR HIS TRAINING CLASS!
WHERE ARE YOU, FRED?
I'm playing truant!
I wish he would put that thing away!
Just look at what he's missing!

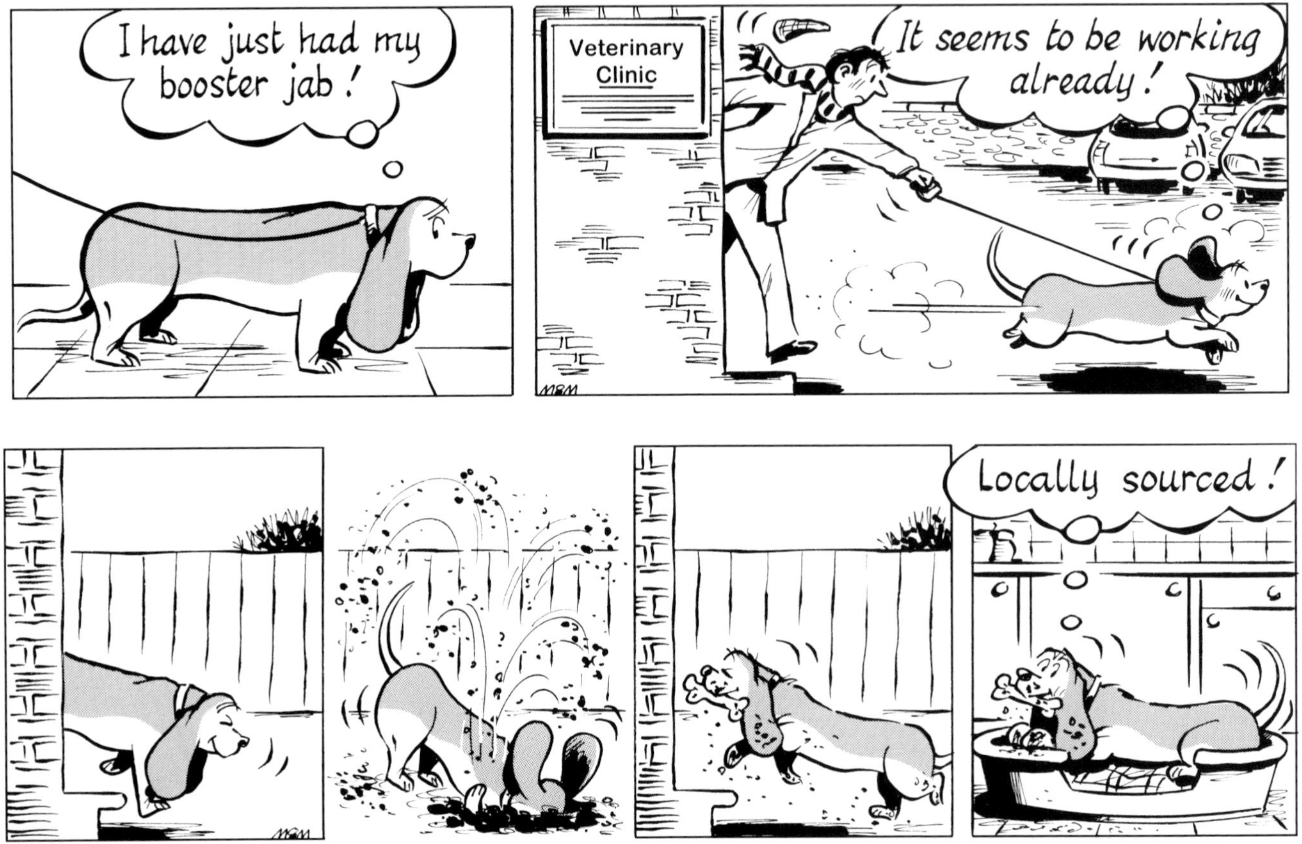
I have just had my booster jab!
Veterinary Clinic
It seems to be working already!
MSM
MSM
Locally sourced!

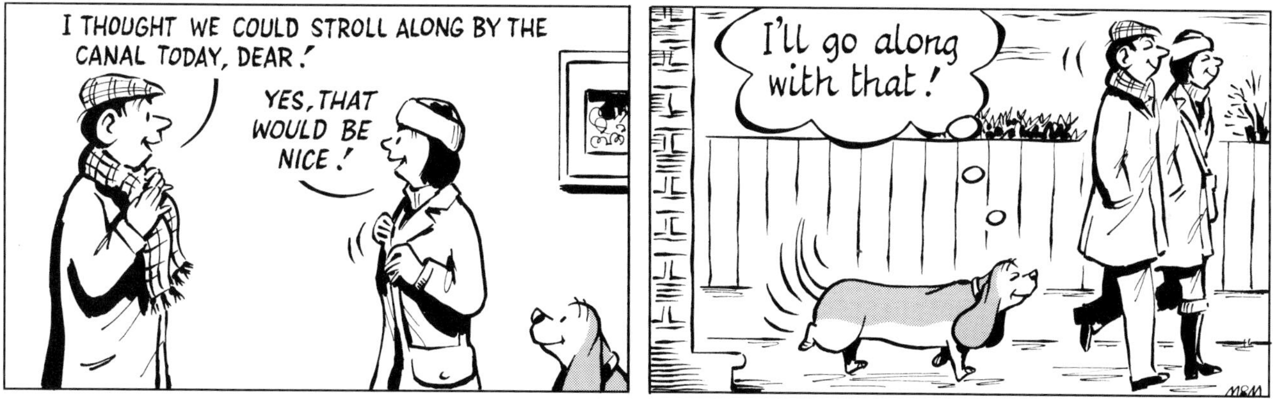
I THOUGHT WE COULD STROLL ALONG BY THE CANAL TODAY, DEAR!
YES, THAT WOULD BE NICE!
I'll go along with that!

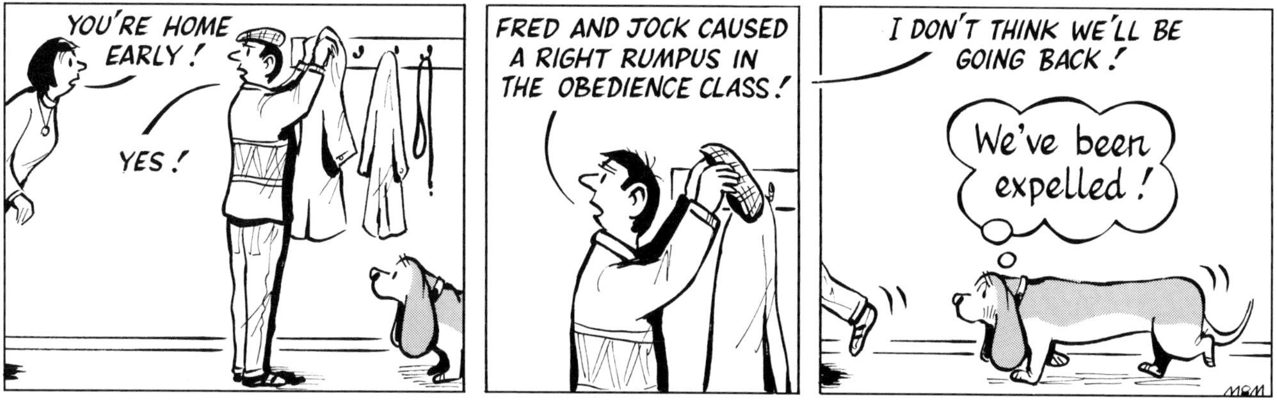
YOU'RE HOME EARLY!
YES!
FRED AND JOCK CAUSED A RIGHT RUMPUS IN THE OBEDIENCE CLASS!
I DON'T THINK WE'LL BE GOING BACK!
We've been expelled!

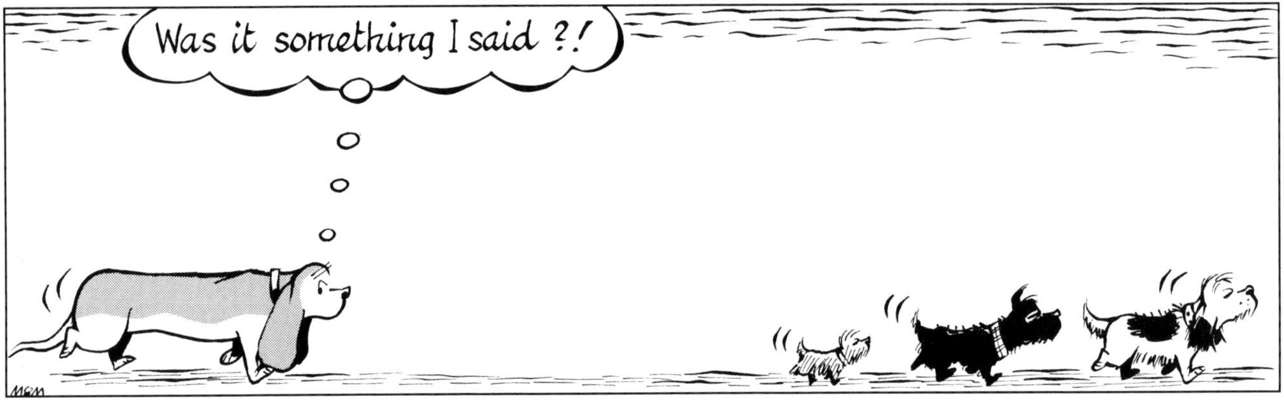
Was it something I said ?!

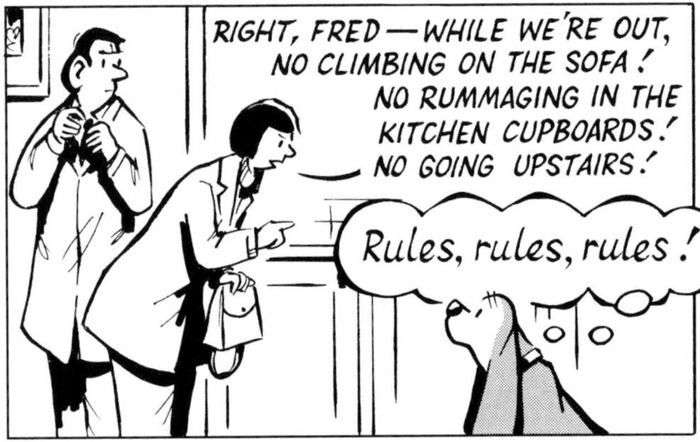
RIGHT, FRED — WHILE WE'RE OUT, NO CLIMBING ON THE SOFA! NO RUMMAGING IN THE KITCHEN CUPBOARDS! NO GOING UPSTAIRS!
Rules, rules, rules!

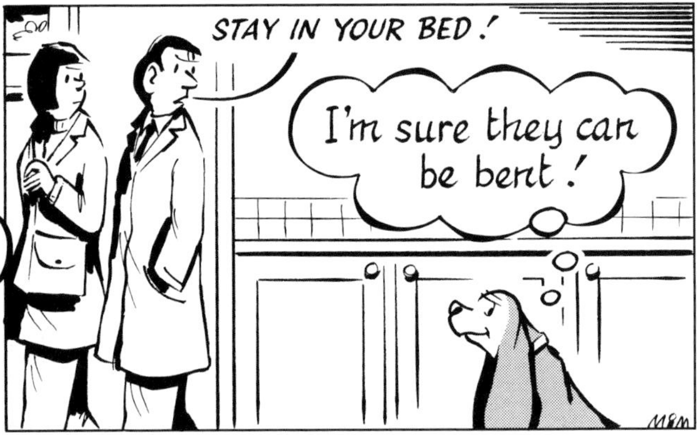
STAY IN YOUR BED!
I'm sure they can be bent!

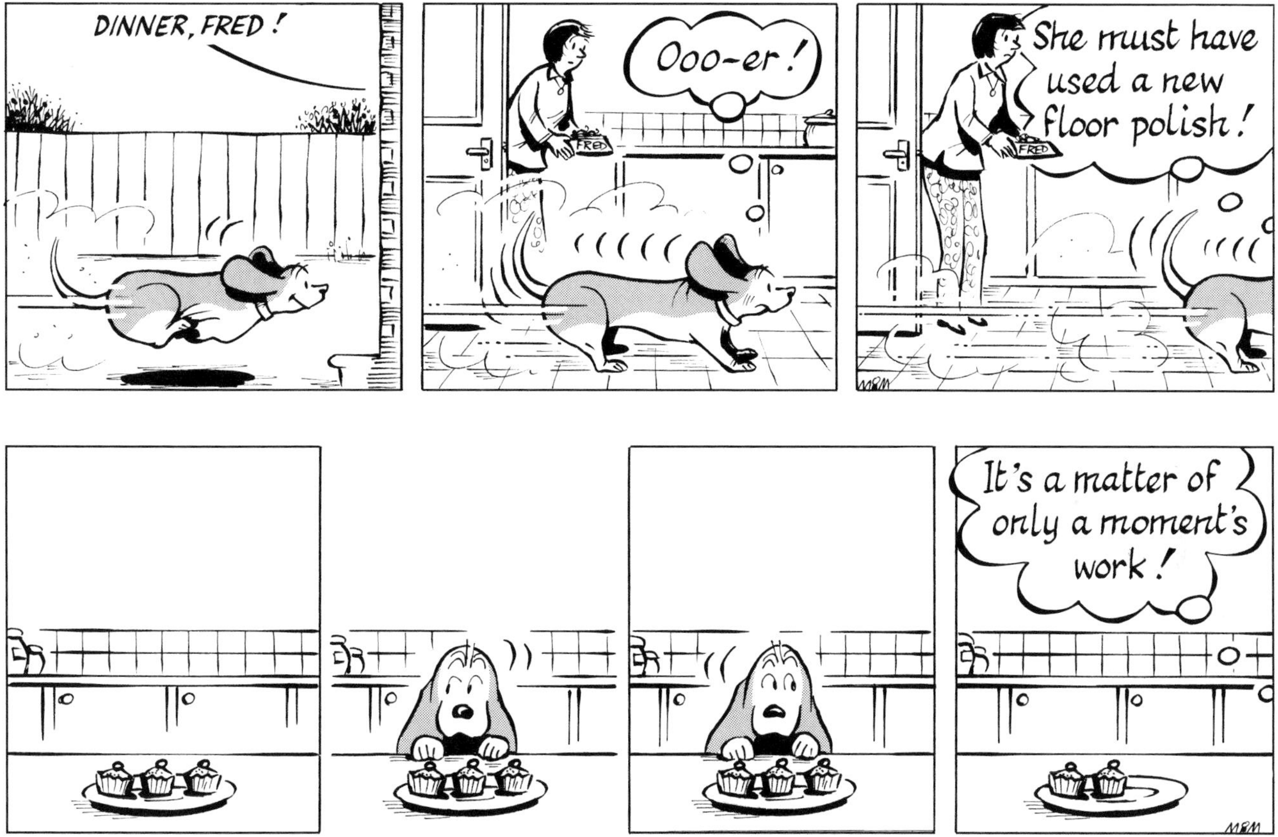
DINNER, FRED!
Ooo-er!
She must have used a new floor polish!
FRED
FRED
MBM
It's a matter of only a moment's work!
MBM

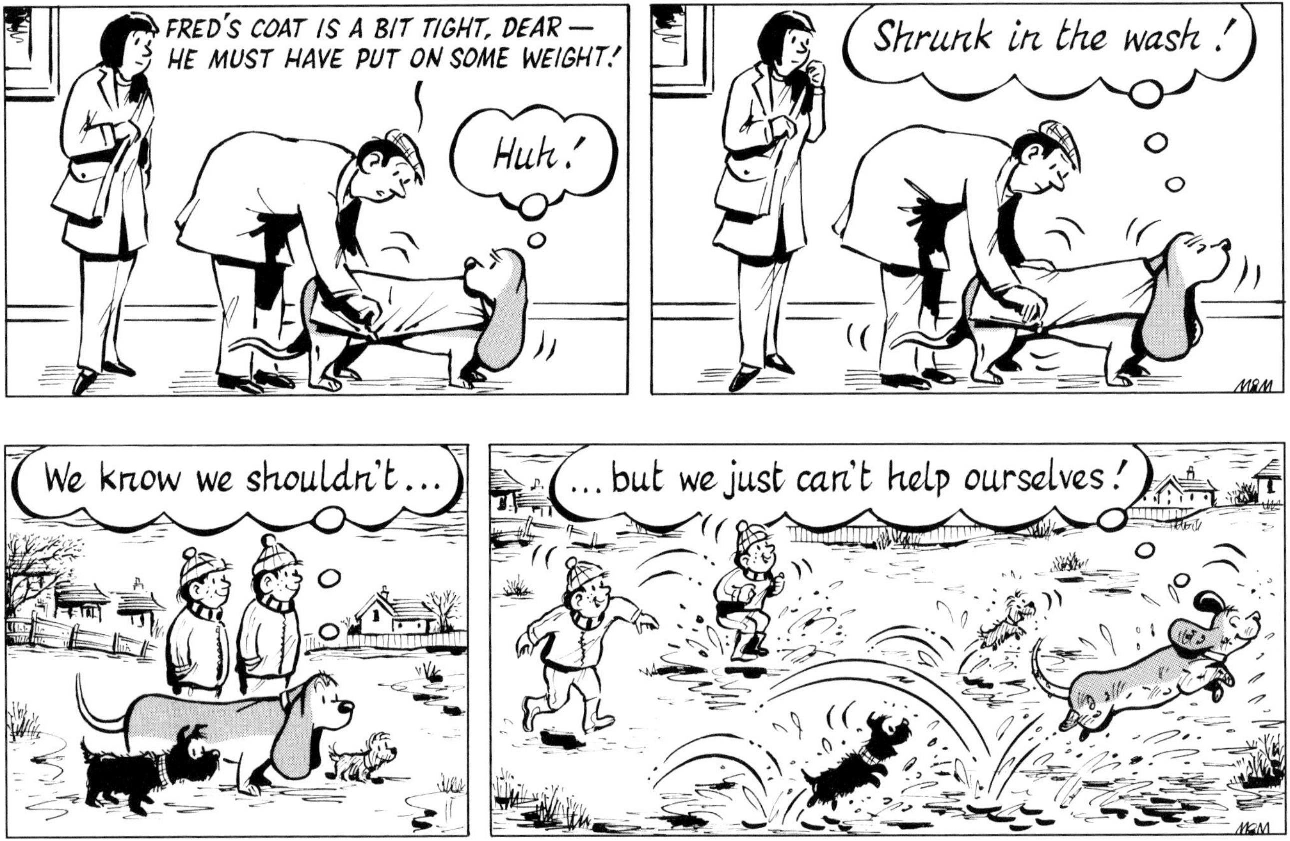
FRED'S COAT IS A BIT TIGHT, DEAR — HE MUST HAVE PUT ON SOME WEIGHT!
Huh!
Shrunk in the wash!
We know we shouldn't...
...but we just can't help ourselves!

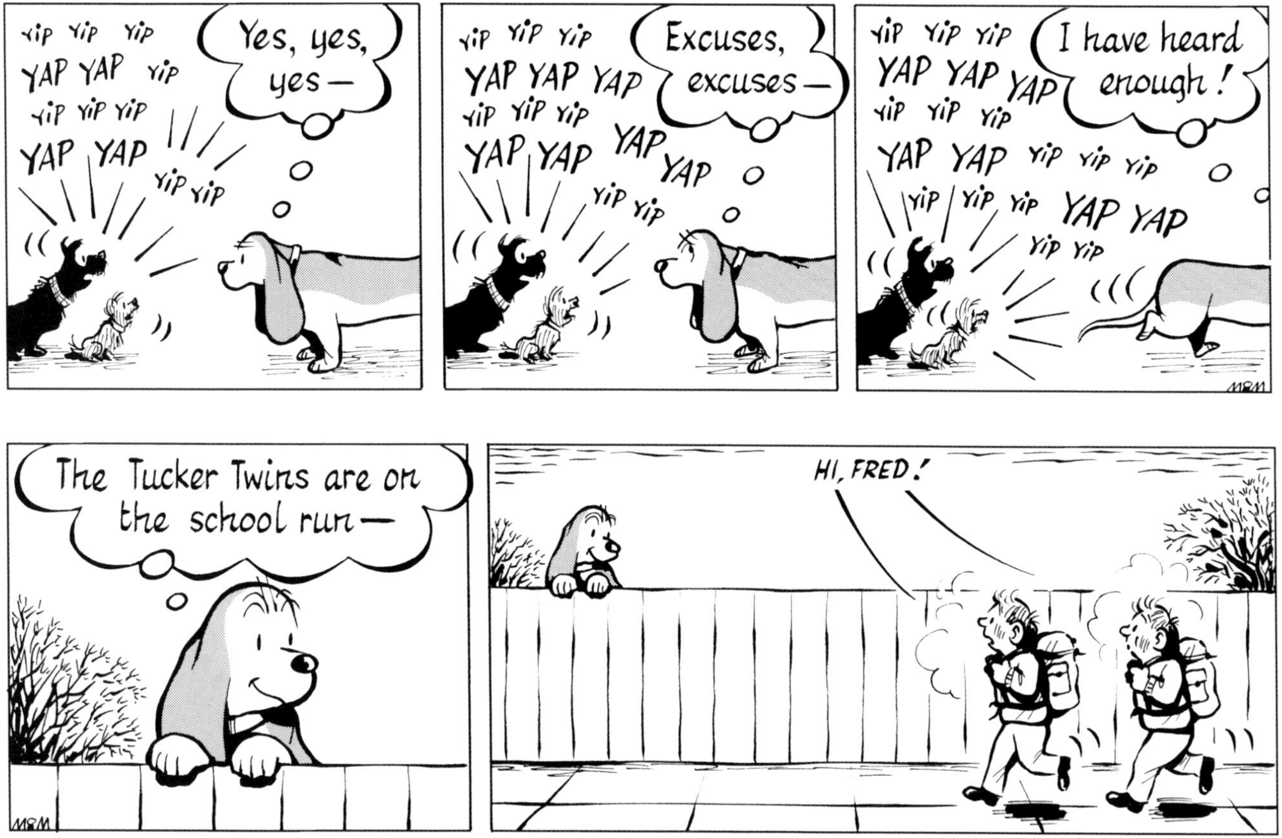
YIP YIP YIP
YAP YAP YIP
YIP YIP YIP
YAP YAP
YIP YIP
Yes, yes, yes—
YIP YIP YIP
YAP YAP YAP
YIP YIP YIP
YAP YAP YAP YAP
YIP YIP
Excuses, excuses—
YIP YIP YIP
YAP YAP YAP
YIP YIP YIP
YAP YAP YIP YIP YIP
YIP YIP YIP YAP YAP
YIP YIP
I have heard enough!
M&M
The Tucker Twins are on the school run—
M&M
HI, FRED!

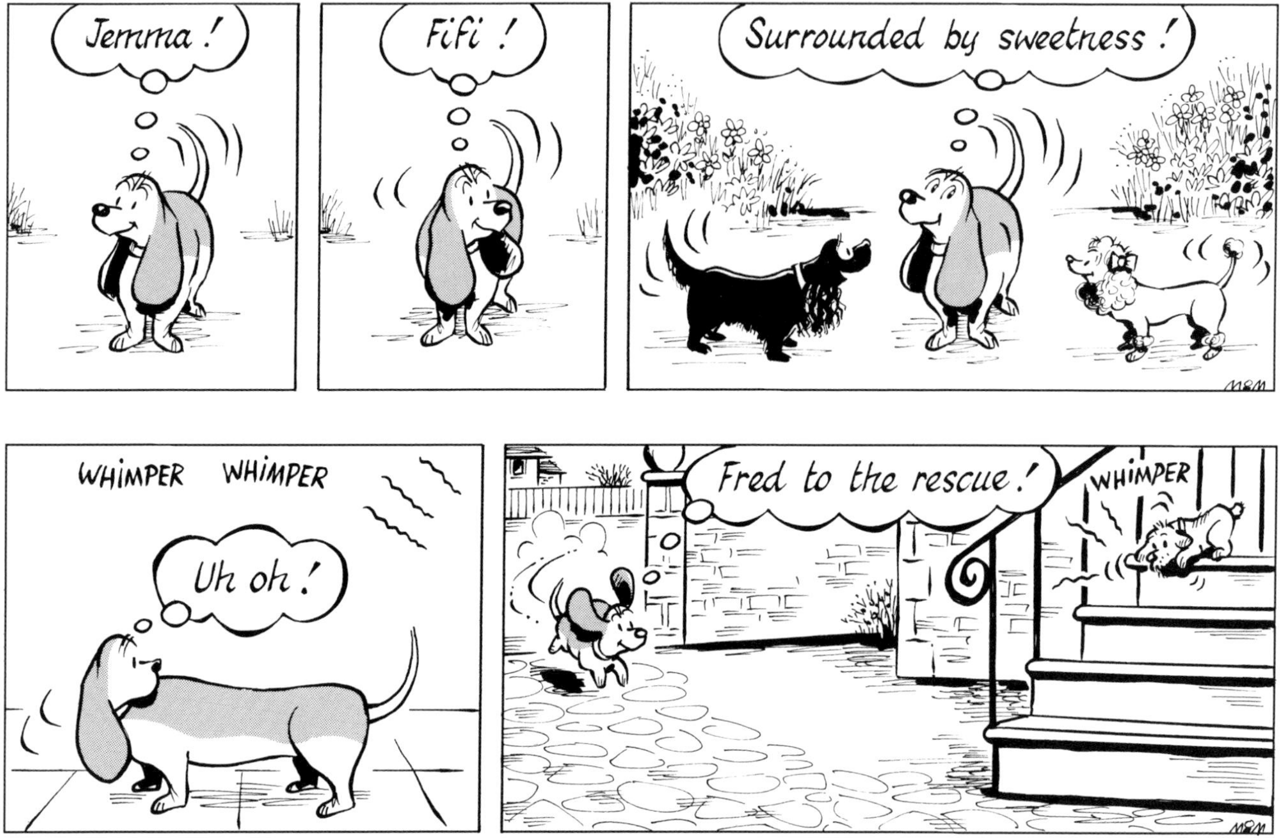
Jemma!
Fifi!
Surrounded by sweetness!
WHIMPER WHIMPER
Uh oh!
Fred to the rescue!
WHIMPER
M&M

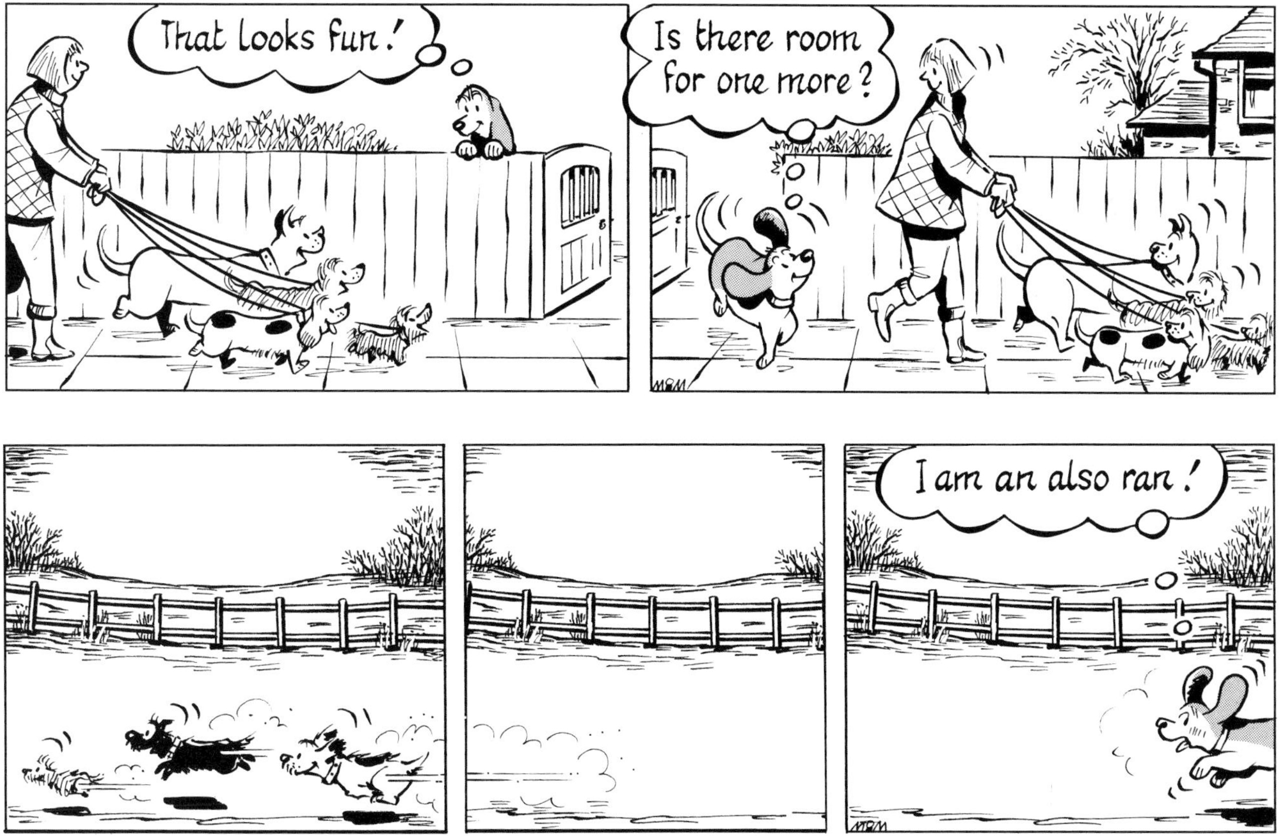
That looks fun!
Is there room for one more?
I am an also ran!

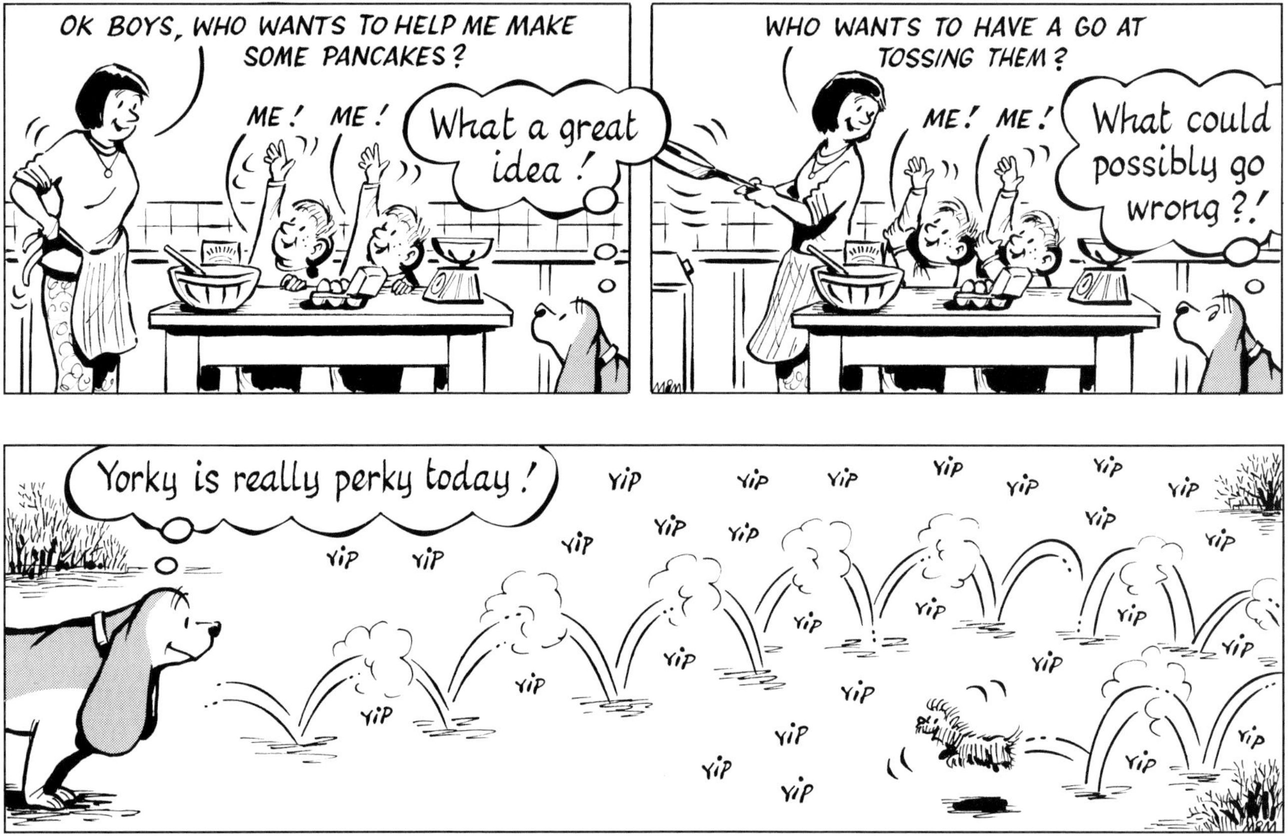
OK BOYS, WHO WANTS TO HELP ME MAKE SOME PANCAKES?
ME! ME!
What a great idea!
WHO WANTS TO HAVE A GO AT TOSSING THEM?
ME! ME!
What could possibly go wrong?!
Yorky is really perky today!
YIP YIP YIP YIP YIP YIP YIP
YIP YIP YIP YIP YIP YIP YIP
YIP YIP YIP YIP YIP YIP YIP
YIP YIP YIP YIP YIP YIP YIP

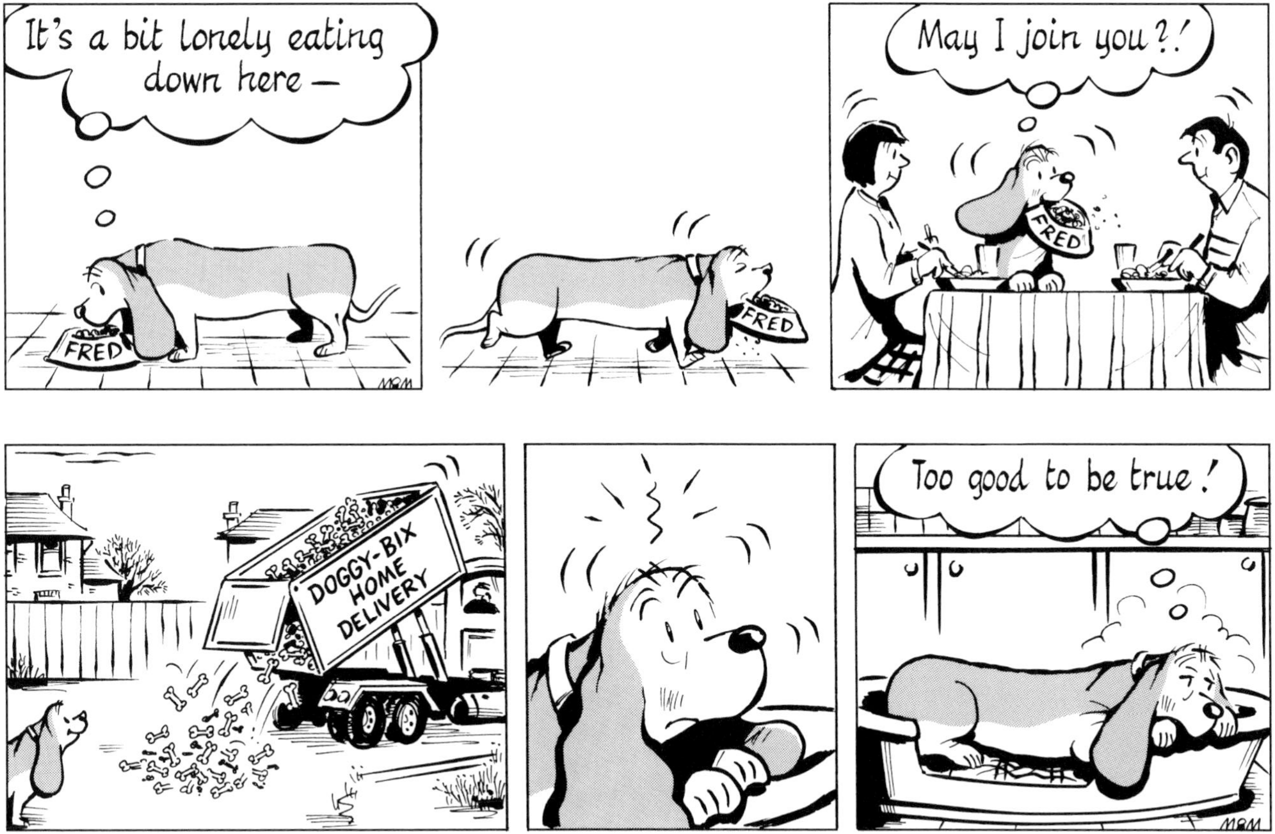
It's a bit lonely eating down here –
FRED
MRM
FRED
May I join you?!
FRED
DOGGY-BIX HOME DELIVERY
Too good to be true!
MRM

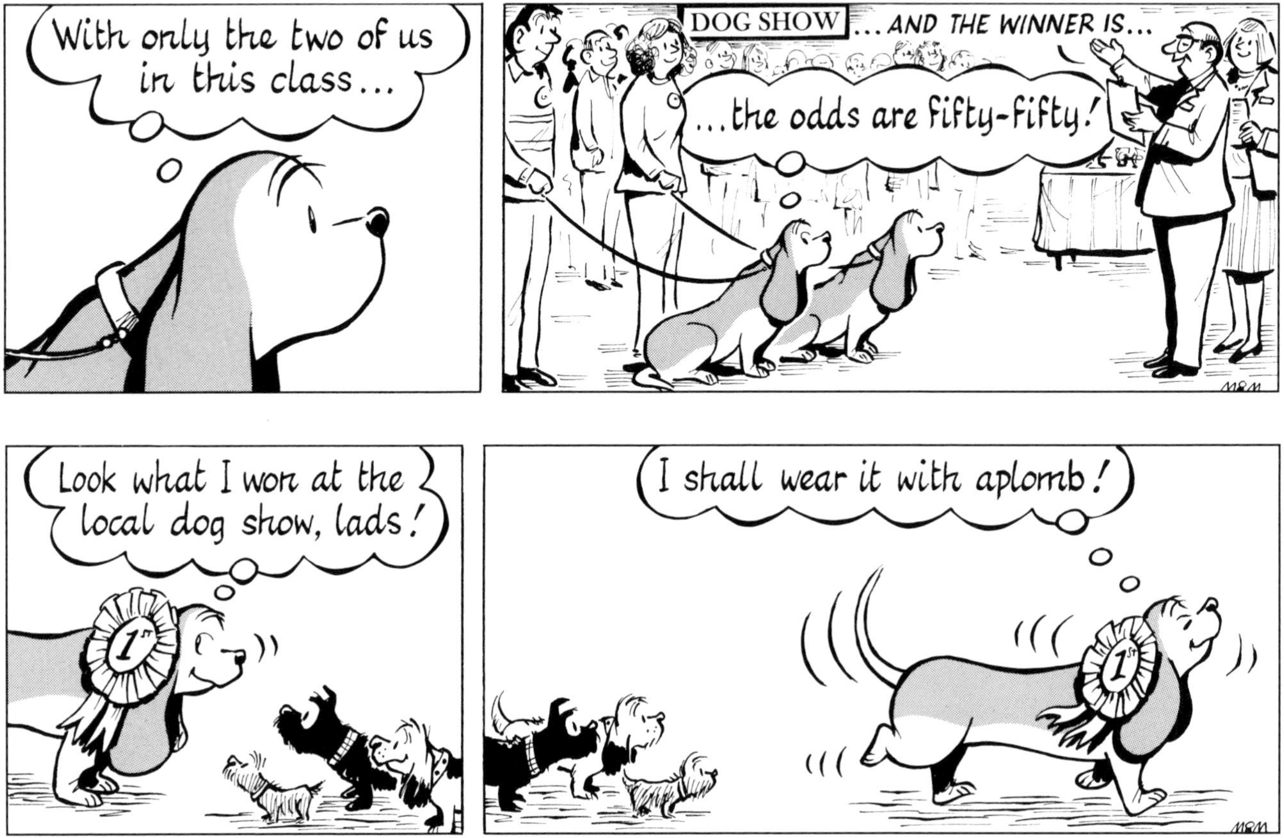
With only the two of us in this class...
DOG SHOW
... AND THE WINNER IS...
...the odds are fifty-fifty!
M&M
Look what I won at the local dog show, lads!
I shall wear it with aplomb!
M&M

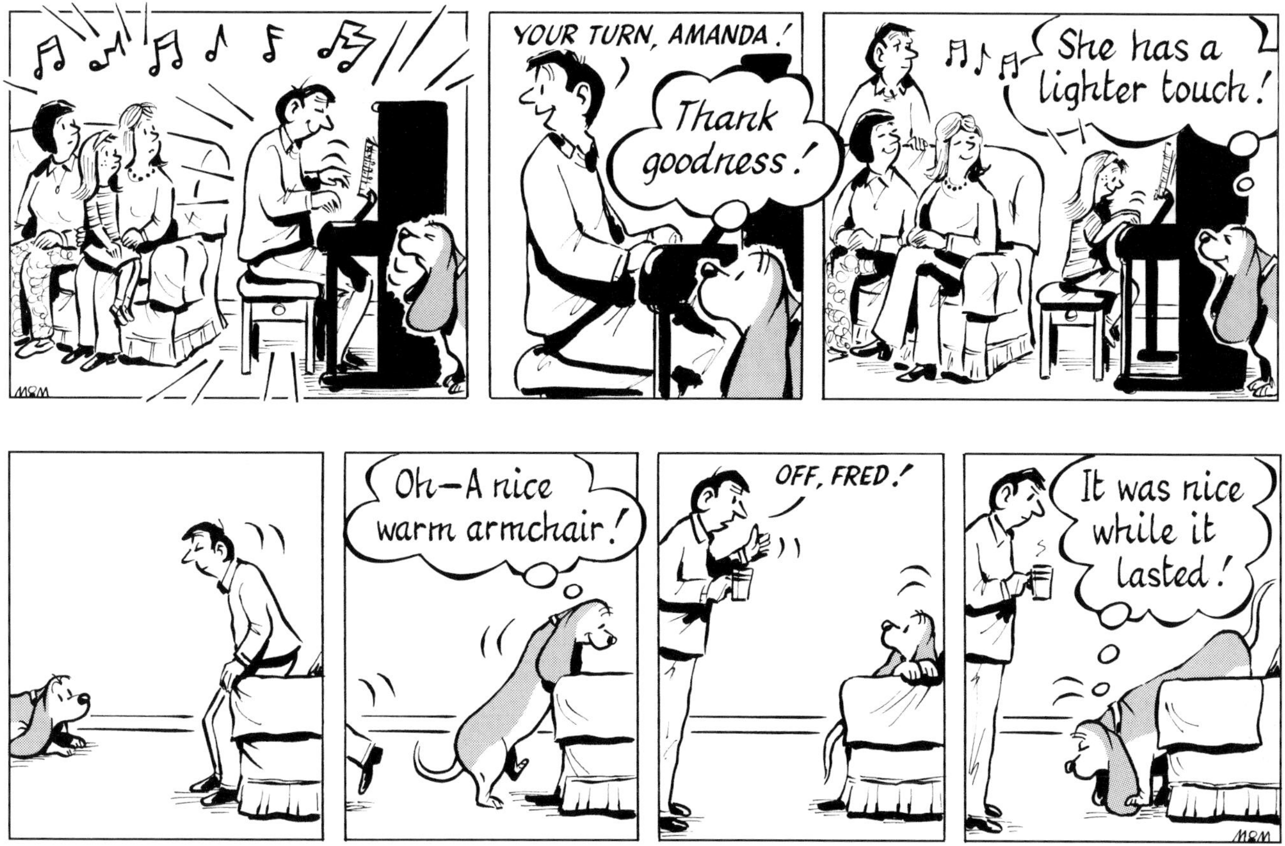
YOUR TURN, AMANDA!
Thank goodness!
She has a lighter touch!
Oh—A nice warm armchair!
OFF, FRED!
It was nice while it lasted!

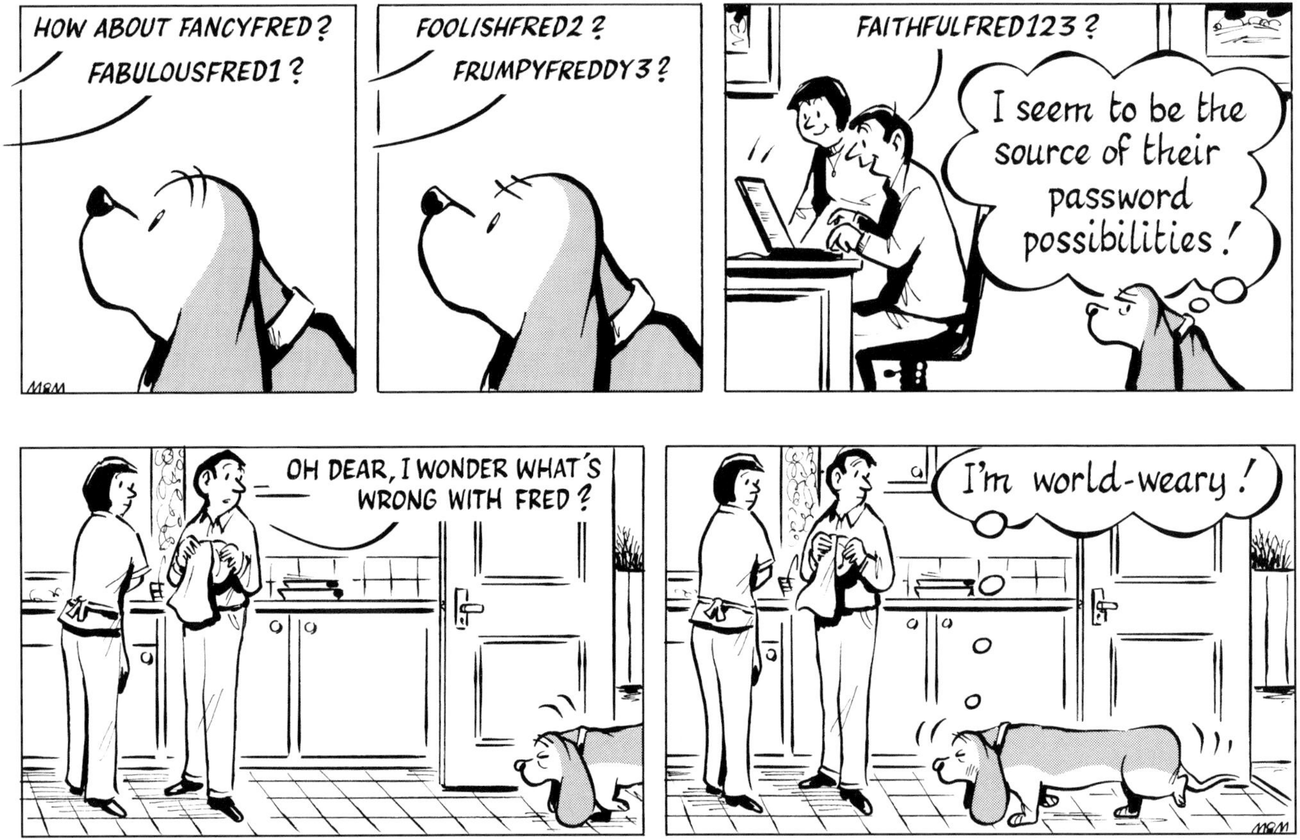
HOW ABOUT FANCYFRED?
FABULOUSFRED1?
FOOLISHFRED2?
FRUMPYFREDDY3?
FAITHFULFRED123?
I seem to be the source of their password possibilities!
OH DEAR, I WONDER WHAT'S WRONG WITH FRED?
I'm world-weary!

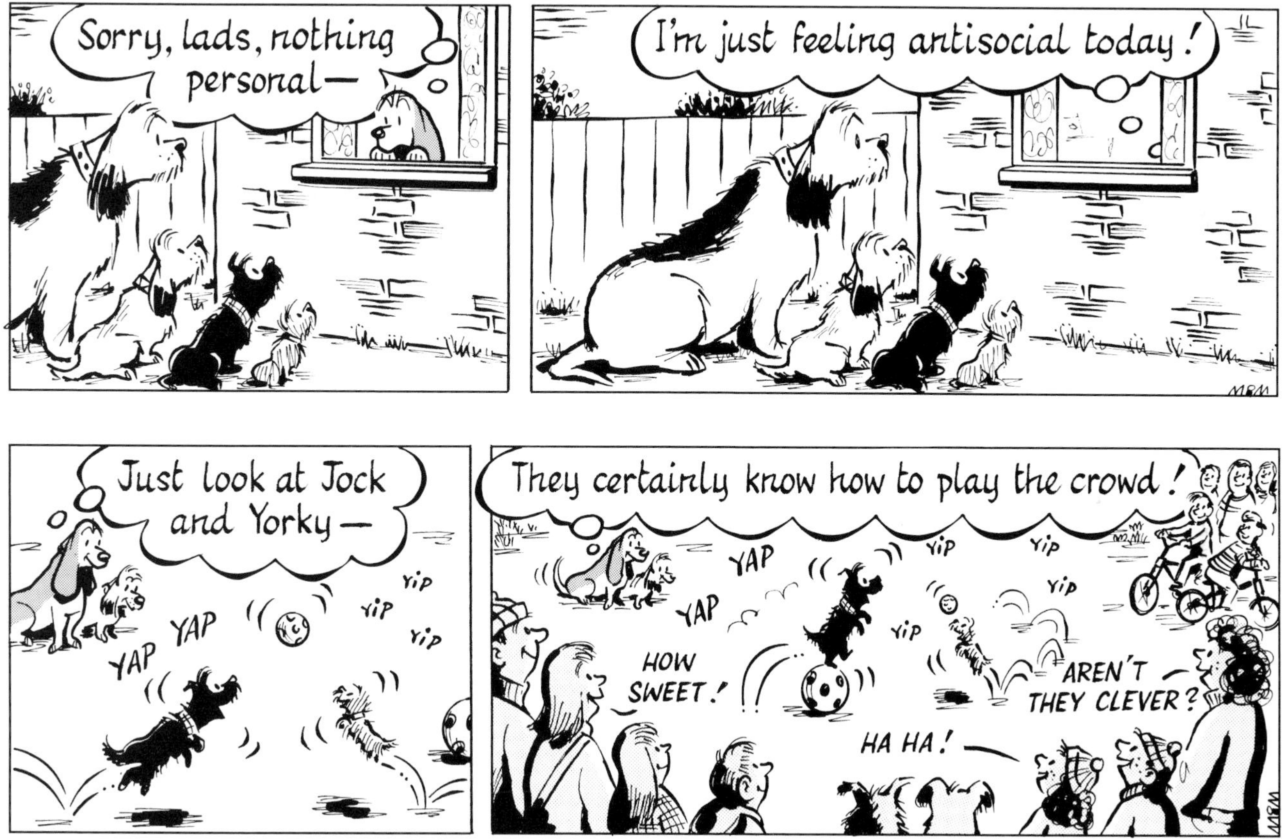
Sorry, lads, nothing personal—
I'm just feeling antisocial today!
Just look at Jock and Yorky—
YAP
YAP
YIP
YIP
YIP
They certainly know how to play the crowd!
YAP
YAP
YIP
YIP
YIP
YIP
HOW SWEET!
AREN'T THEY CLEVER?
HA HA!

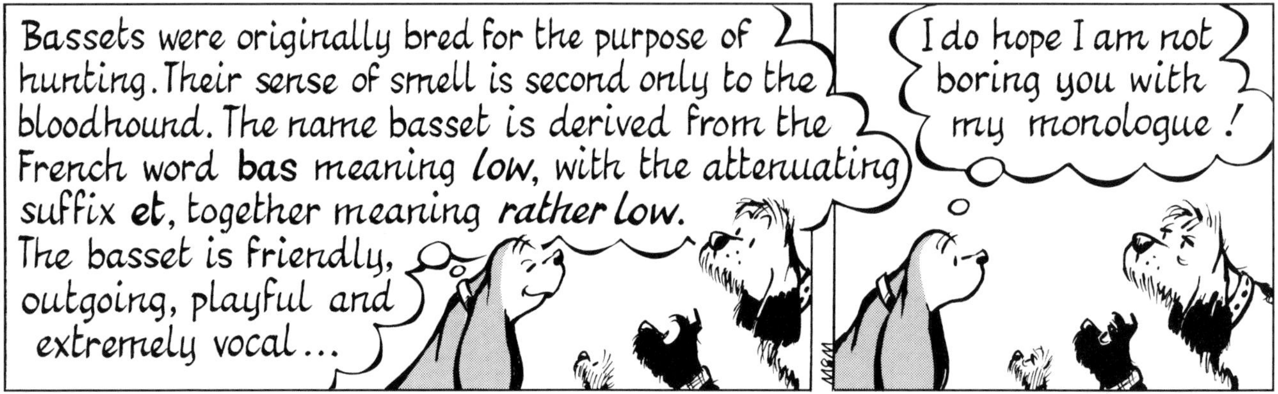
Bassets were originally bred for the purpose of hunting. Their sense of smell is second only to the bloodhound. The name basset is derived from the French word **bas** meaning *low*, with the attenuating suffix **et**, together meaning ***rather low***. The basset is friendly, outgoing, playful and extremely vocal...
I do hope I am not boring you with my monologue!

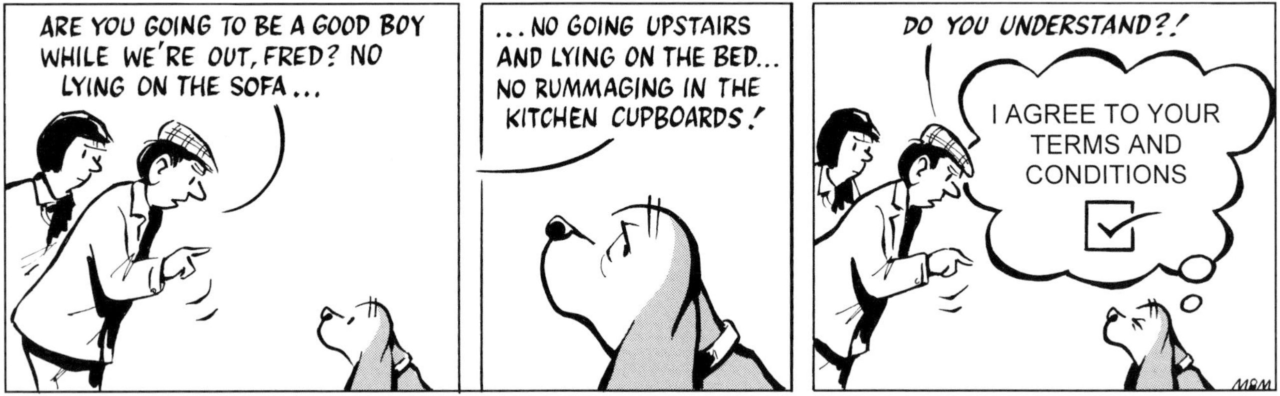
ARE YOU GOING TO BE A GOOD BOY WHILE WE'RE OUT, FRED? NO LYING ON THE SOFA...
...NO GOING UPSTAIRS AND LYING ON THE BED... NO RUMMAGING IN THE KITCHEN CUPBOARDS!
DO YOU UNDERSTAND?!
I AGREE TO YOUR TERMS AND CONDITIONS

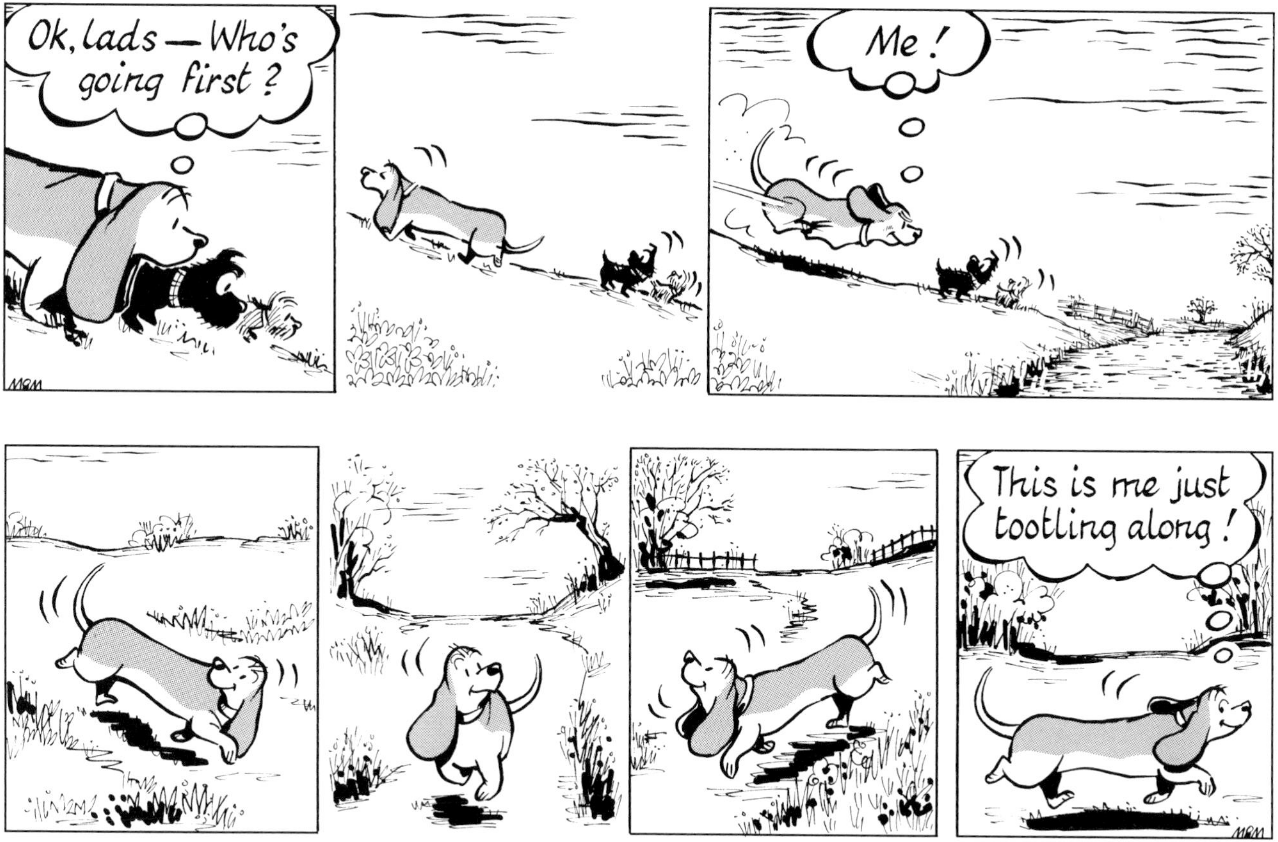
Ok, lads — Who's going first ?
Me !
This is me just tootling along !
MCM
MCM

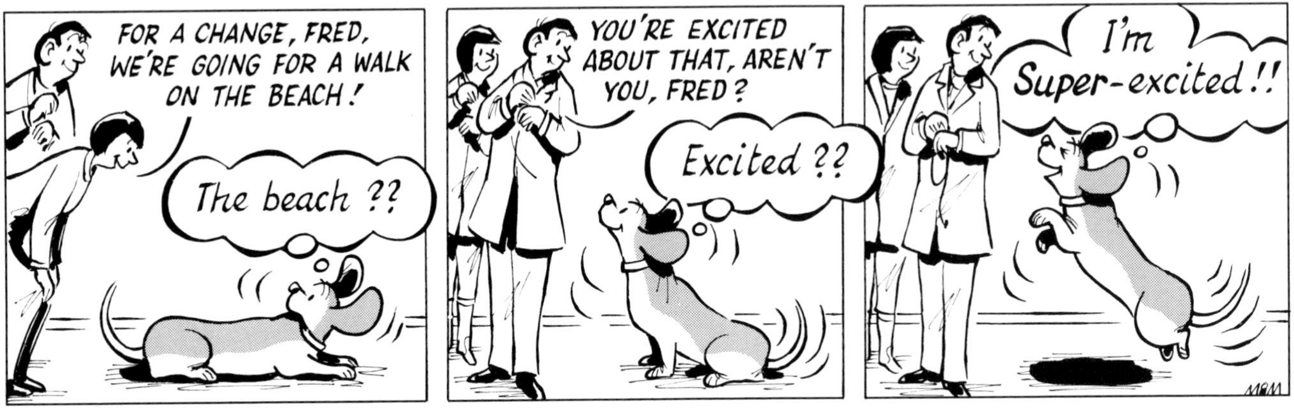
FOR A CHANGE, FRED, WE'RE GOING FOR A WALK ON THE BEACH!
The beach ??
YOU'RE EXCITED ABOUT THAT, AREN'T YOU, FRED?
Excited ??
I'm Super-excited!!

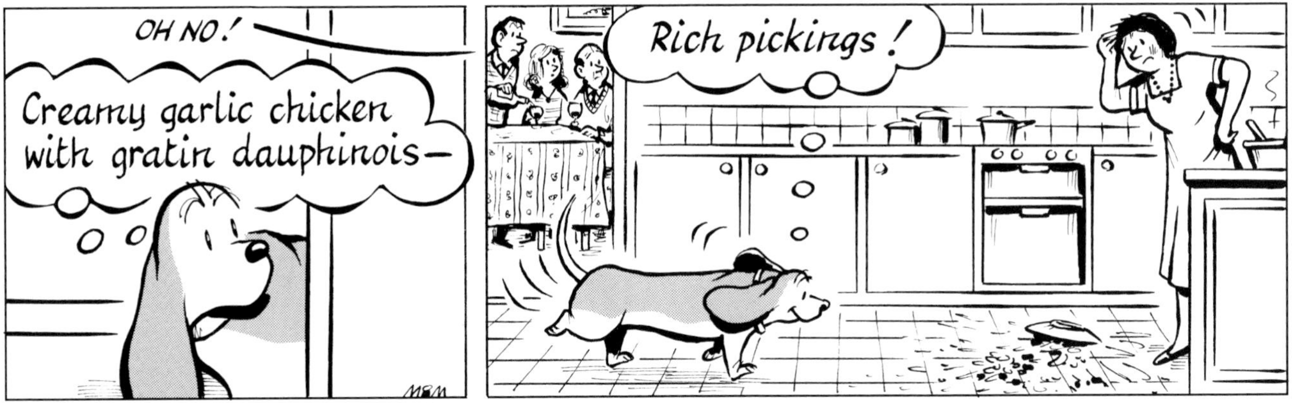
OH NO!
Creamy garlic chicken with gratin dauphinois–
Rich pickings!

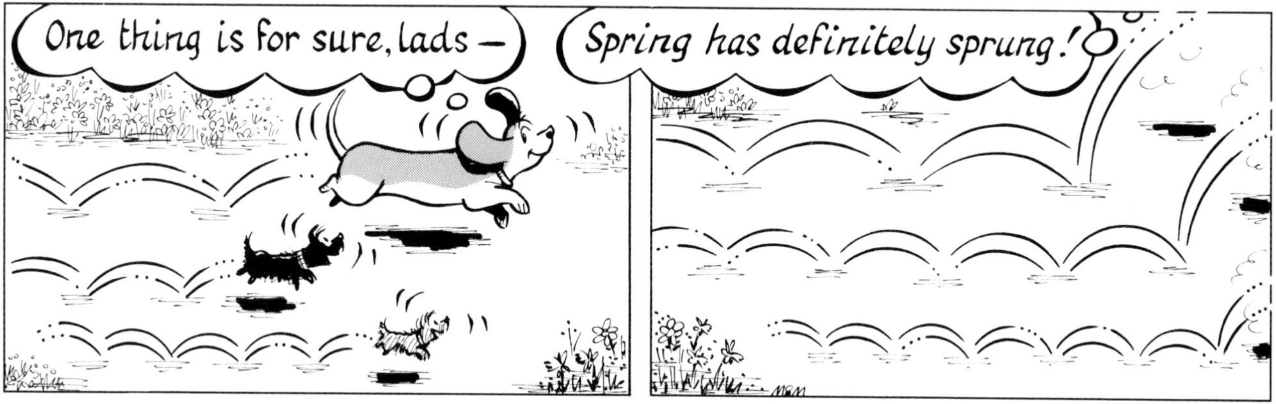
One thing is for sure, lads —
Spring has definitely sprung!
M&M

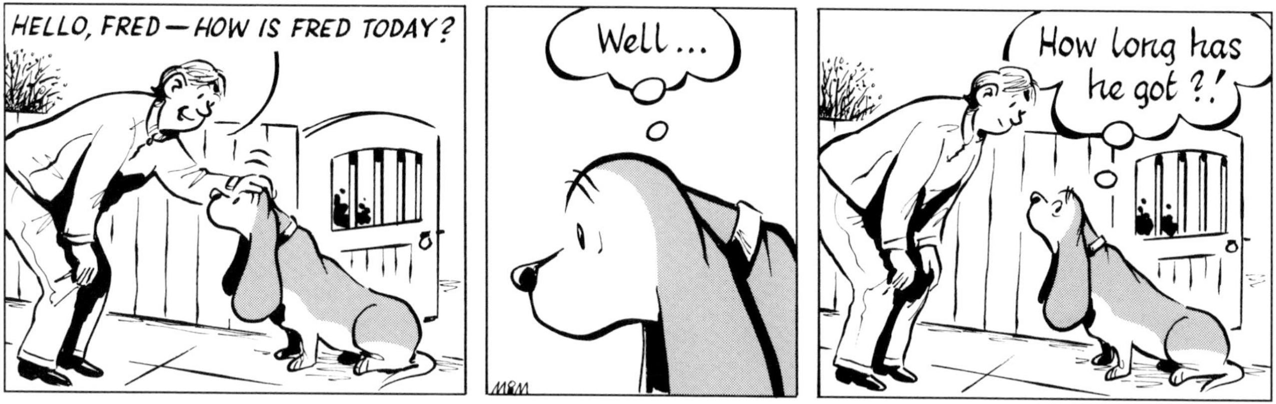
HELLO, FRED — HOW IS FRED TODAY?
Well ...
M&M
How long has he got?!

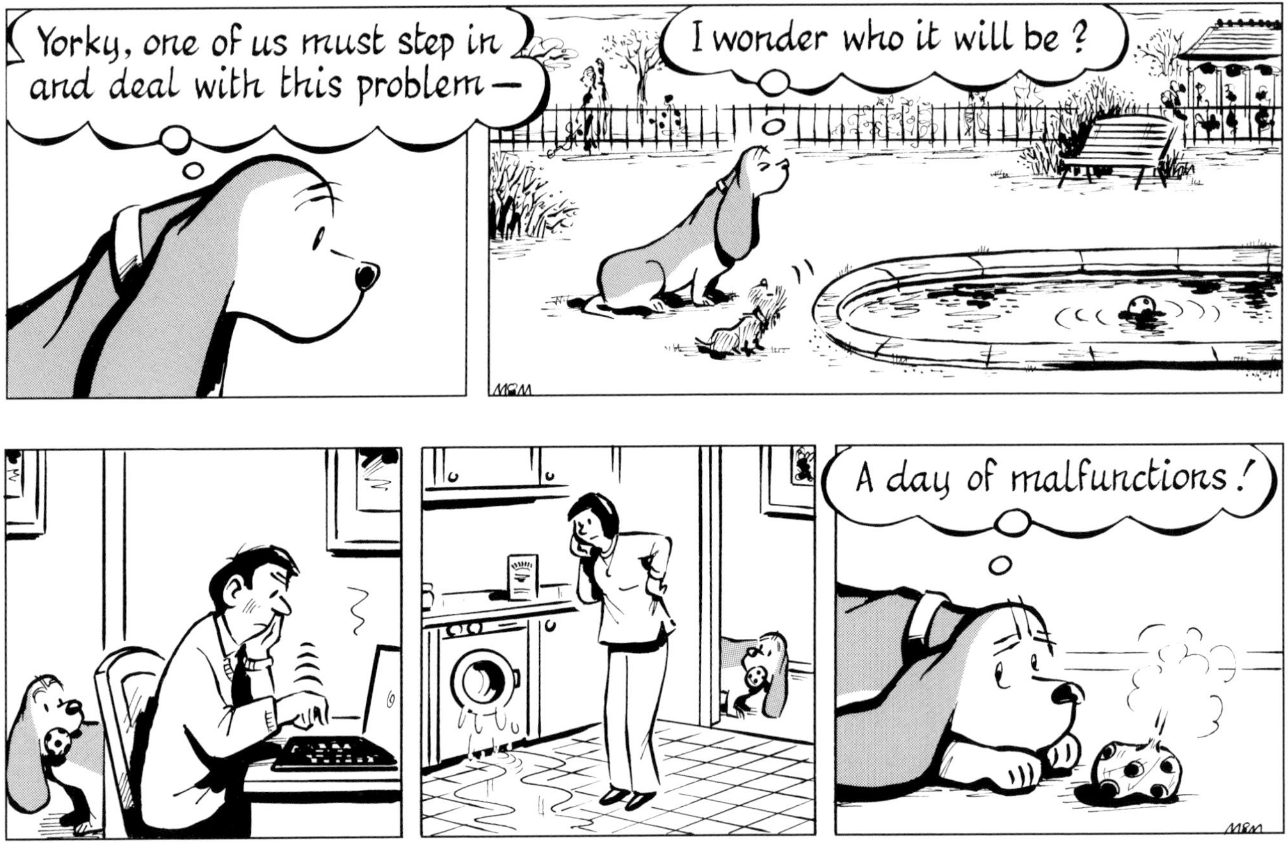
Yorky, one of us must step in and deal with this problem —
I wonder who it will be ?
M&M
A day of malfunctions !
M&M

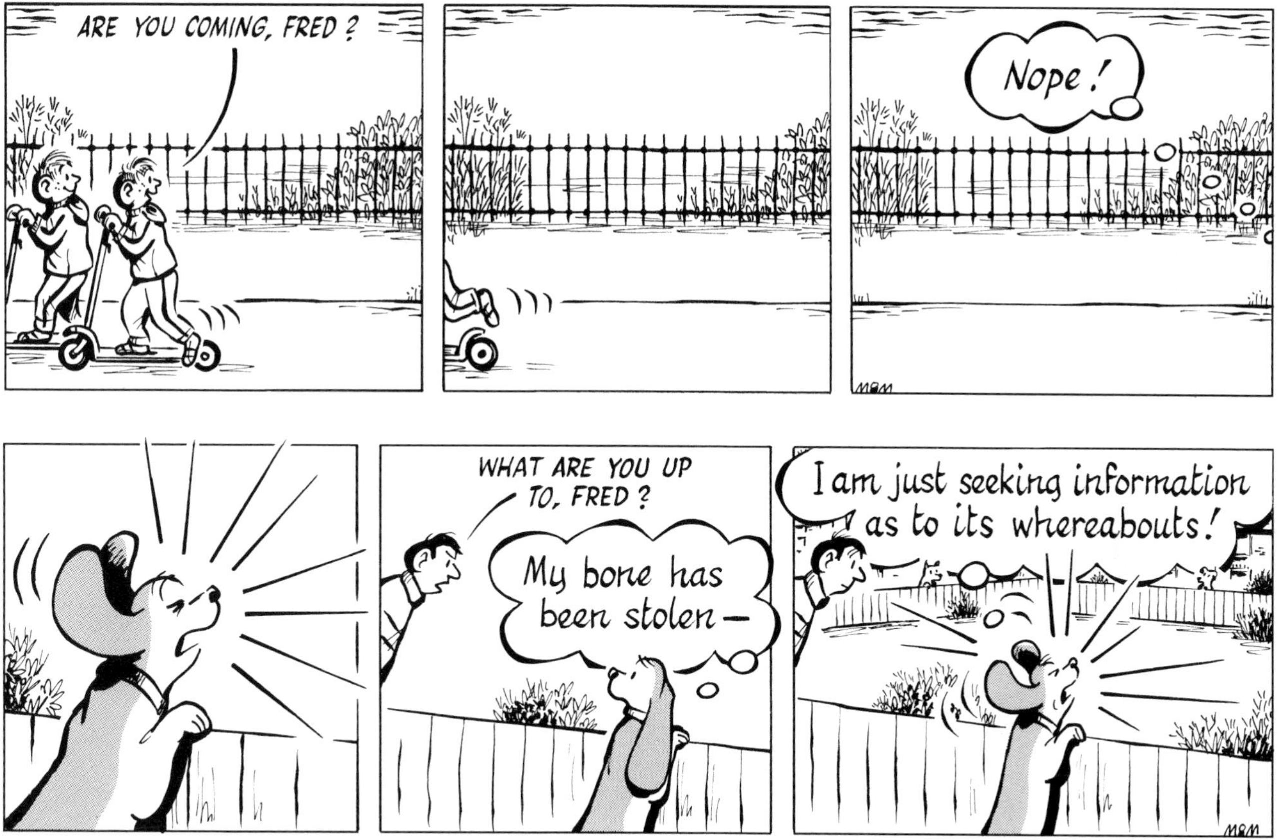
ARE YOU COMING, FRED ?
Nope !
MGM
WHAT ARE YOU UP TO, FRED ?
My bone has been stolen –
I am just seeking information as to its whereabouts !
MGM

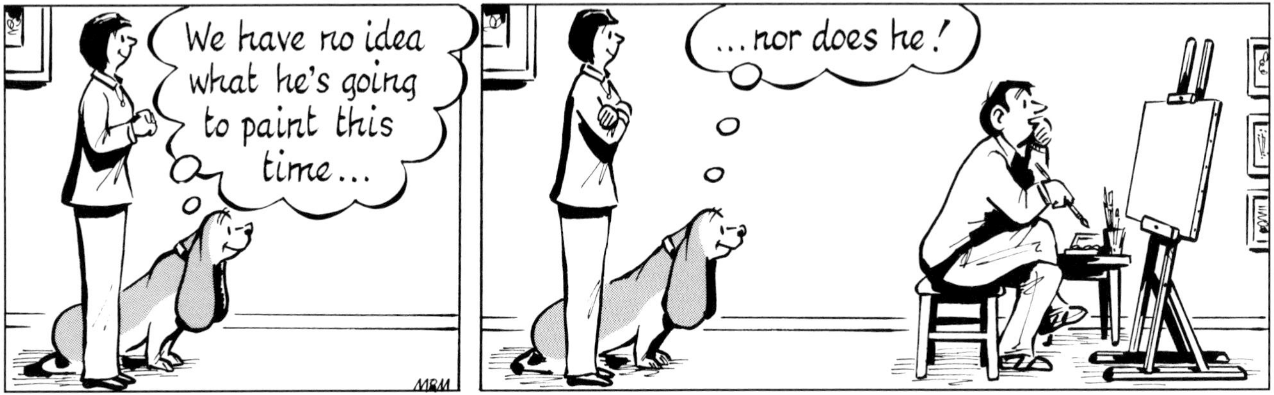
We have no idea what he's going to paint this time...
...nor does he!

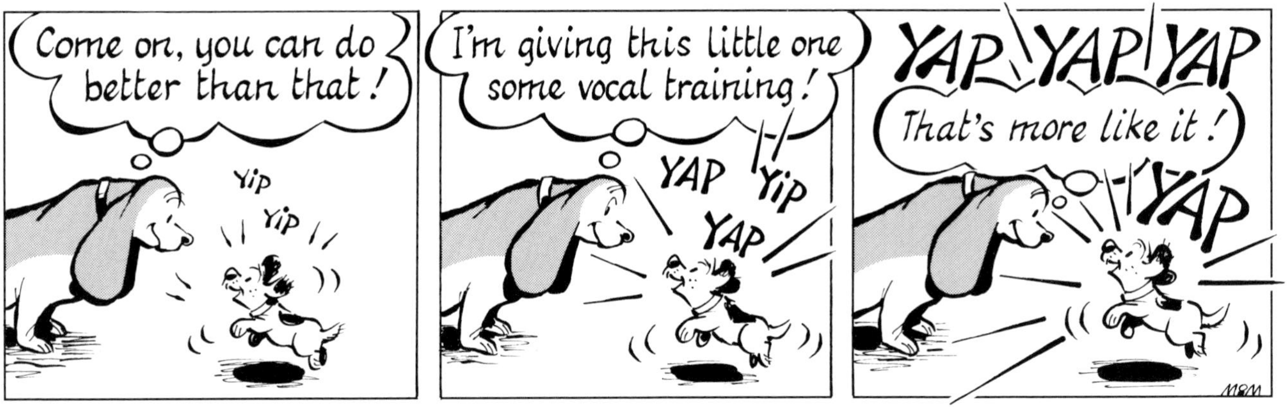
Come on, you can do better than that!
Yip
Yip
I'm giving this little one some vocal training!
YAP
Yip
YAP
YAP YAP YAP
That's more like it!
YAP

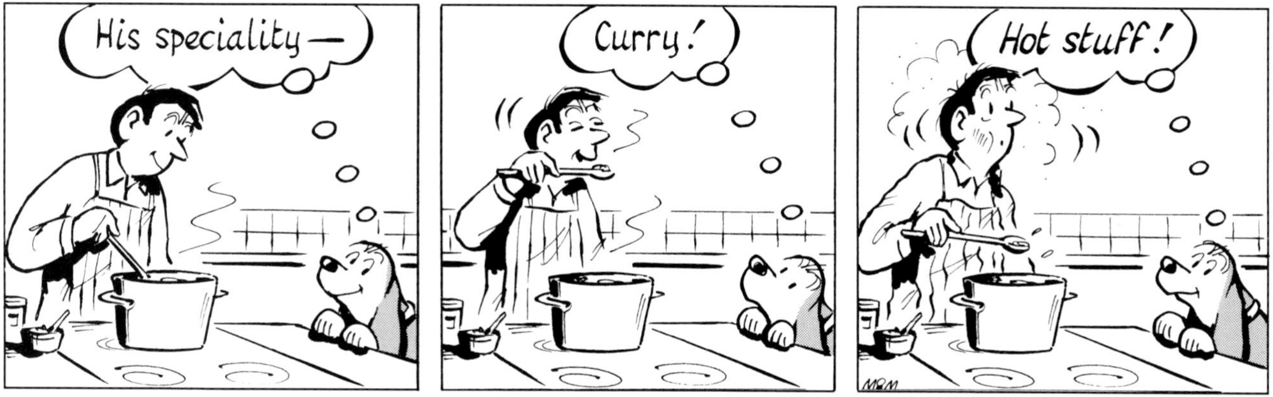
His speciality—
Curry!
Hot stuff!

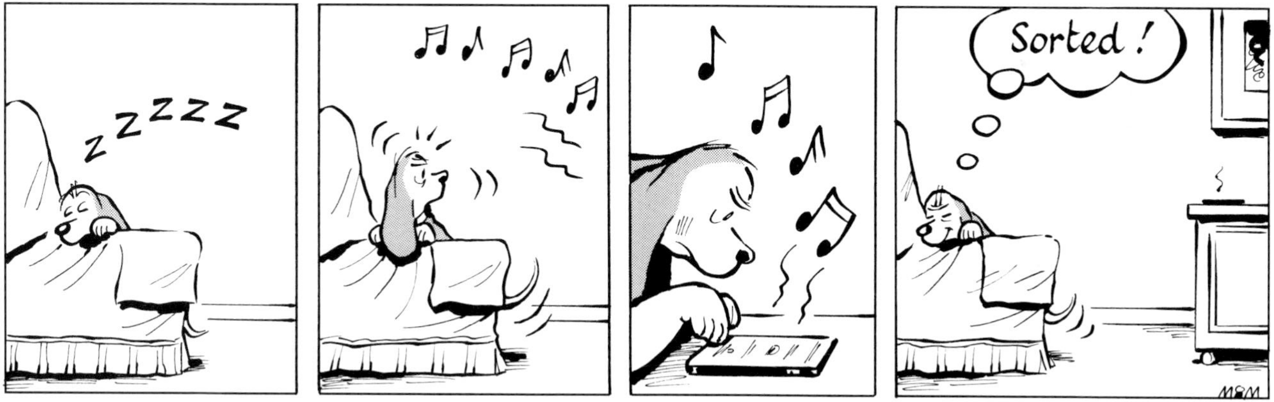
zzZZZ
Sorted!

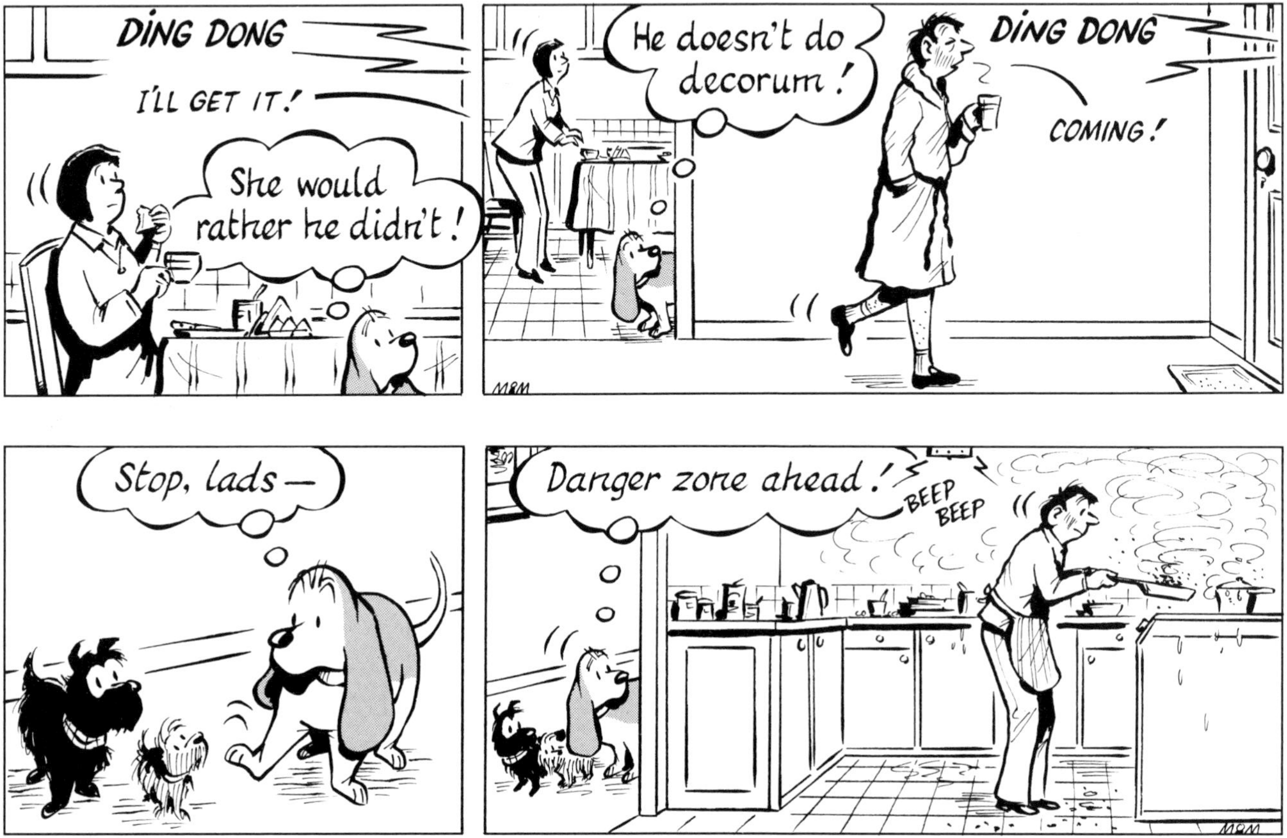
DING DONG
I'LL GET IT!
She would rather he didn't!
He doesn't do decorum!
DING DONG
COMING!
M&M
Stop, lads —
Danger zone ahead!
BEEP BEEP
M&M

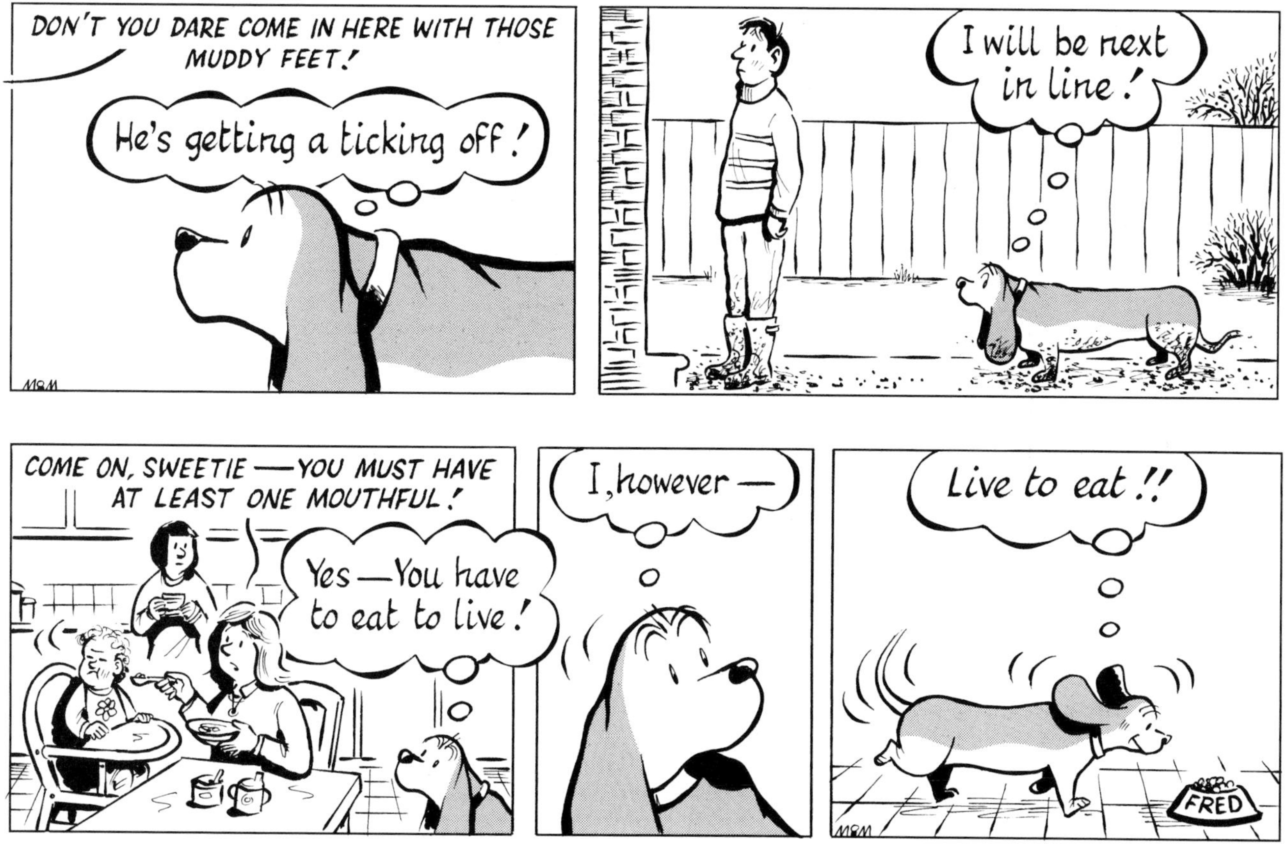
DON'T YOU DARE COME IN HERE WITH THOSE MUDDY FEET!
He's getting a ticking off!
I will be next in line!
COME ON, SWEETIE — YOU MUST HAVE AT LEAST ONE MOUTHFUL!
Yes — You have to eat to live!
I, however —
Live to eat!!
FRED

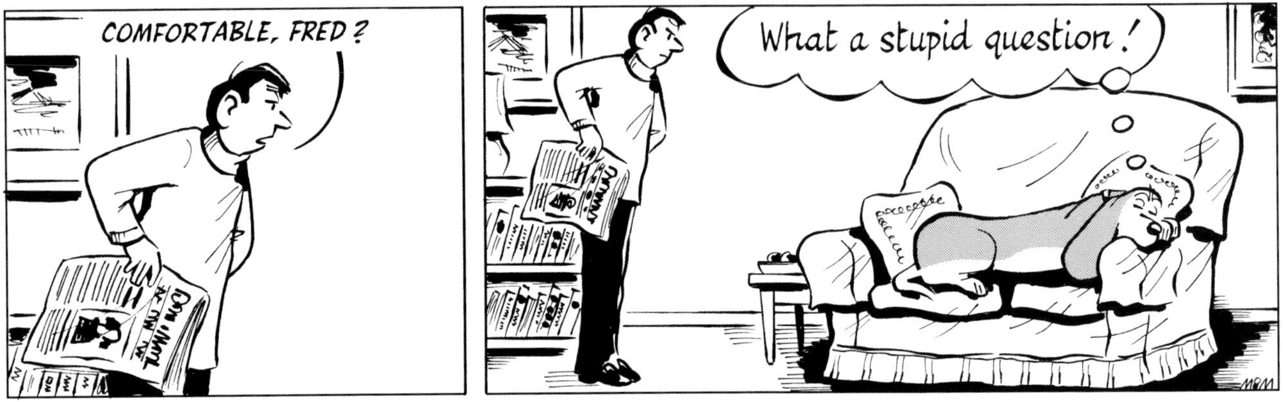
COMFORTABLE, FRED?
What a stupid question!

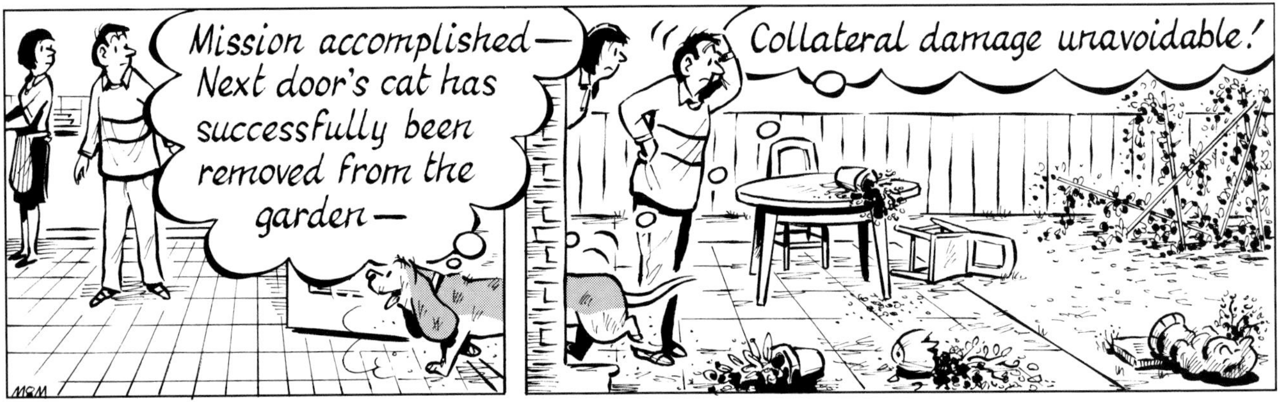
Mission accomplished— Next door's cat has successfully been removed from the garden—
Collateral damage unavoidable!

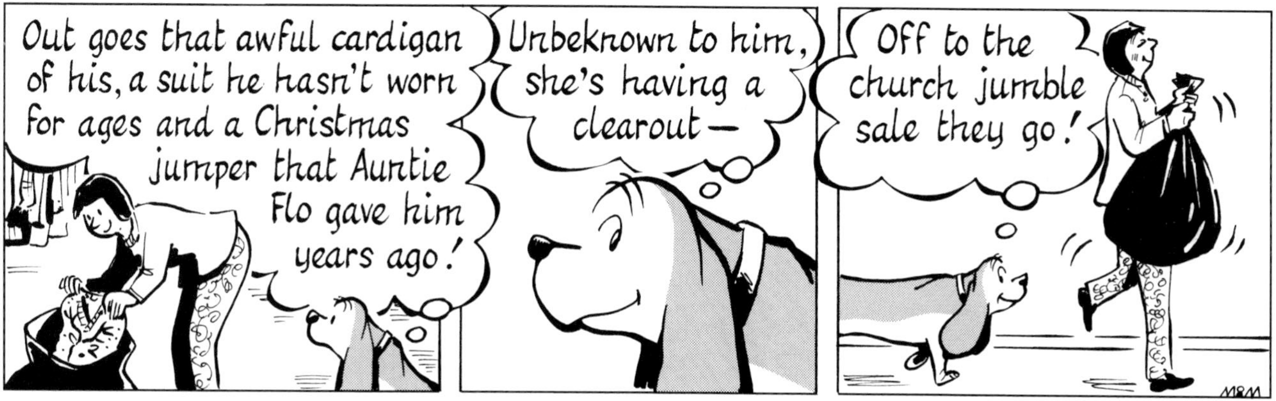
Out goes that awful cardigan of his, a suit he hasn't worn for ages and a Christmas jumper that Auntie Flo gave him years ago!
Unbeknown to him, she's having a clearout—
Off to the church jumble sale they go!
M&M

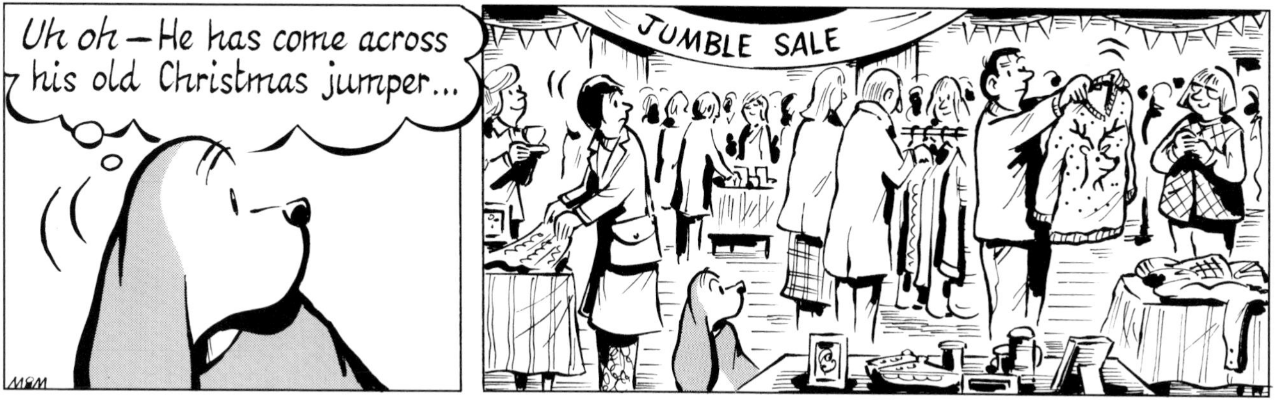
Uh oh—He has come across his old Christmas jumper...
M&M
JUMBLE SALE

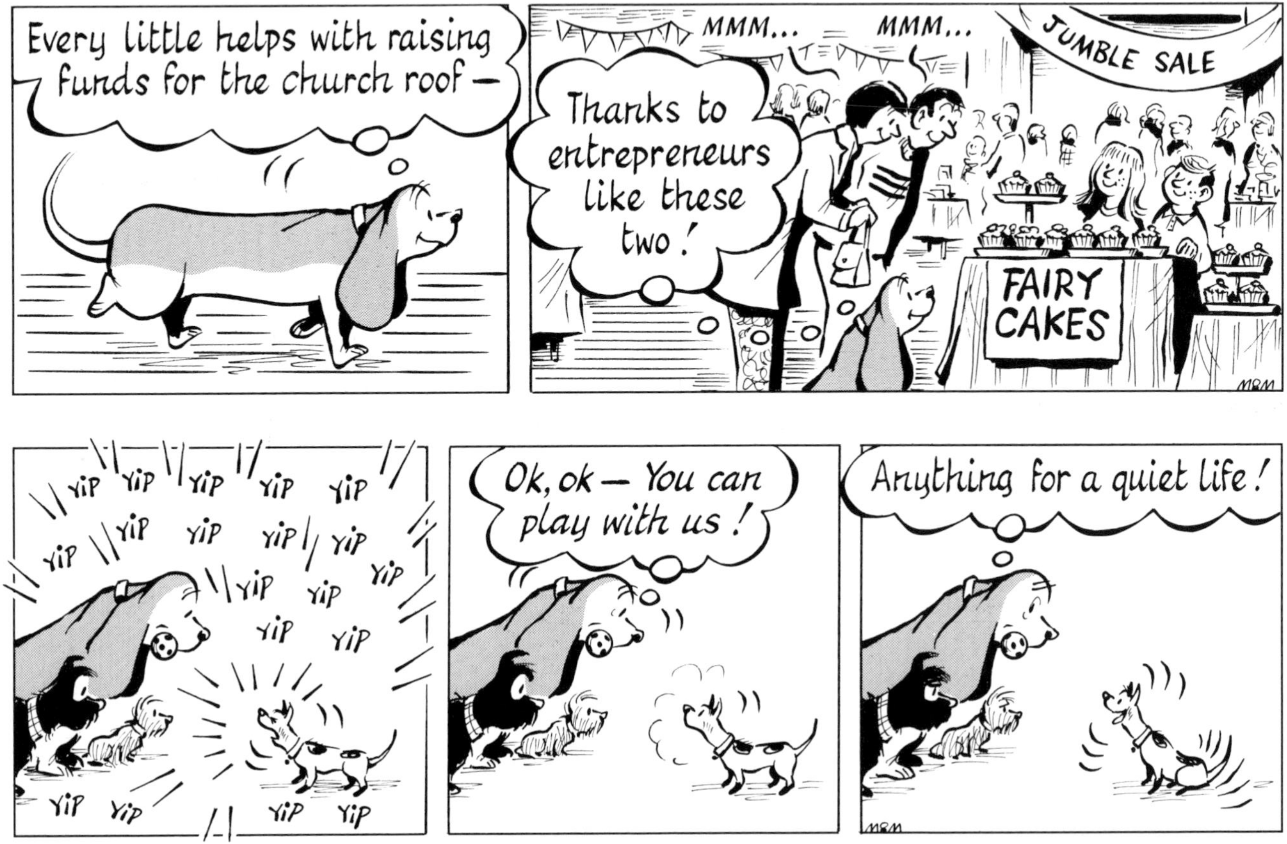
Every little helps with raising funds for the church roof –
MMM...
MMM...
JUMBLE SALE
Thanks to entrepreneurs like these two!
FAIRY CAKES
M&M
YIP YIP YIP YIP YIP
YIP YIP YIP YIP YIP
YIP YIP YIP
YIP YIP
YIP YIP YIP YIP
Ok, ok – You can play with us!
Anything for a quiet life!
M&M

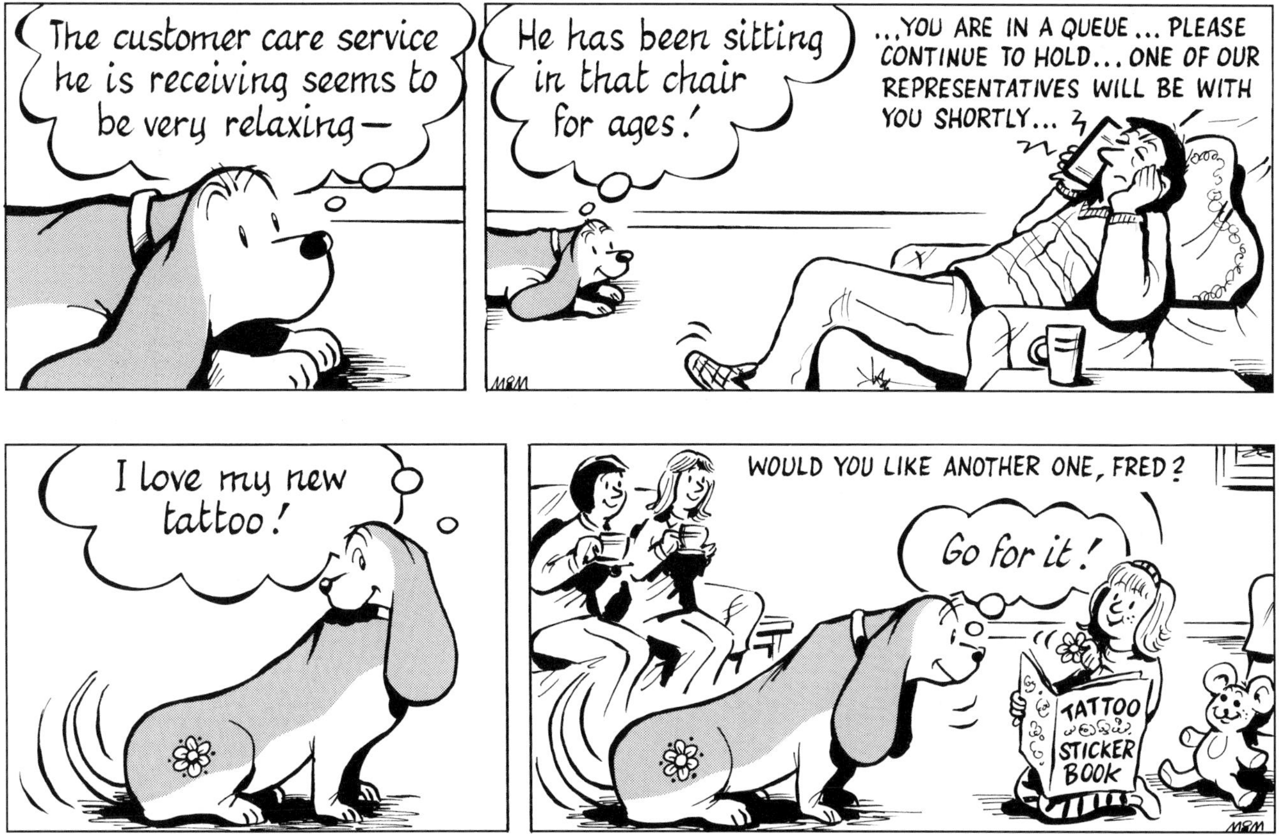

The customer care service he is receiving seems to be very relaxing—
He has been sitting in that chair for ages!
...YOU ARE IN A QUEUE ... PLEASE CONTINUE TO HOLD... ONE OF OUR REPRESENTATIVES WILL BE WITH YOU SHORTLY...
M&M
I love my new tattoo!
WOULD YOU LIKE ANOTHER ONE, FRED?
Go for it!
TATTOO STICKER BOOK
M&M

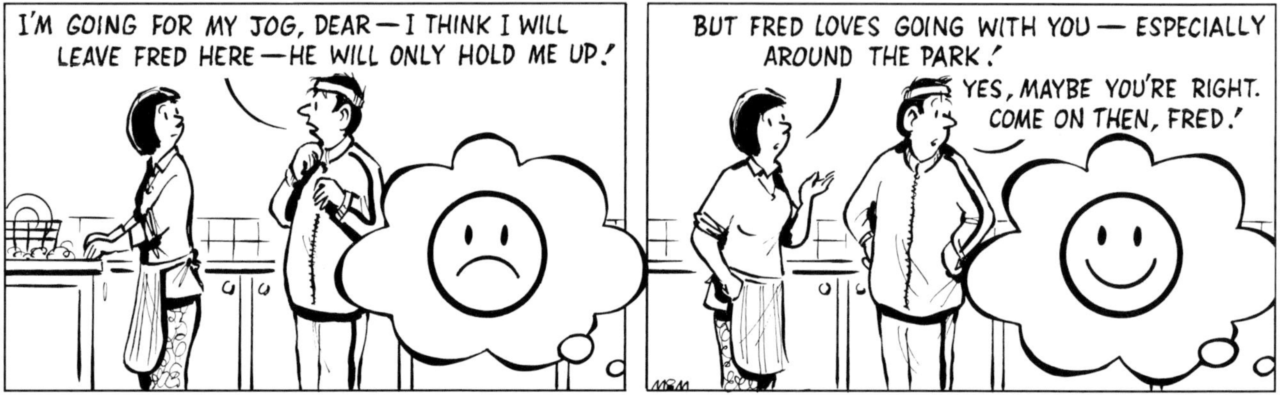
I'M GOING FOR MY JOG, DEAR — I THINK I WILL LEAVE FRED HERE — HE WILL ONLY HOLD ME UP!
BUT FRED LOVES GOING WITH YOU — ESPECIALLY AROUND THE PARK!
YES, MAYBE YOU'RE RIGHT. COME ON THEN, FRED!

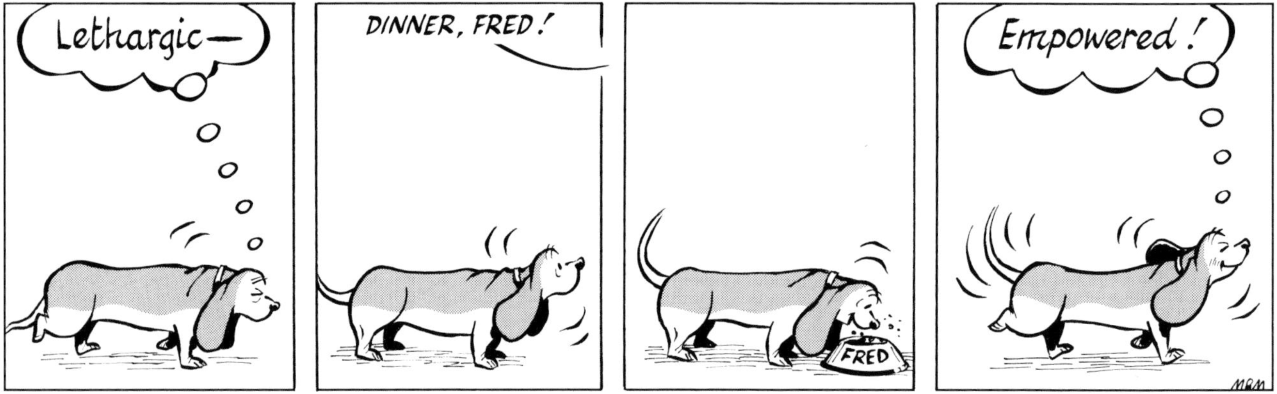
Lethargic —
DINNER, FRED!
FRED
Empowered!

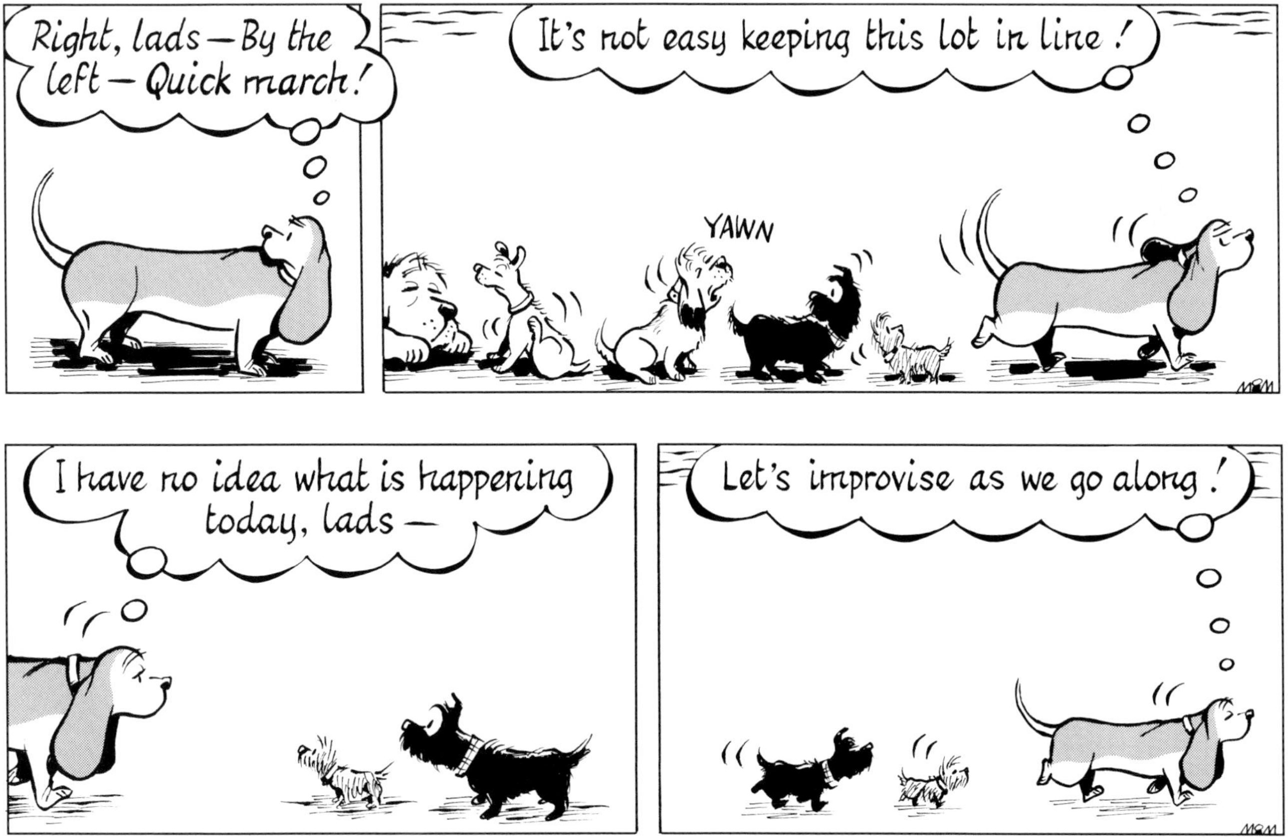
Right, lads — By the left — Quick march!
It's not easy keeping this lot in line!
YAWN
MGM
I have no idea what is happening today, lads —
Let's improvise as we go along!
MGM

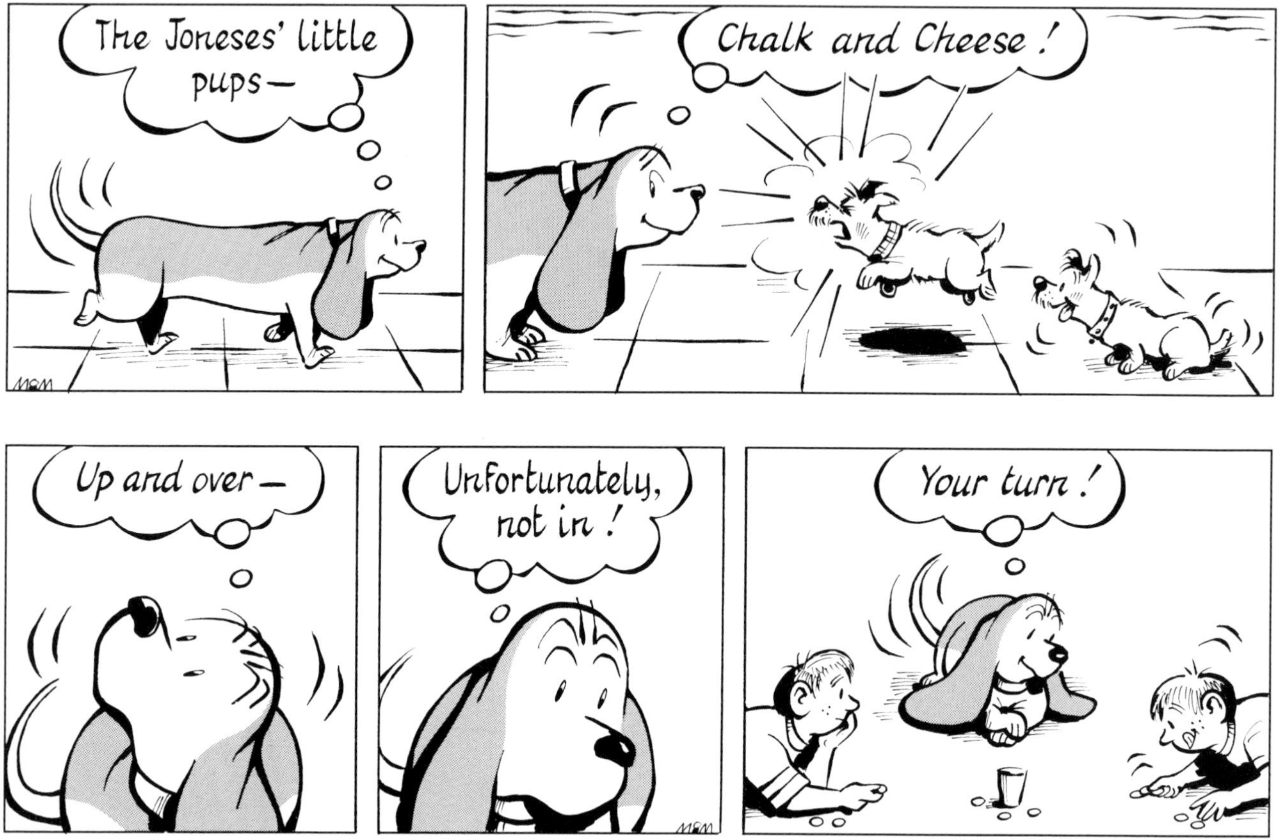
The Joneses' little pups—
Chalk and Cheese!
Up and over—
Unfortunately, not in!
Your turn!

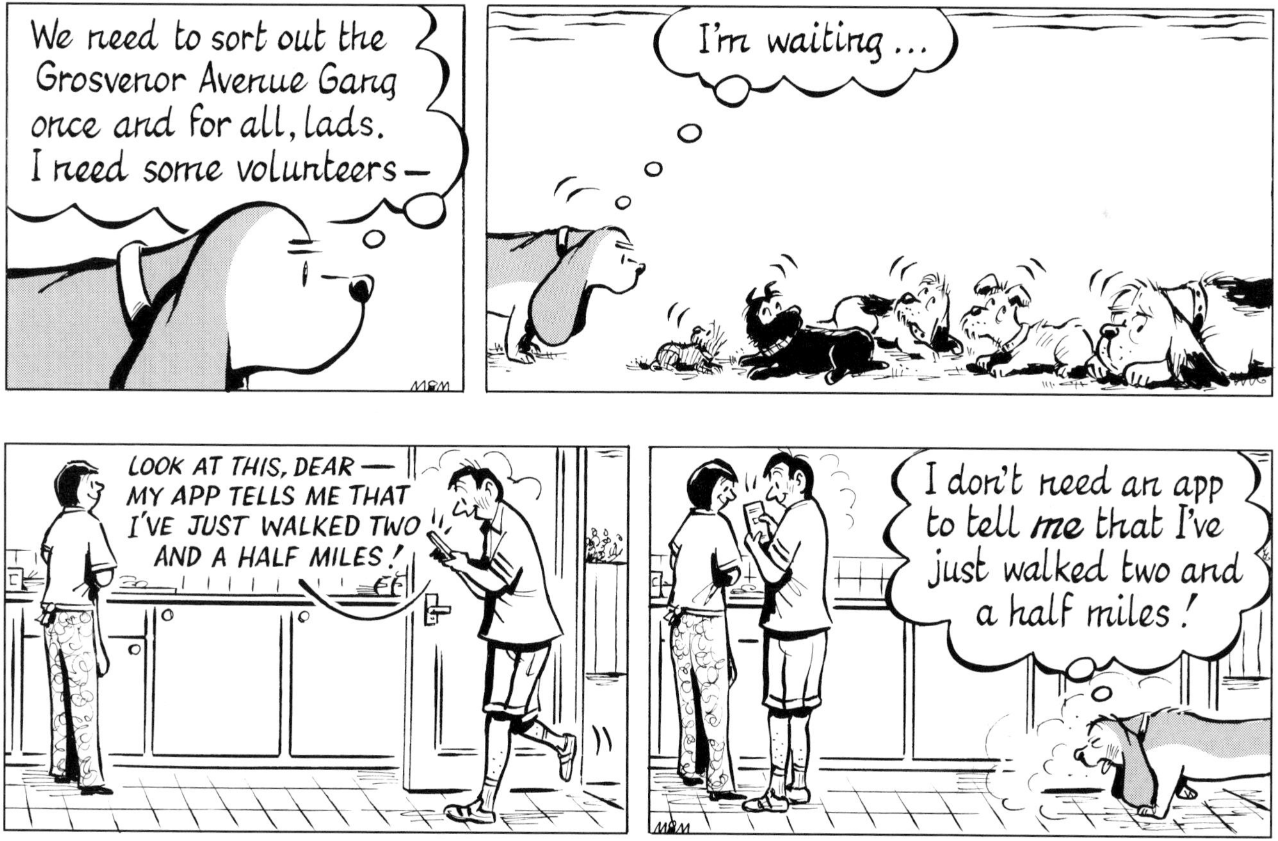
We need to sort out the Grosvenor Avenue Gang once and for all, lads. I need some volunteers—
M&M
I'm waiting ...
LOOK AT THIS, DEAR — MY APP TELLS ME THAT I'VE JUST WALKED TWO AND A HALF MILES!
I don't need an app to tell *me* that I've just walked two and a half miles!
M&M

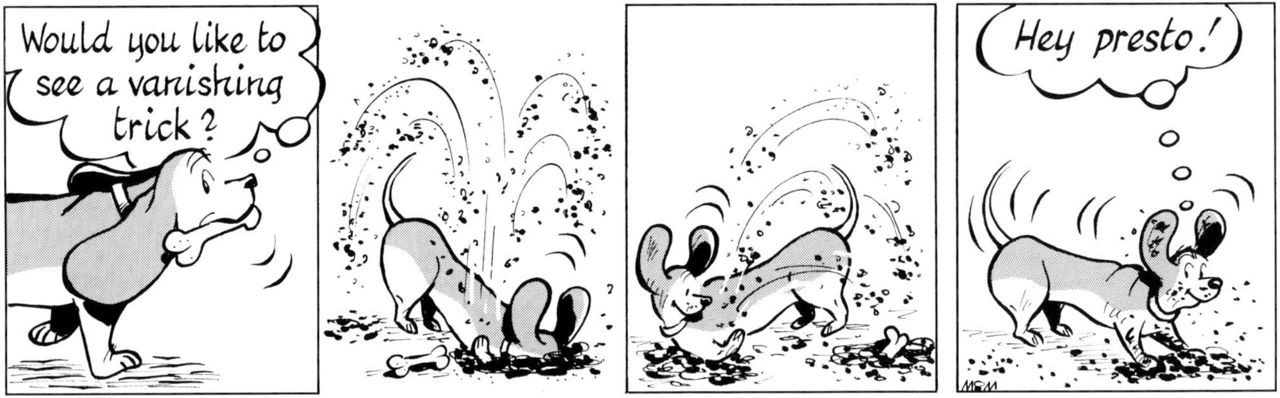
Would you like to see a varishing trick?
Hey presto!
M&M

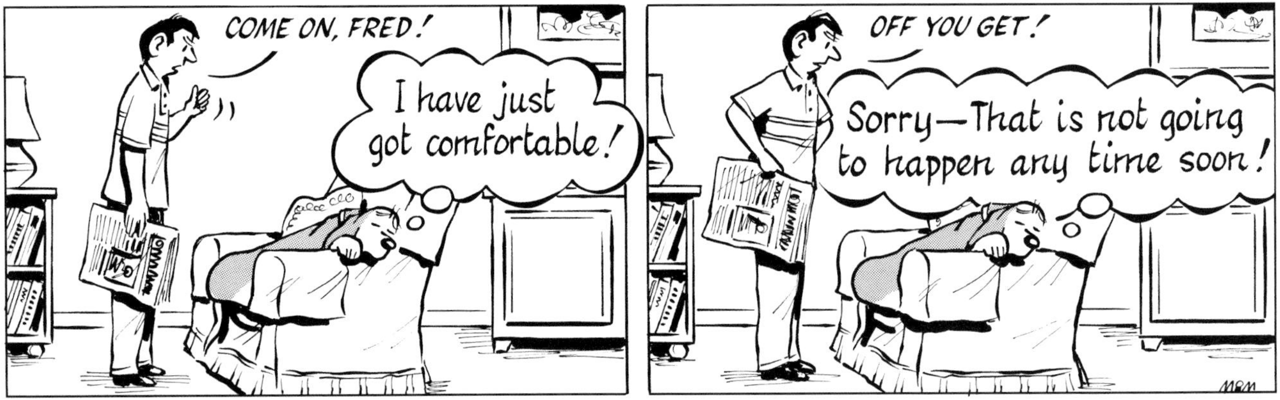
COME ON, FRED!
I have just got comfortable!
OFF YOU GET!
Sorry—That is not going to happen any time soon!
M&M

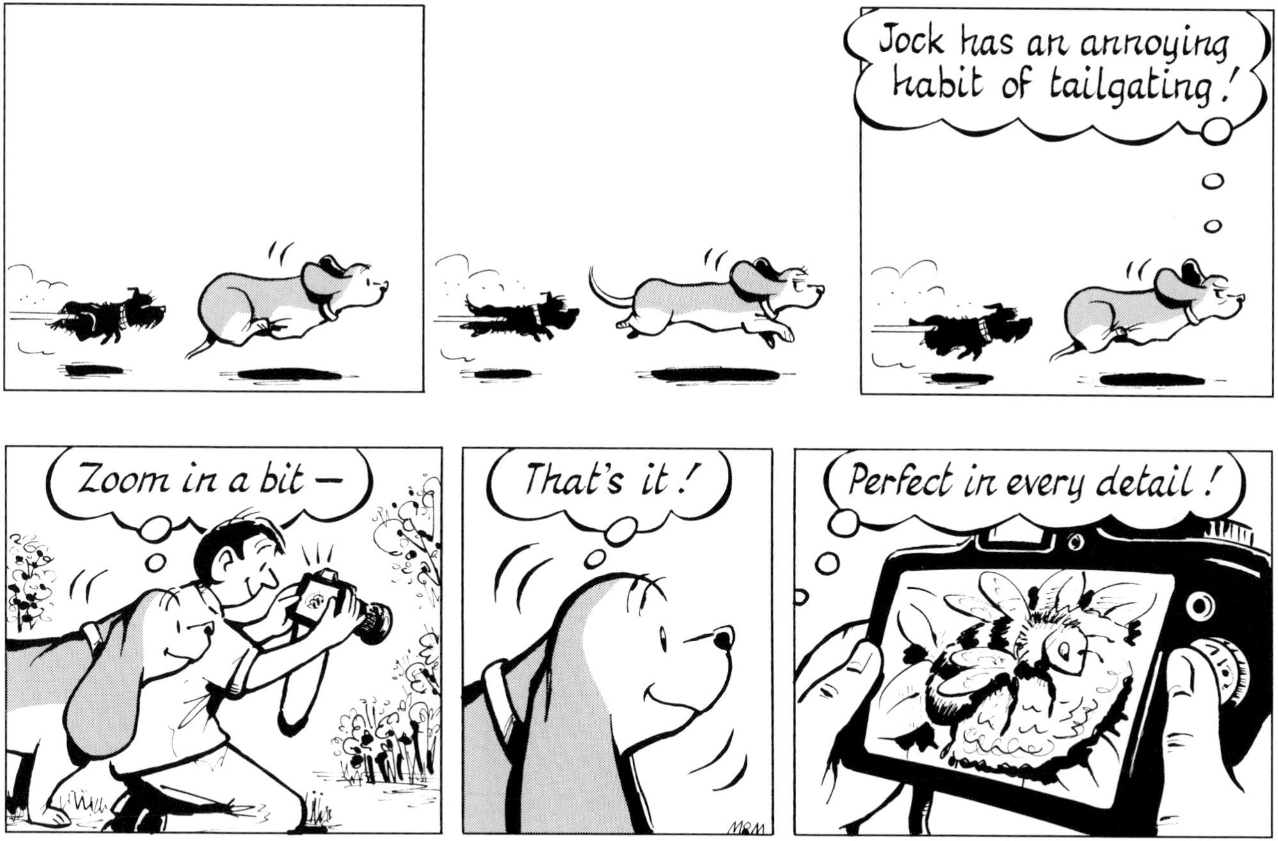
Jock has an annoying habit of tailgating!
Zoom in a bit —
That's it!
Perfect in every detail!
M&M

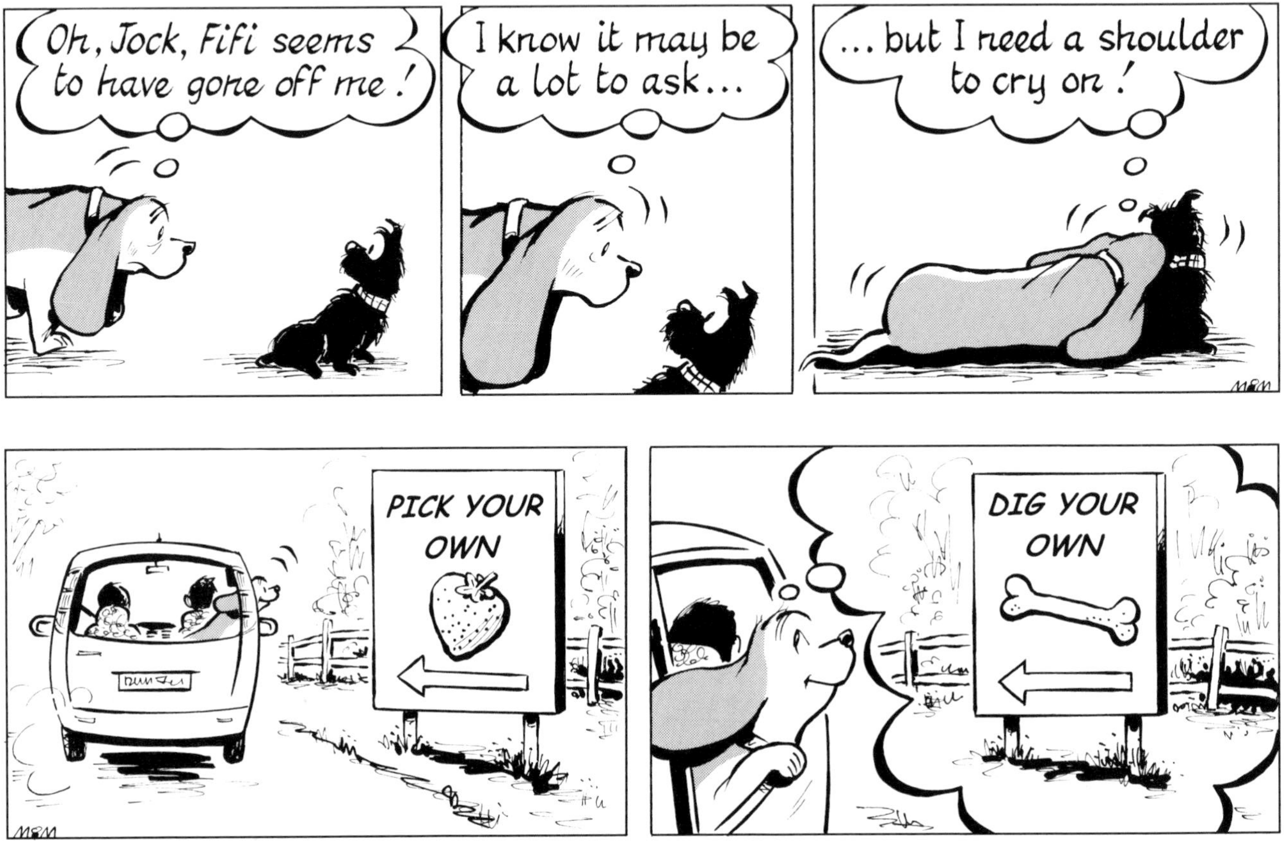
Oh, Jock, Fifi seems to have gone off me!
I know it may be a lot to ask...
...but I need a shoulder to cry on!
PICK YOUR OWN
DIG YOUR OWN

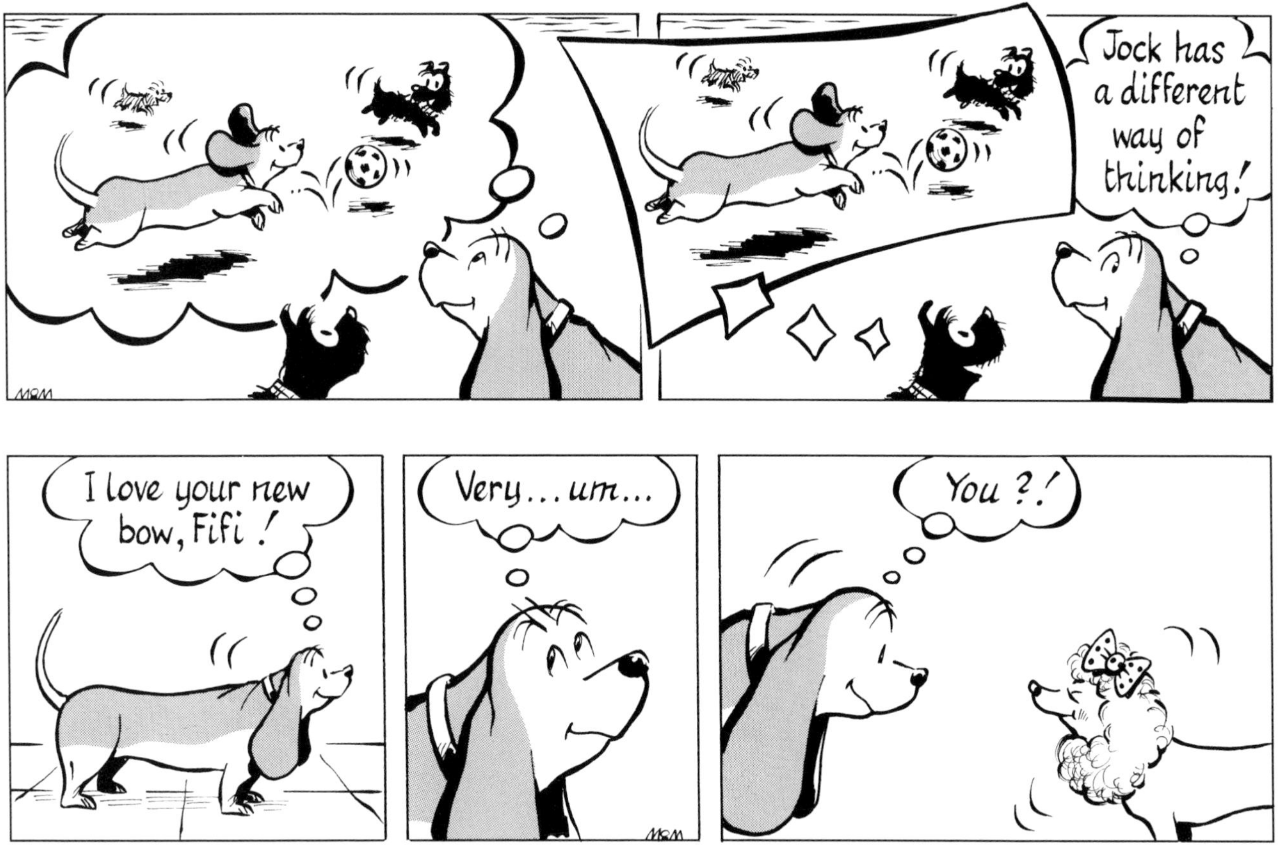

Jock has a different way of thinking!
I love your new bow, Fifi!
Very...um...
You?!

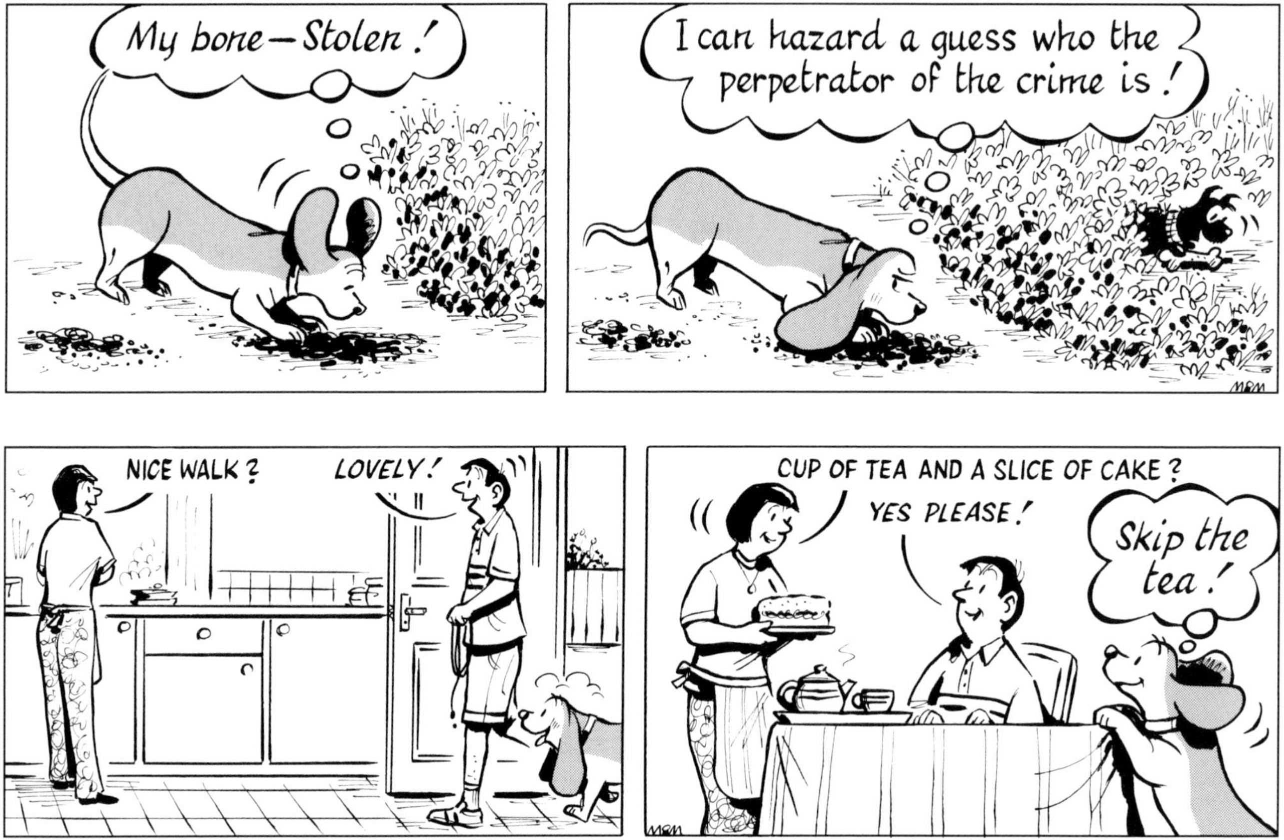
My bone—Stolen!
I can hazard a guess who the perpetrator of the crime is!
MBM
NICE WALK?
LOVELY!
CUP OF TEA AND A SLICE OF CAKE?
YES PLEASE!
Skip the tea!
MBM

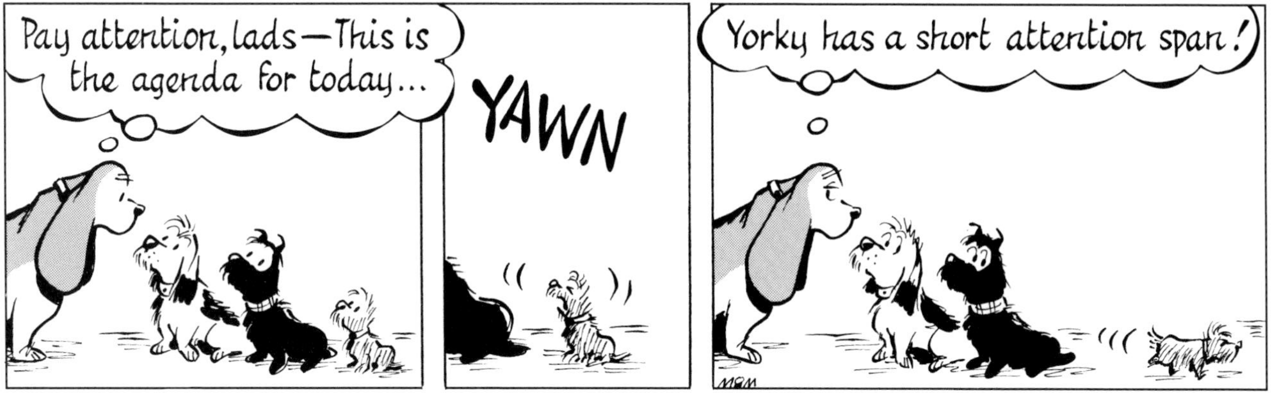

Pay attention, lads—This is the agenda for today...
YAWN
Yorky has a short attention span!
MGM

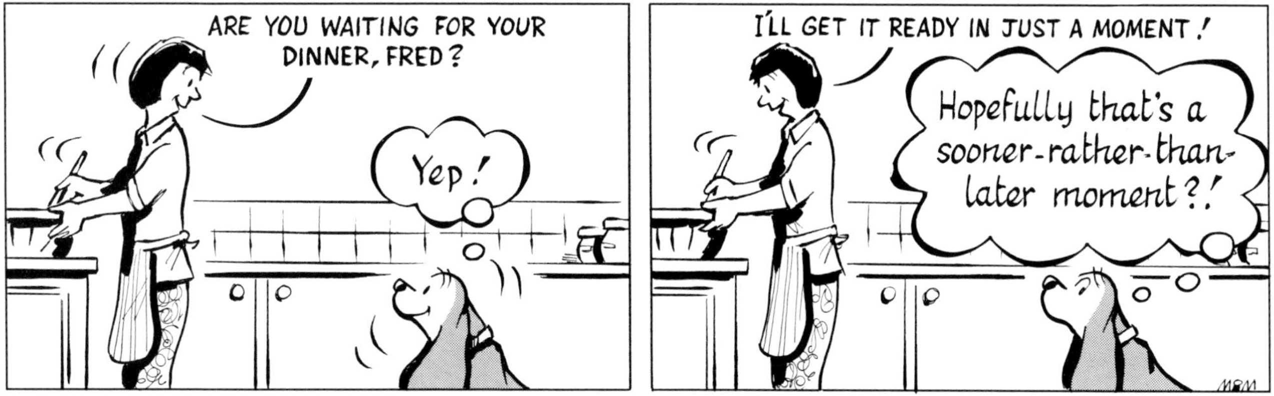

ARE YOU WAITING FOR YOUR DINNER, FRED?
Yep!
I'LL GET IT READY IN JUST A MOMENT!
Hopefully that's a sooner-rather-than-later moment?!
MGM

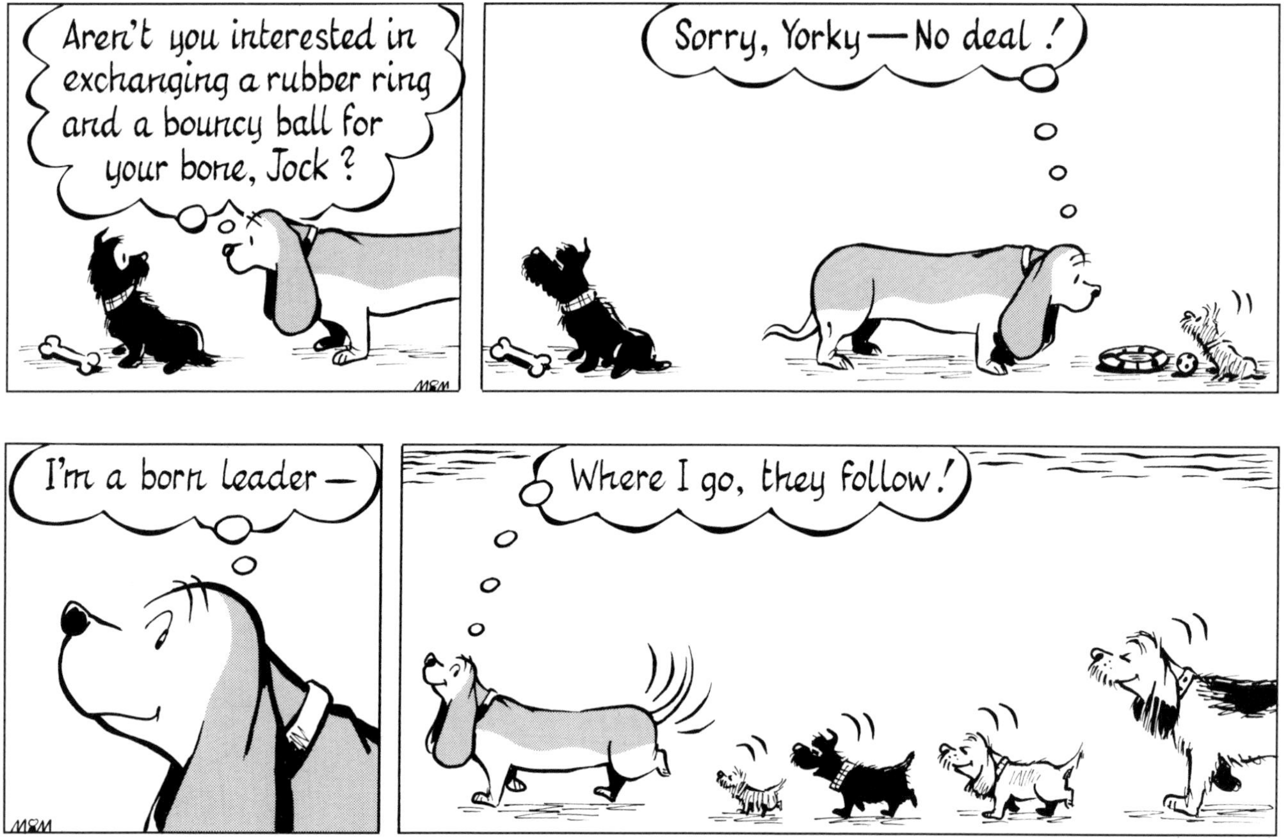
Aren't you interested in exchanging a rubber ring and a bouncy ball for your bone, Jock?
Sorry, Yorky — No deal!
I'm a born leader —
Where I go, they follow!

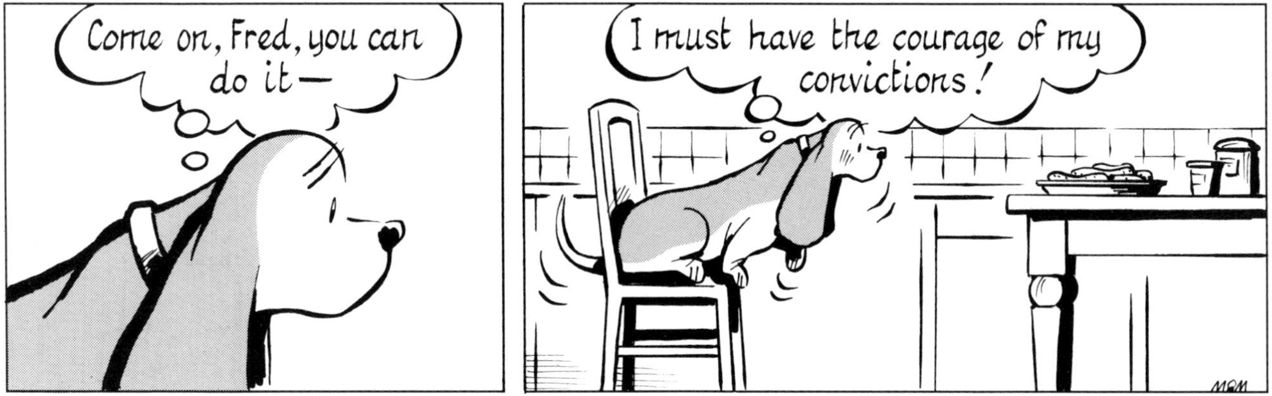
Come on, Fred, you can do it—
I must have the courage of my convictions!

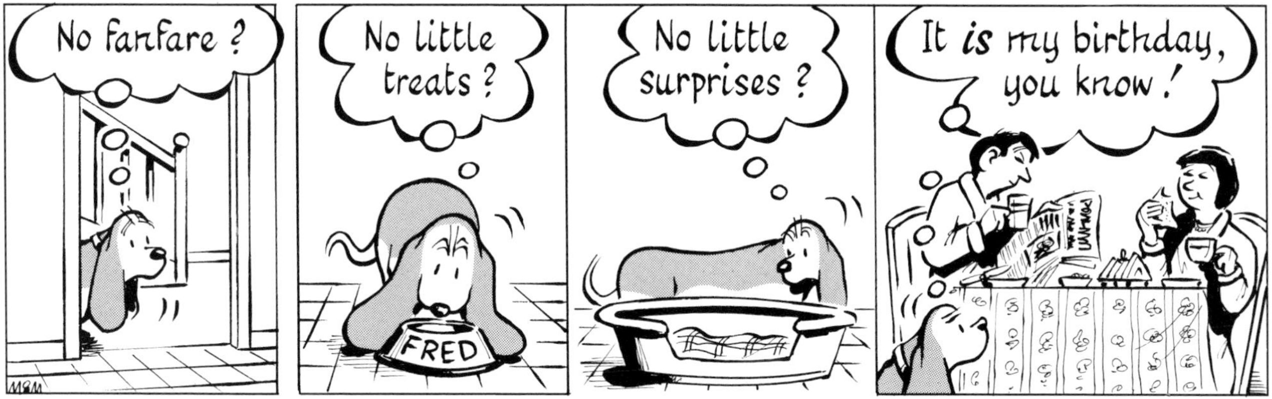
No fanfare?
No little treats?
FRED
No little surprises?
It *is* my birthday, you know!

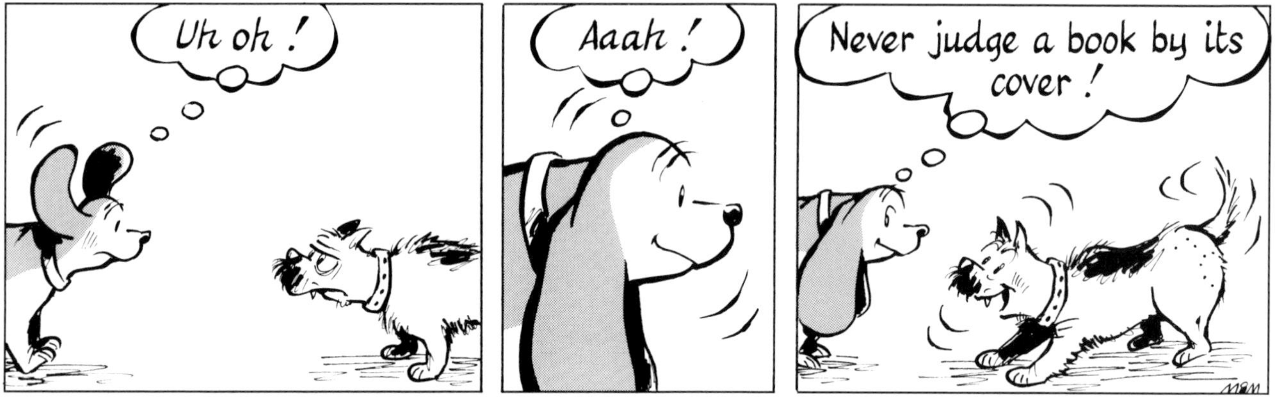
Uh oh!
Aaah!
Never judge a book by its cover!
MGM

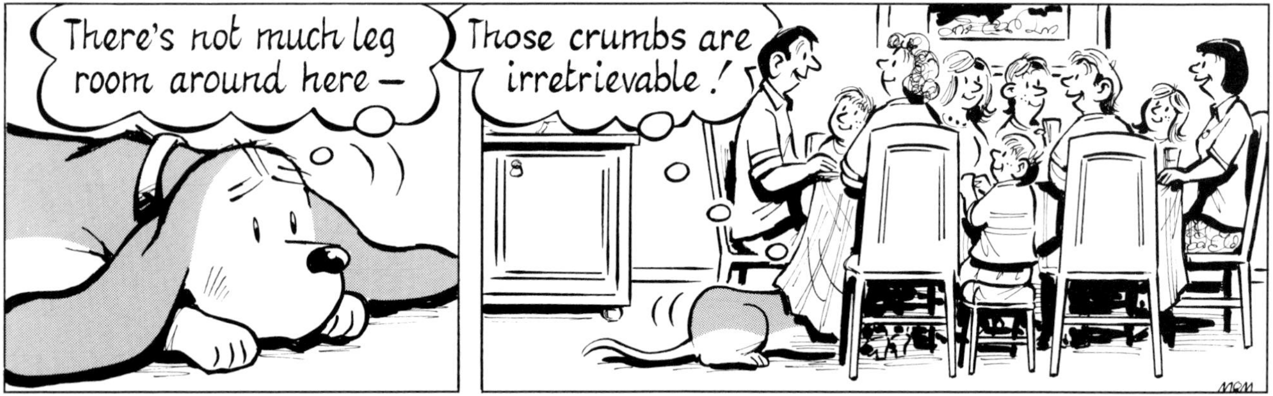
There's not much leg room around here –
Those crumbs are irretrievable!
MGM

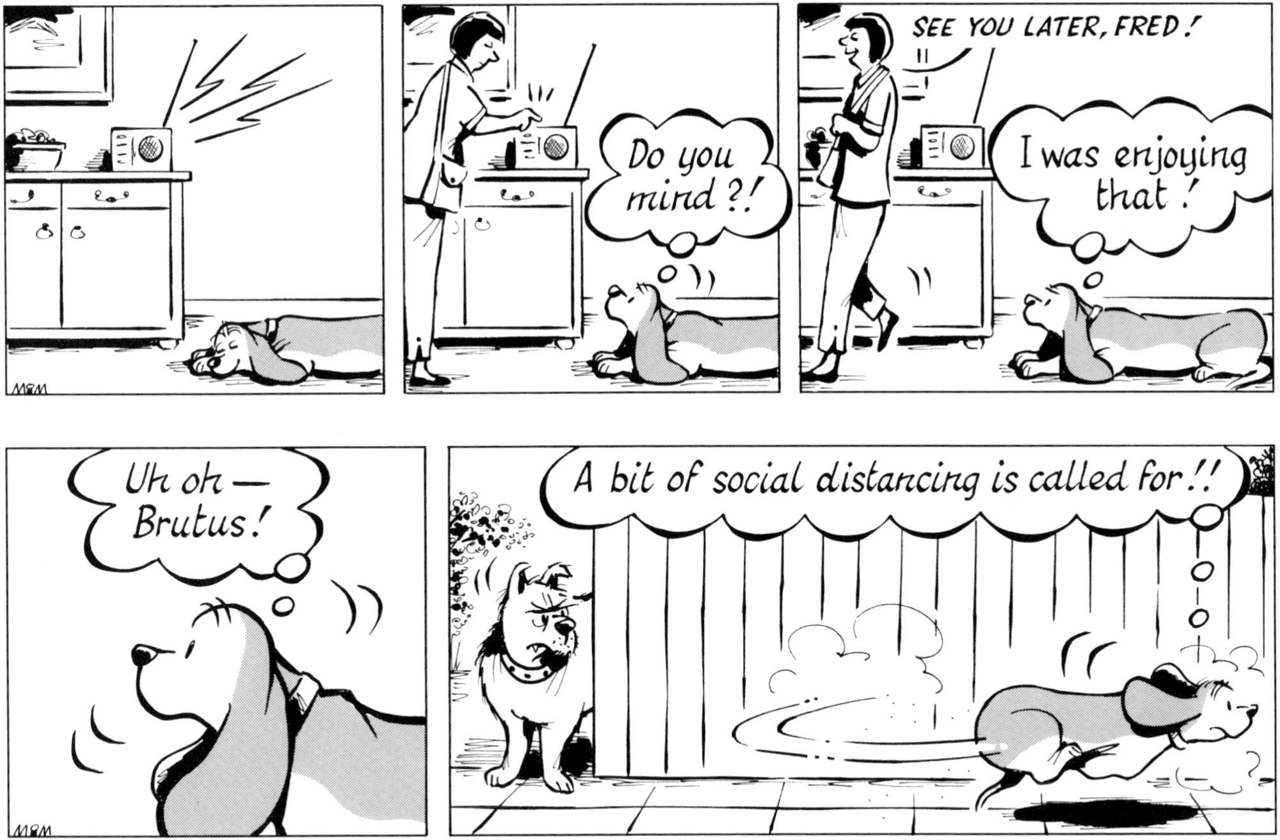
Do you mind?!
SEE YOU LATER, FRED!
I was enjoying that!
Uh oh — Brutus!
A bit of social distancing is called for!!

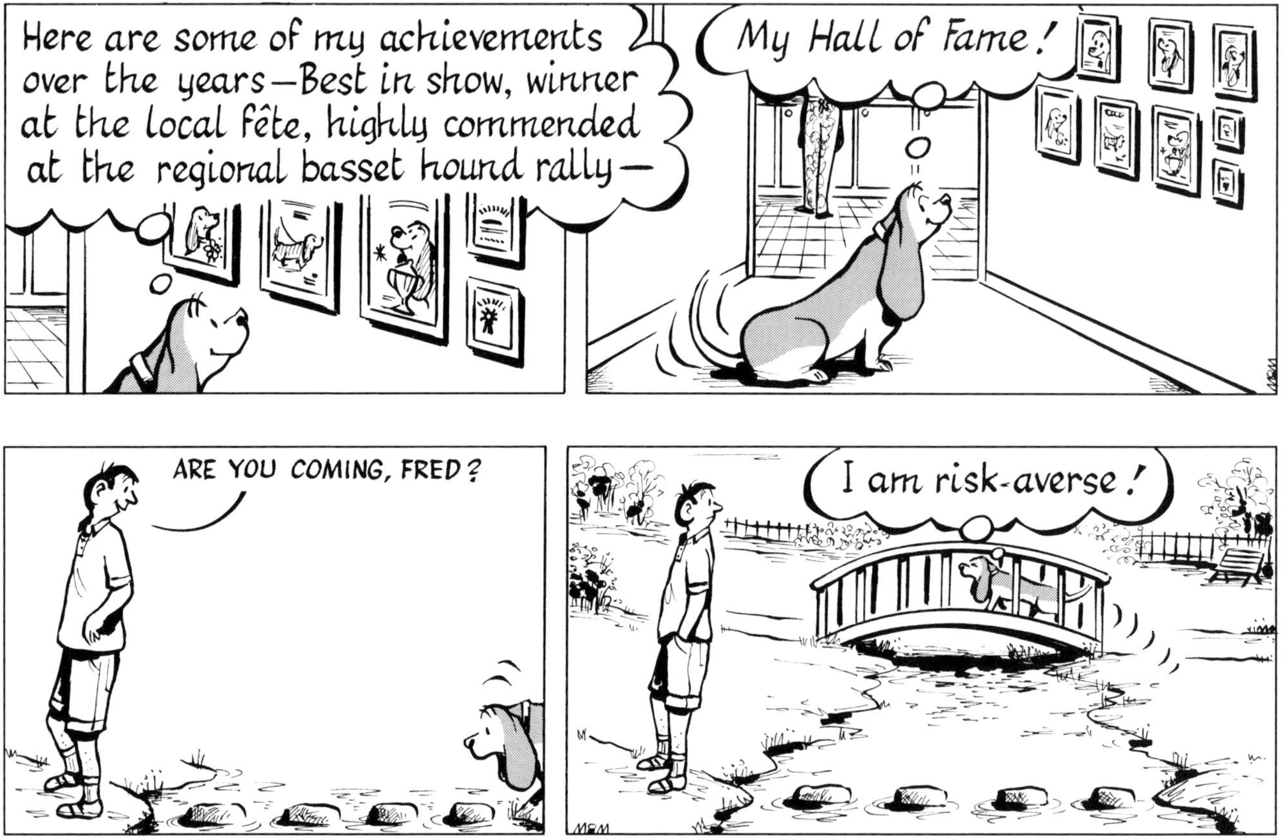
Here are some of my achievements over the years—Best in show, winner at the local fête, highly commended at the regional basset hound rally—
My Hall of Fame!
ARE YOU COMING, FRED?
I am risk-averse!

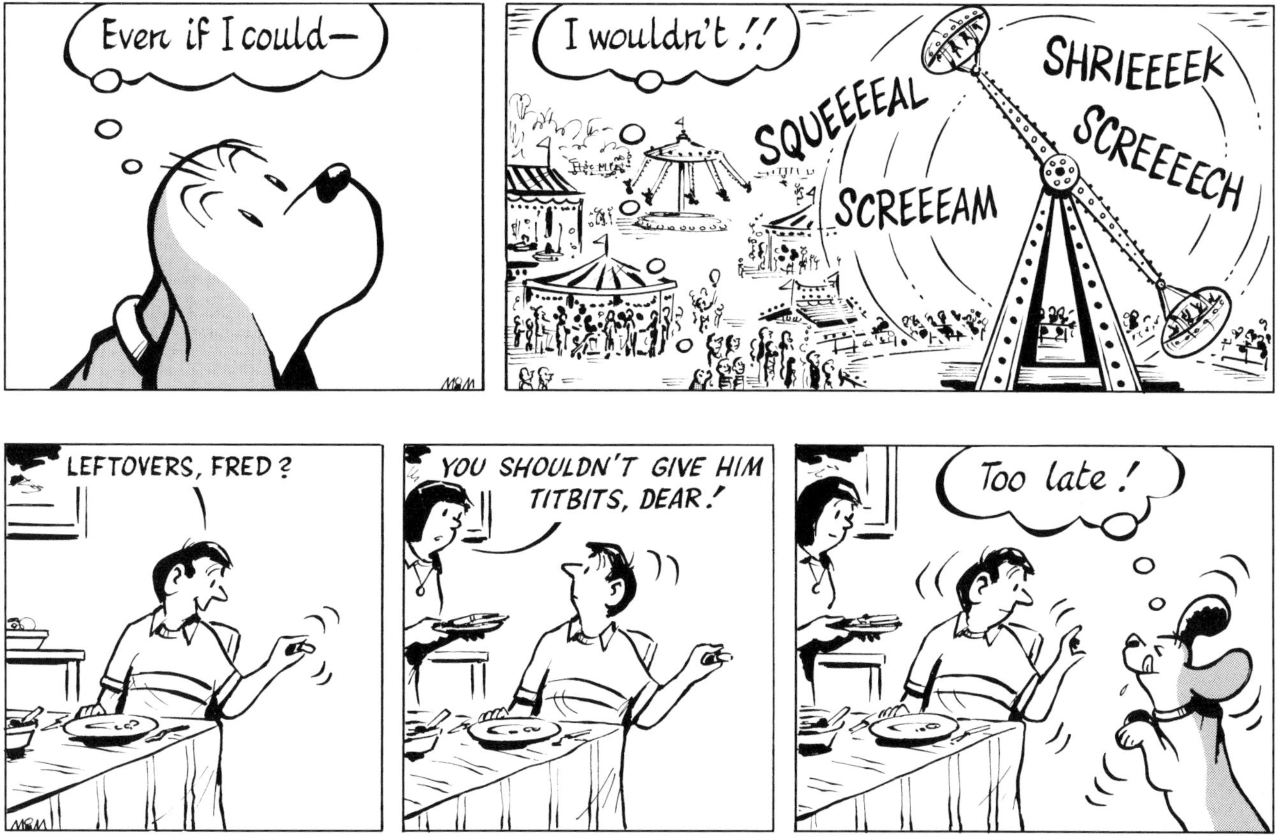
Even if I could—
I wouldn't !!
SQUEEEEAL
SHRIEEEEK
SCREEEEECH
SCREEEEAM
LEFTOVERS, FRED ?
YOU SHOULDN'T GIVE HIM TITBITS, DEAR !
Too late !

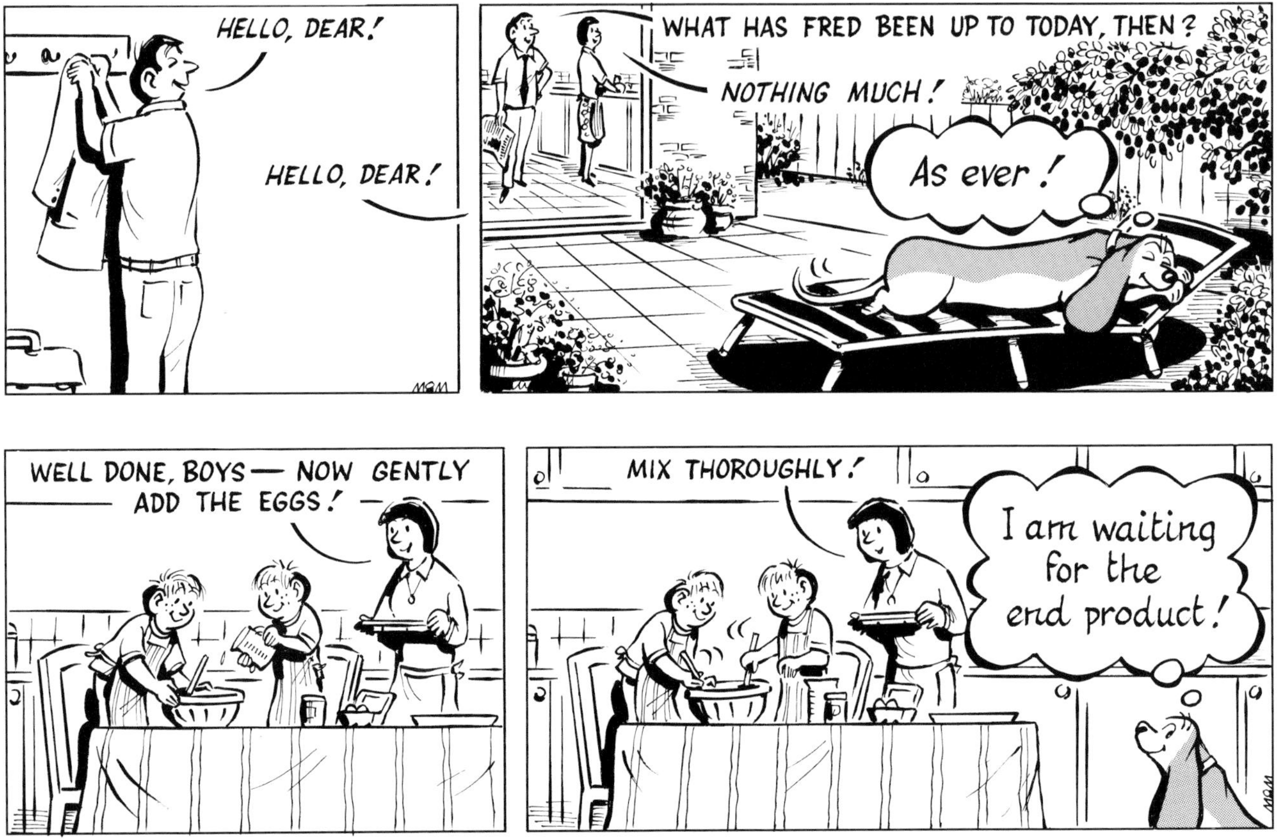

HELLO, DEAR!
HELLO, DEAR!
WHAT HAS FRED BEEN UP TO TODAY, THEN?
NOTHING MUCH!
As ever!
WELL DONE, BOYS — NOW GENTLY ADD THE EGGS!
MIX THOROUGHLY!
I am waiting for the end product!

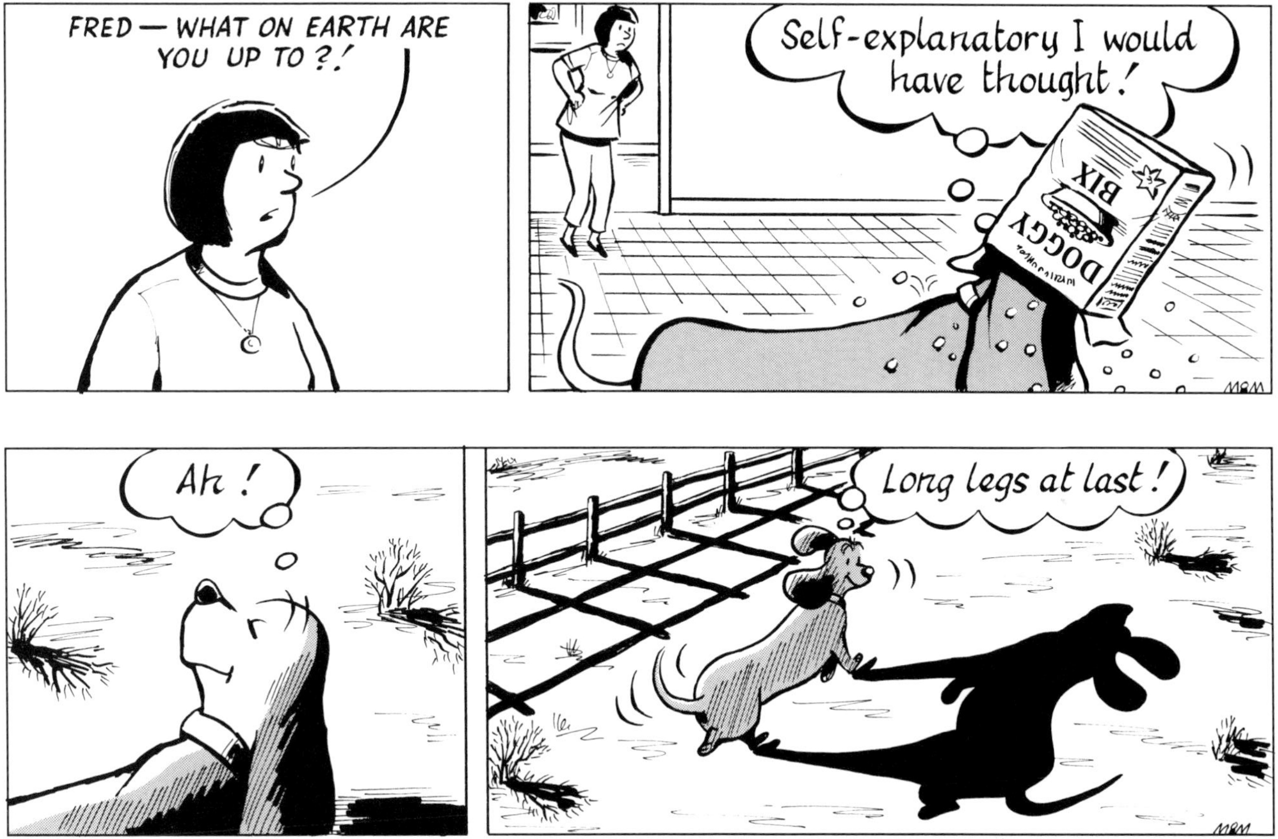
FRED — WHAT ON EARTH ARE YOU UP TO ?!
Self-explanatory I would have thought!
DOGGY BIX
Ah!
Long legs at last!

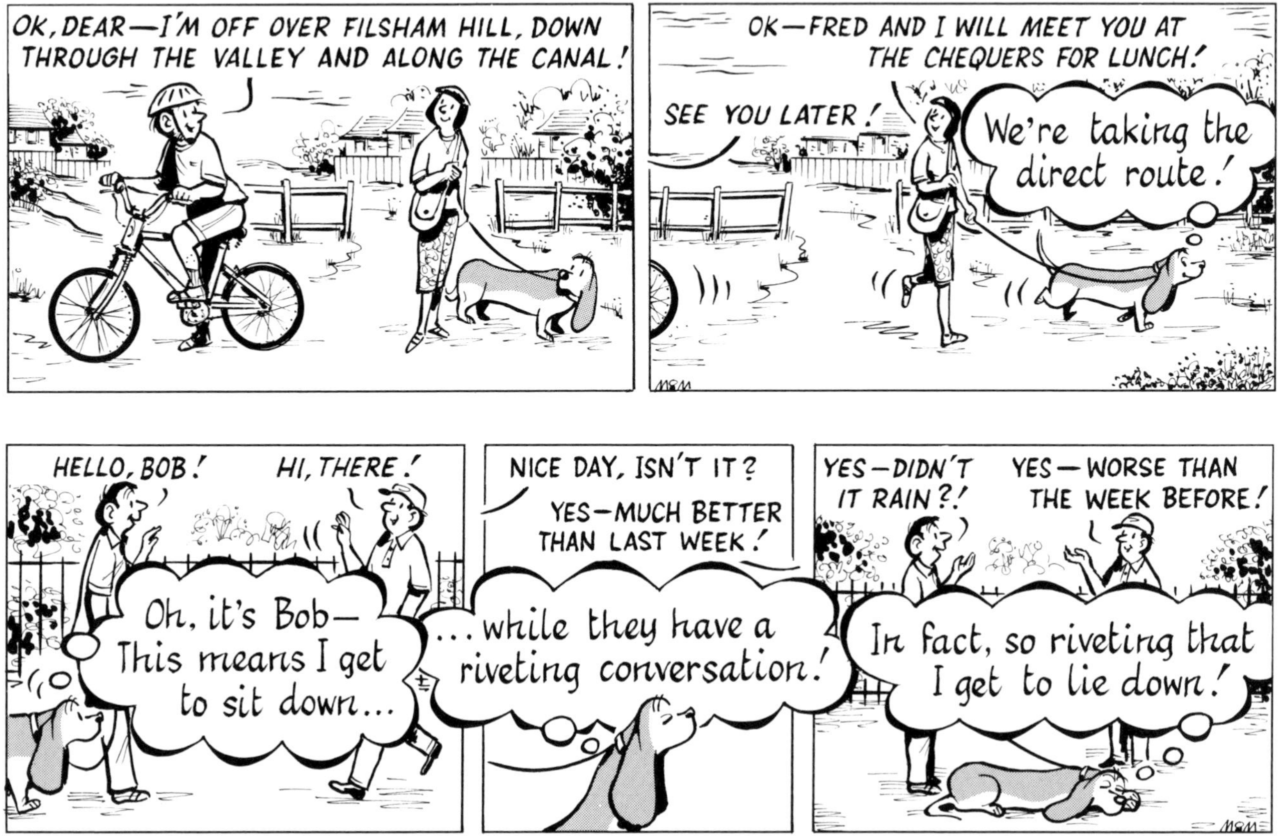
OK, DEAR—I'M OFF OVER FILSHAM HILL, DOWN THROUGH THE VALLEY AND ALONG THE CANAL!
OK—FRED AND I WILL MEET YOU AT THE CHEQUERS FOR LUNCH!
SEE YOU LATER!
We're taking the direct route!
HELLO, BOB!
HI, THERE!
Oh, it's Bob— This means I get to sit down...
NICE DAY, ISN'T IT?
YES—MUCH BETTER THAN LAST WEEK!
...while they have a riveting conversation!
YES—DIDN'T IT RAIN?!
YES—WORSE THAN THE WEEK BEFORE!
In fact, so riveting that I get to lie down!

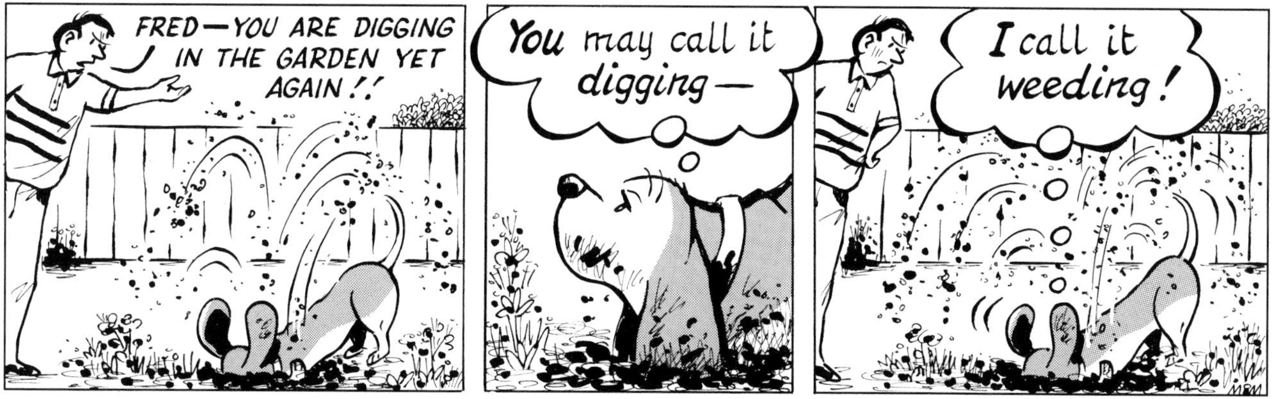
FRED—YOU ARE DIGGING IN THE GARDEN YET AGAIN!!
You may call it digging—
I call it weeding!

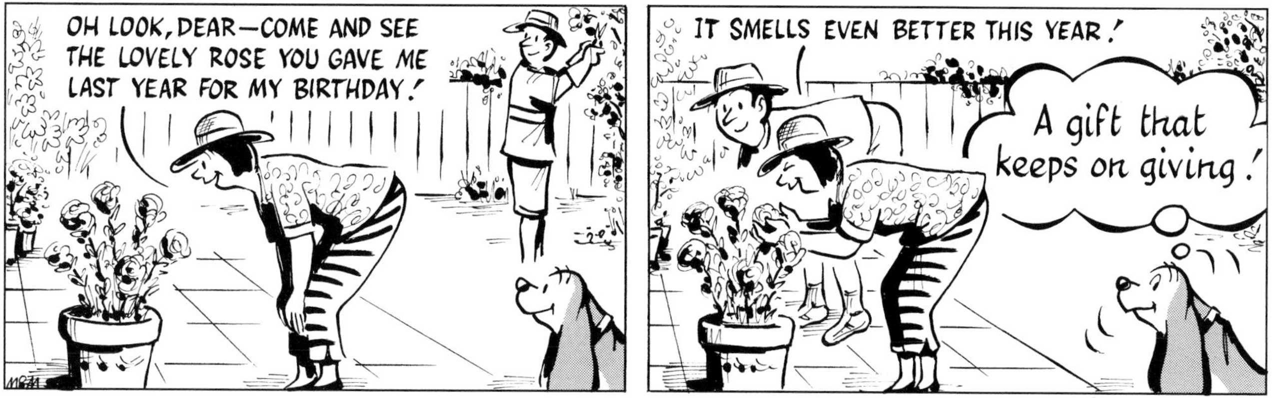
OH LOOK, DEAR—COME AND SEE THE LOVELY ROSE YOU GAVE ME LAST YEAR FOR MY BIRTHDAY!
IT SMELLS EVEN BETTER THIS YEAR!
A gift that keeps on giving!

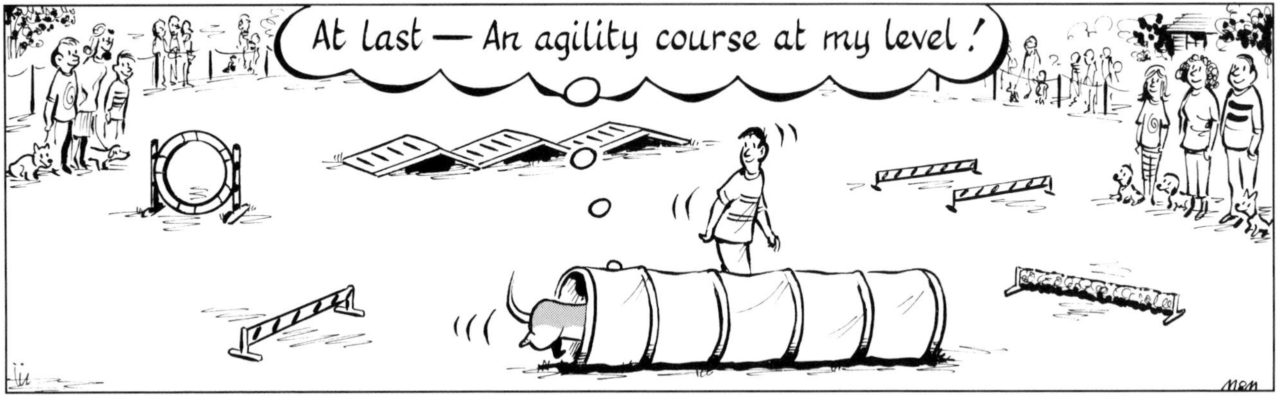
At last — An agility course at my level!

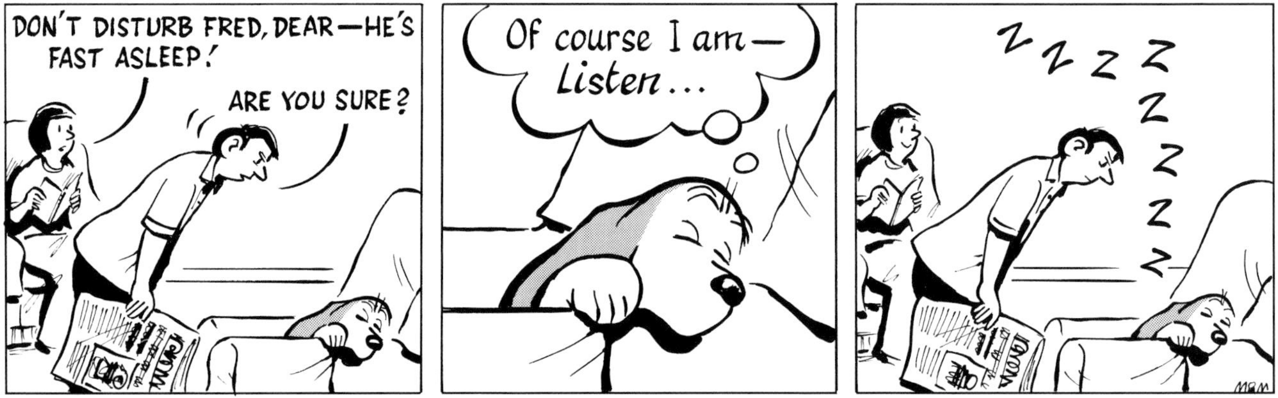
DON'T DISTURB FRED, DEAR—HE'S FAST ASLEEP!
ARE YOU SURE?
Of course I am— Listen...
Z Z Z Z Z Z Z Z Z

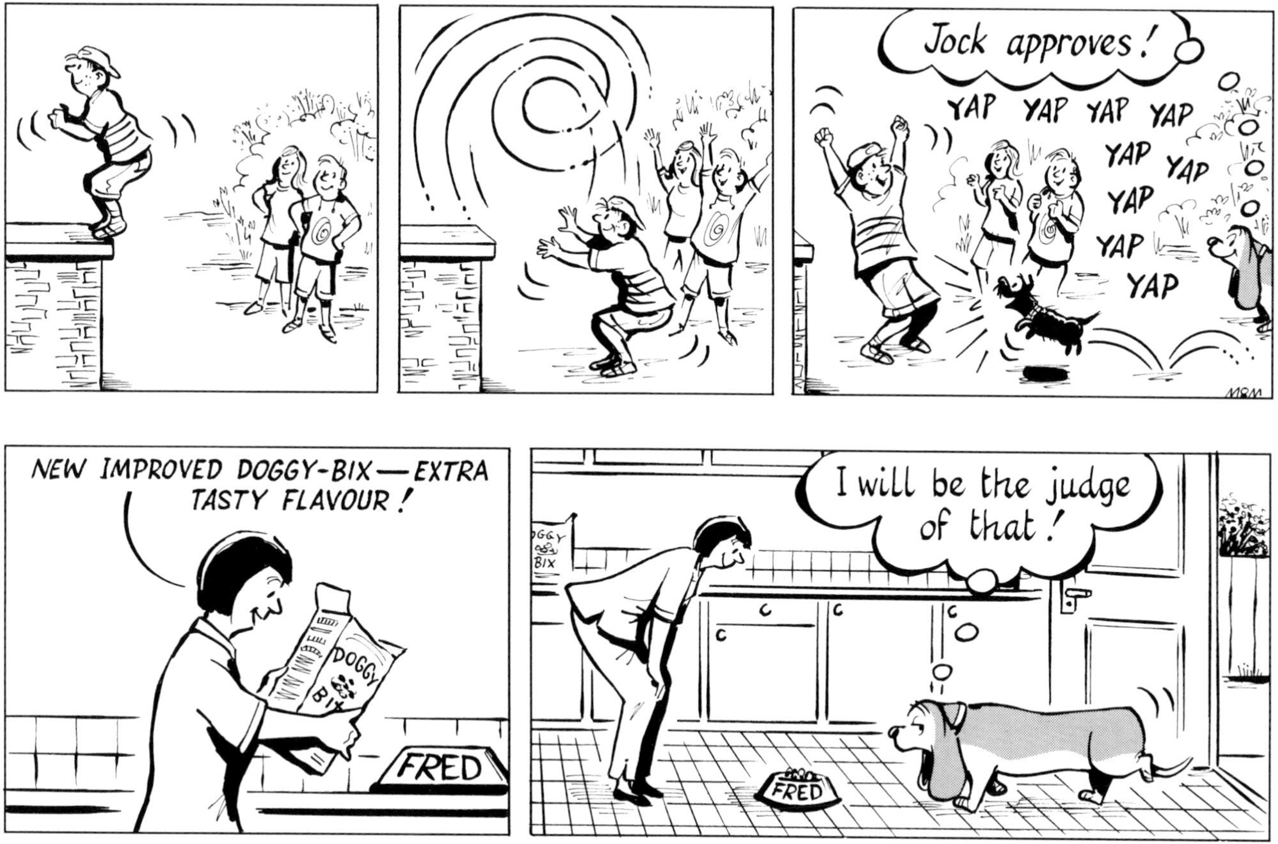

Jock approves!
YAP YAP YAP YAP YAP YAP YAP YAP YAP
NEW IMPROVED DOGGY-BIX — EXTRA TASTY FLAVOUR!
DOGGY BIX
FRED
I will be the judge of that!
DOGGY BIX
FRED

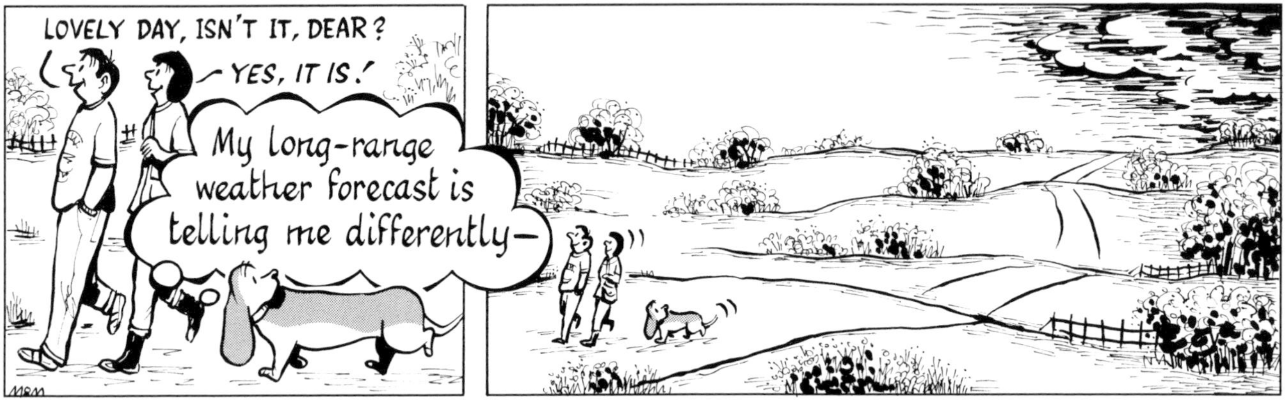
LOVELY DAY, ISN'T IT, DEAR?
YES, IT IS!
My long-range weather forecast is telling me differently—

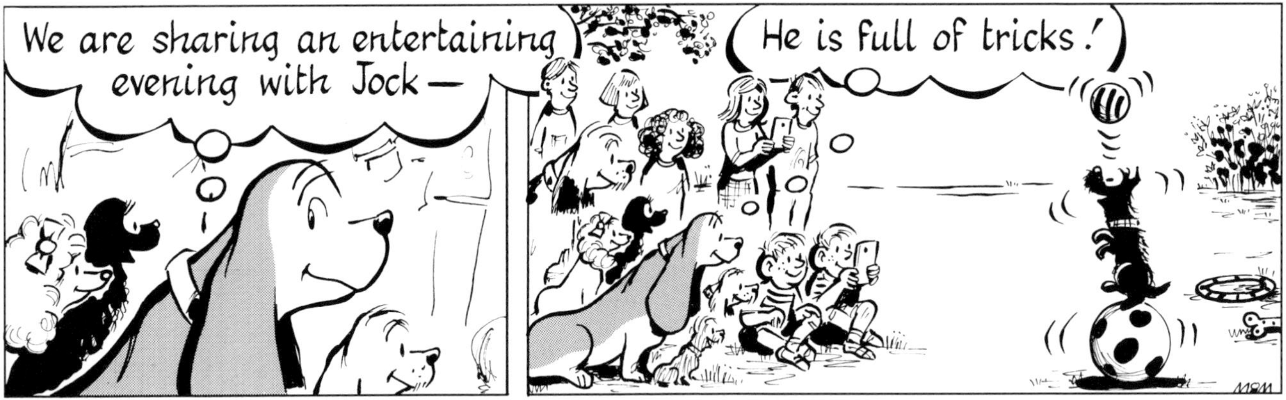
We are sharing an entertaining evening with Jock—
He is full of tricks!

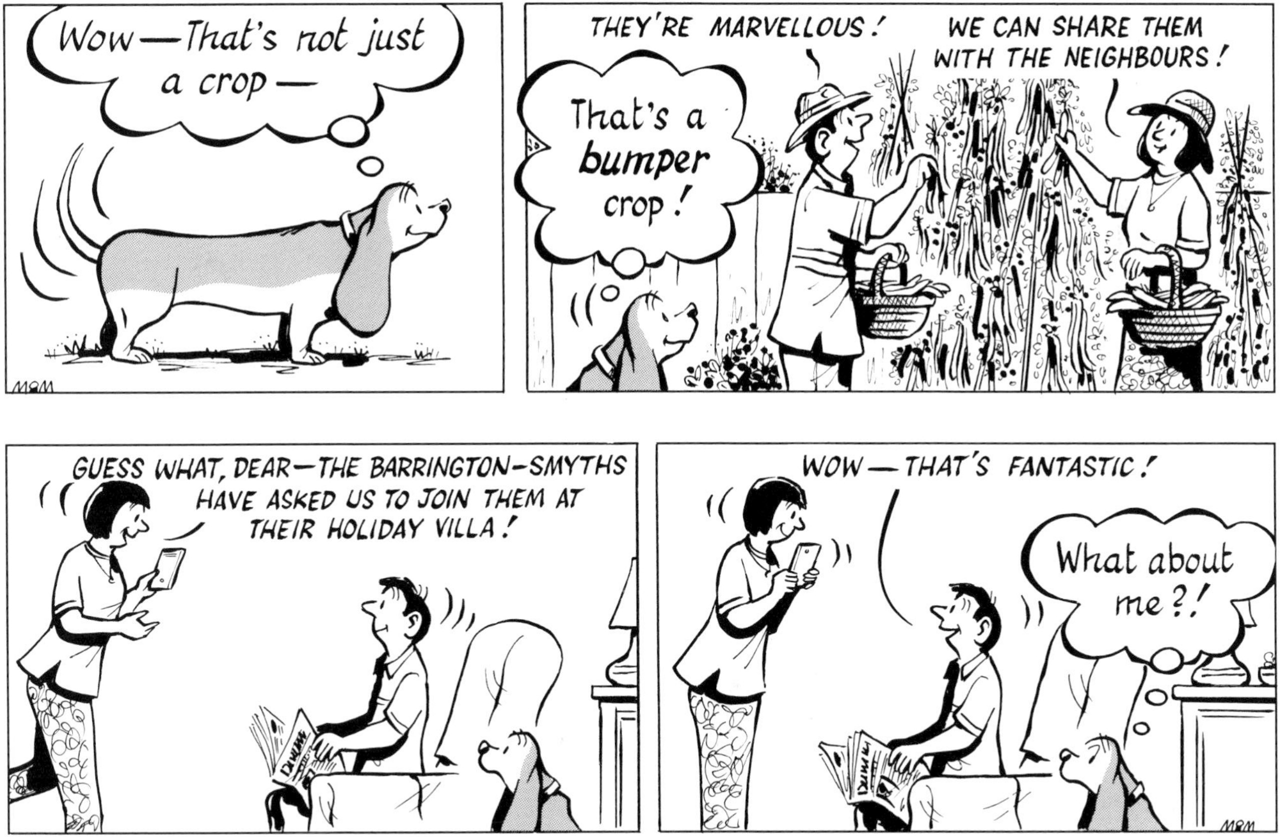
Wow—That's not just a crop—
THEY'RE MARVELLOUS!
WE CAN SHARE THEM WITH THE NEIGHBOURS!
That's a bumper crop!
GUESS WHAT, DEAR—THE BARRINGTON-SMYTHS HAVE ASKED US TO JOIN THEM AT THEIR HOLIDAY VILLA!
WOW—THAT'S FANTASTIC!
What about me?!

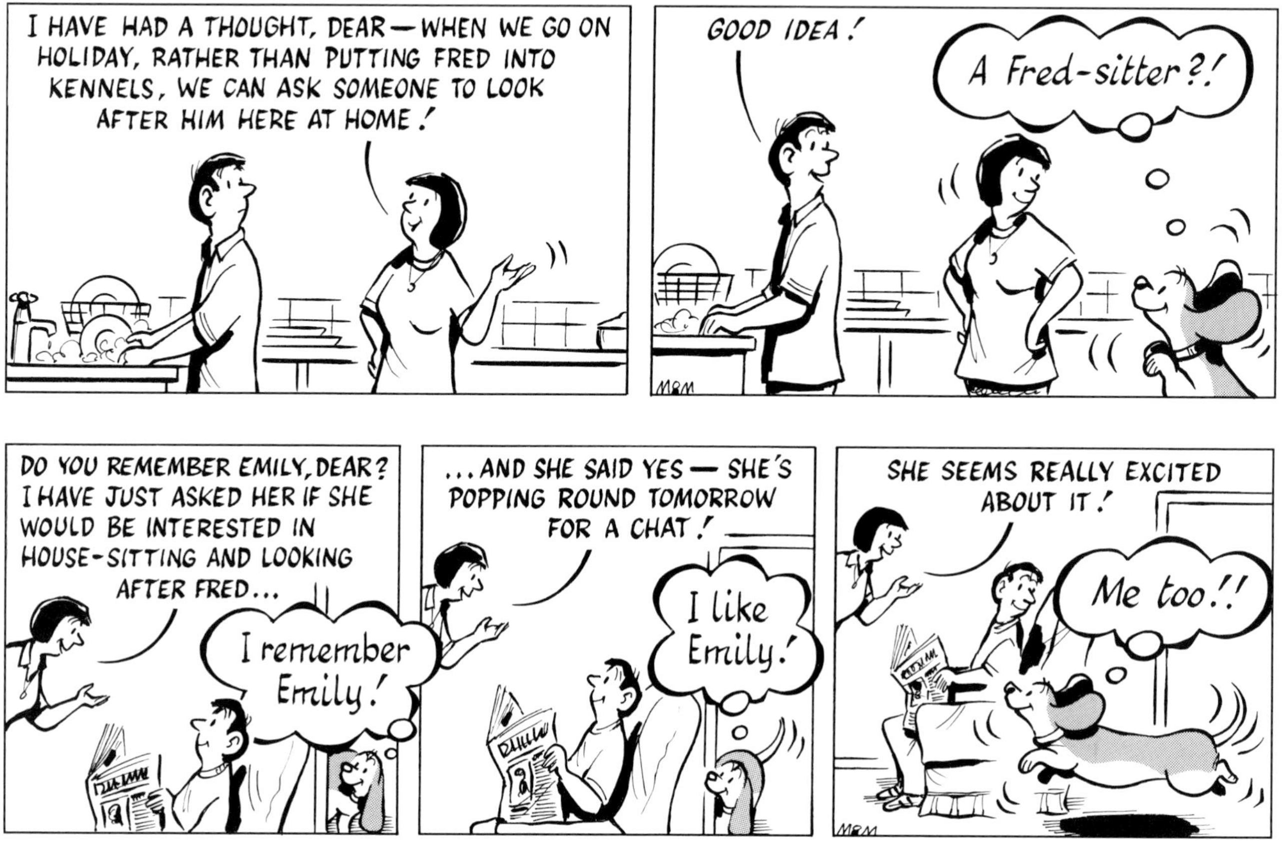
I HAVE HAD A THOUGHT, DEAR — WHEN WE GO ON HOLIDAY, RATHER THAN PUTTING FRED INTO KENNELS, WE CAN ASK SOMEONE TO LOOK AFTER HIM HERE AT HOME!
GOOD IDEA!
A Fred-sitter?!
MBM
DO YOU REMEMBER EMILY, DEAR? I HAVE JUST ASKED HER IF SHE WOULD BE INTERESTED IN HOUSE-SITTING AND LOOKING AFTER FRED...
I remember Emily!
...AND SHE SAID YES — SHE'S POPPING ROUND TOMORROW FOR A CHAT!
I like Emily!
SHE SEEMS REALLY EXCITED ABOUT IT!
Me too!!
MBM

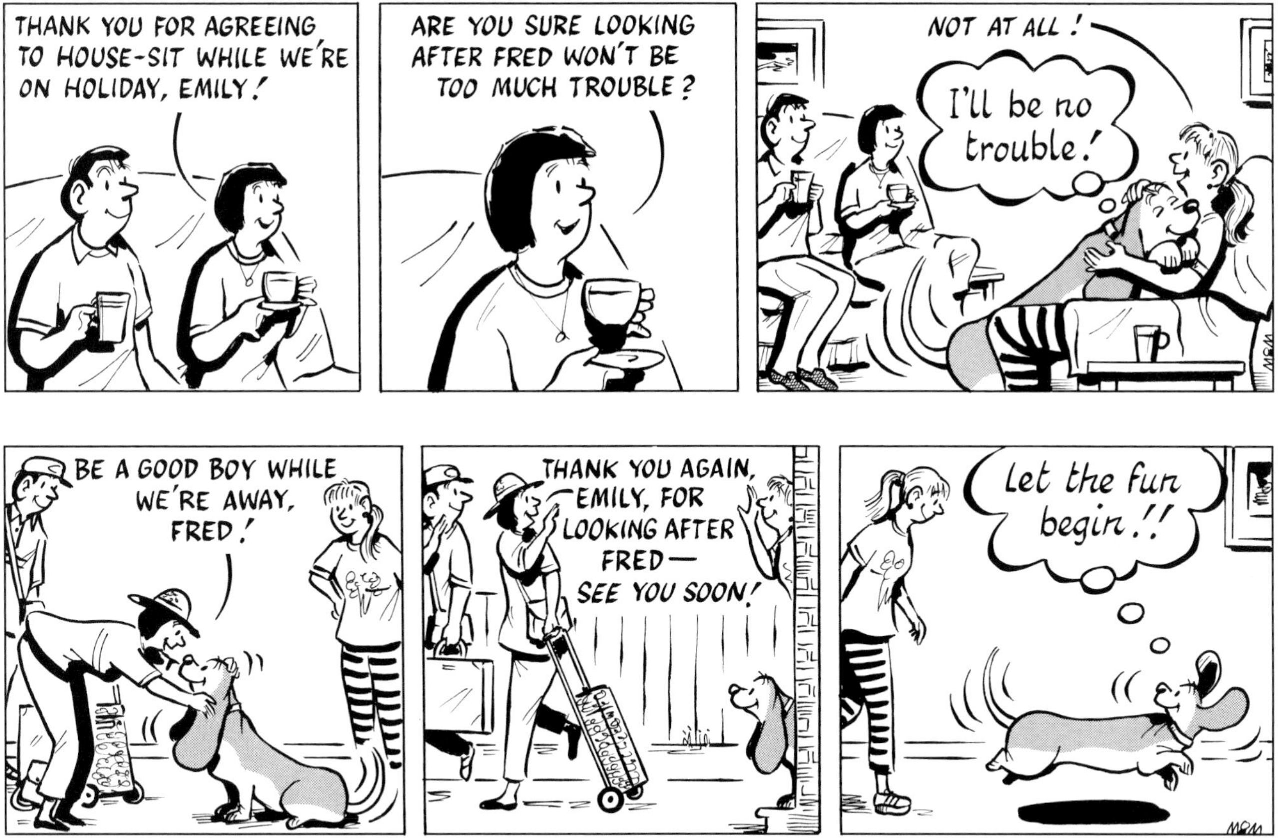
THANK YOU FOR AGREEING TO HOUSE-SIT WHILE WE'RE ON HOLIDAY, EMILY!
ARE YOU SURE LOOKING AFTER FRED WON'T BE TOO MUCH TROUBLE?
NOT AT ALL!
I'll be no trouble!
BE A GOOD BOY WHILE WE'RE AWAY, FRED!
THANK YOU AGAIN, EMILY, FOR LOOKING AFTER FRED— SEE YOU SOON!
Let the fun begin!!

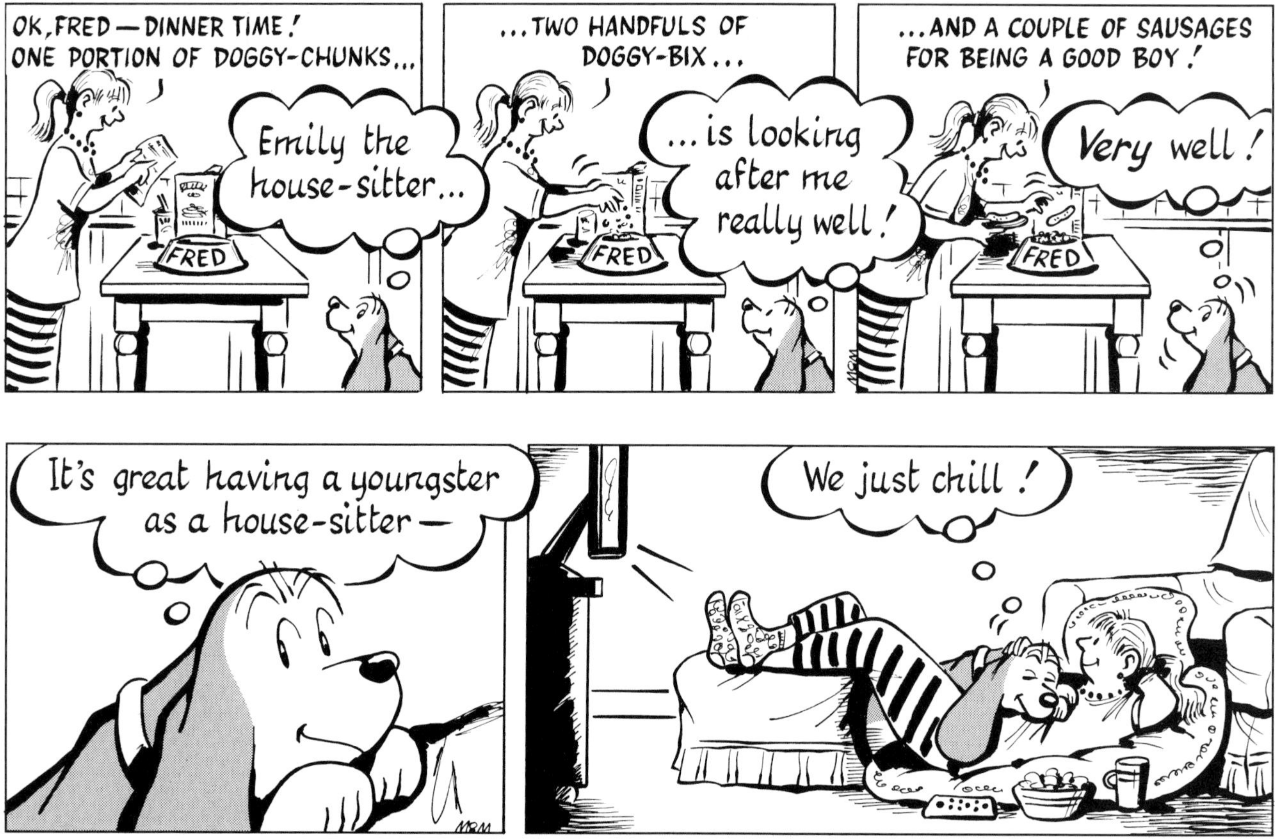
OK, FRED — DINNER TIME! ONE PORTION OF DOGGY-CHUNKS...
Emily the house-sitter...
FRED
...TWO HANDFULS OF DOGGY-BIX...
...is looking after me really well!
FRED
...AND A COUPLE OF SAUSAGES FOR BEING A GOOD BOY!
Very well!
FRED
It's great having a youngster as a house-sitter —
We just chill!

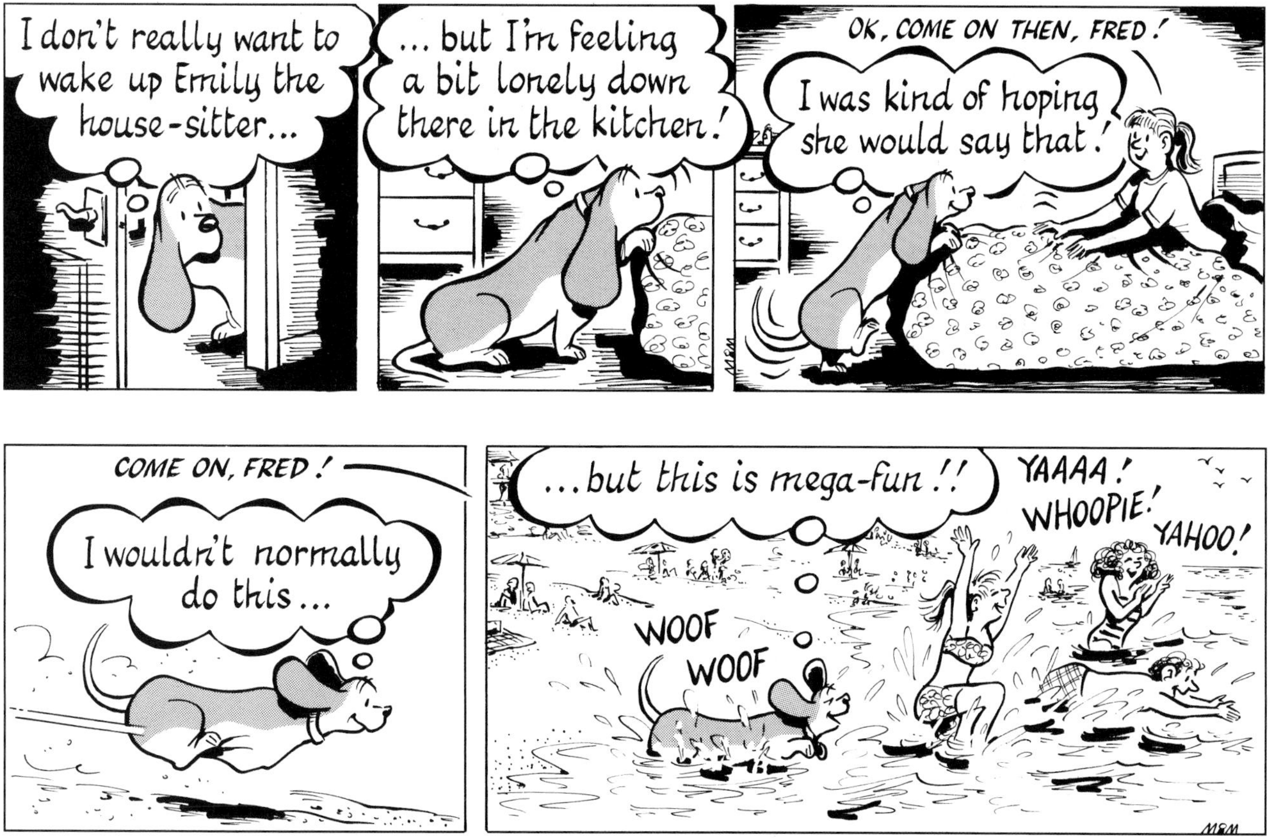
I don't really want to wake up Emily the house-sitter...
... but I'm feeling a bit lonely down there in the kitchen!
OK, COME ON THEN, FRED!
I was kind of hoping she would say that!
COME ON, FRED!
I wouldn't normally do this...
...but this is mega-fun!!
YAAAA!
WHOOPIE!
YAHOO!
WOOF
WOOF

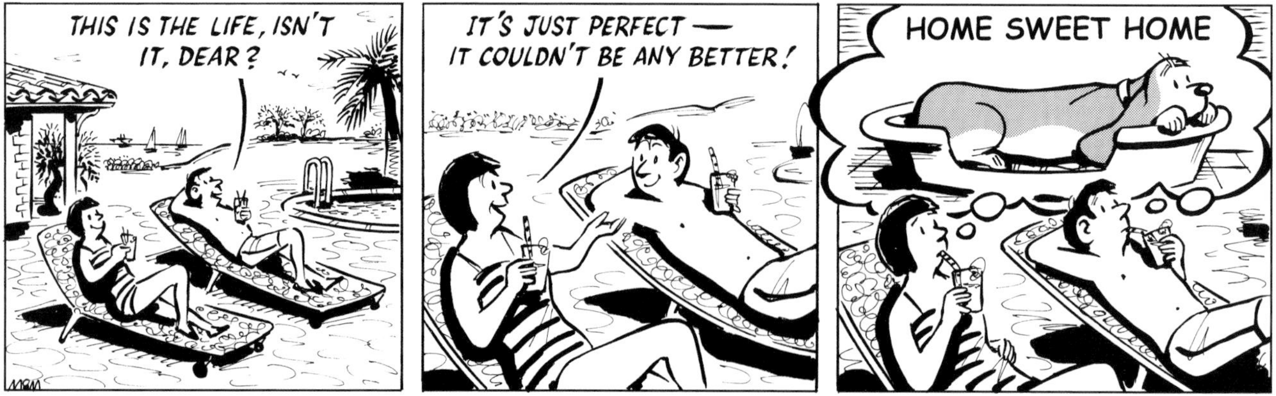
THIS IS THE LIFE, ISN'T IT, DEAR?
IT'S JUST PERFECT — IT COULDN'T BE ANY BETTER!
HOME SWEET HOME

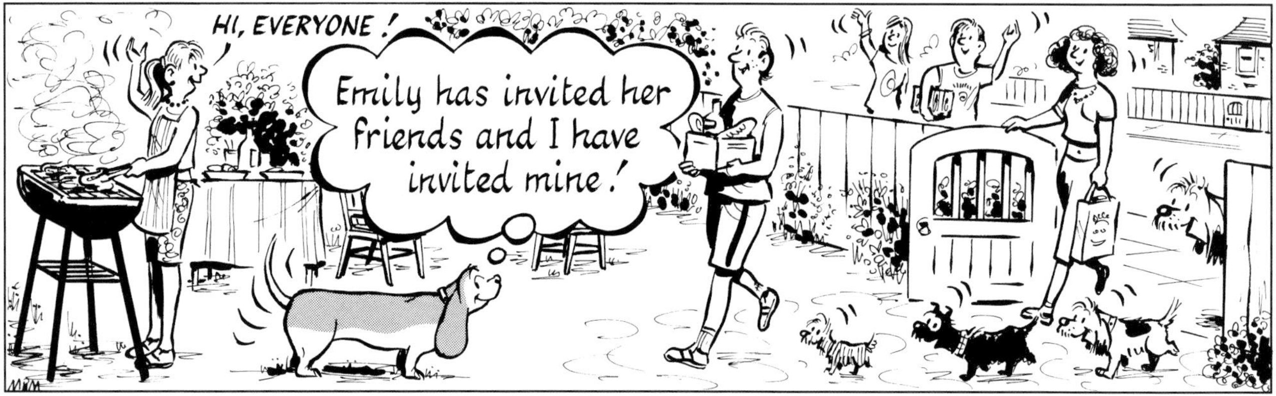
HI, EVERYONE!
Emily has invited her friends and I have invited mine!

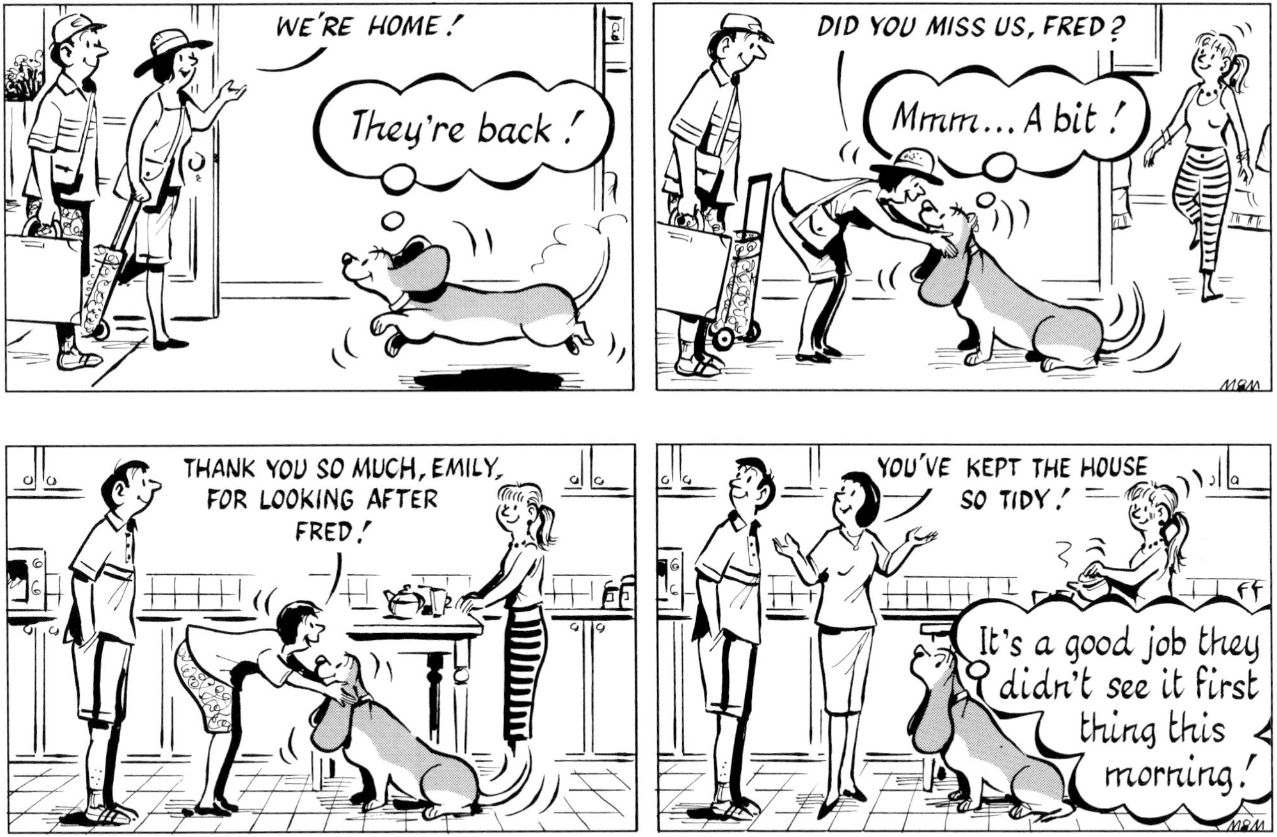
WE'RE HOME!
They're back!
DID YOU MISS US, FRED?
Mmm.... A bit!
THANK YOU SO MUCH, EMILY, FOR LOOKING AFTER FRED!
YOU'VE KEPT THE HOUSE SO TIDY!
It's a good job they didn't see it first thing this morning!

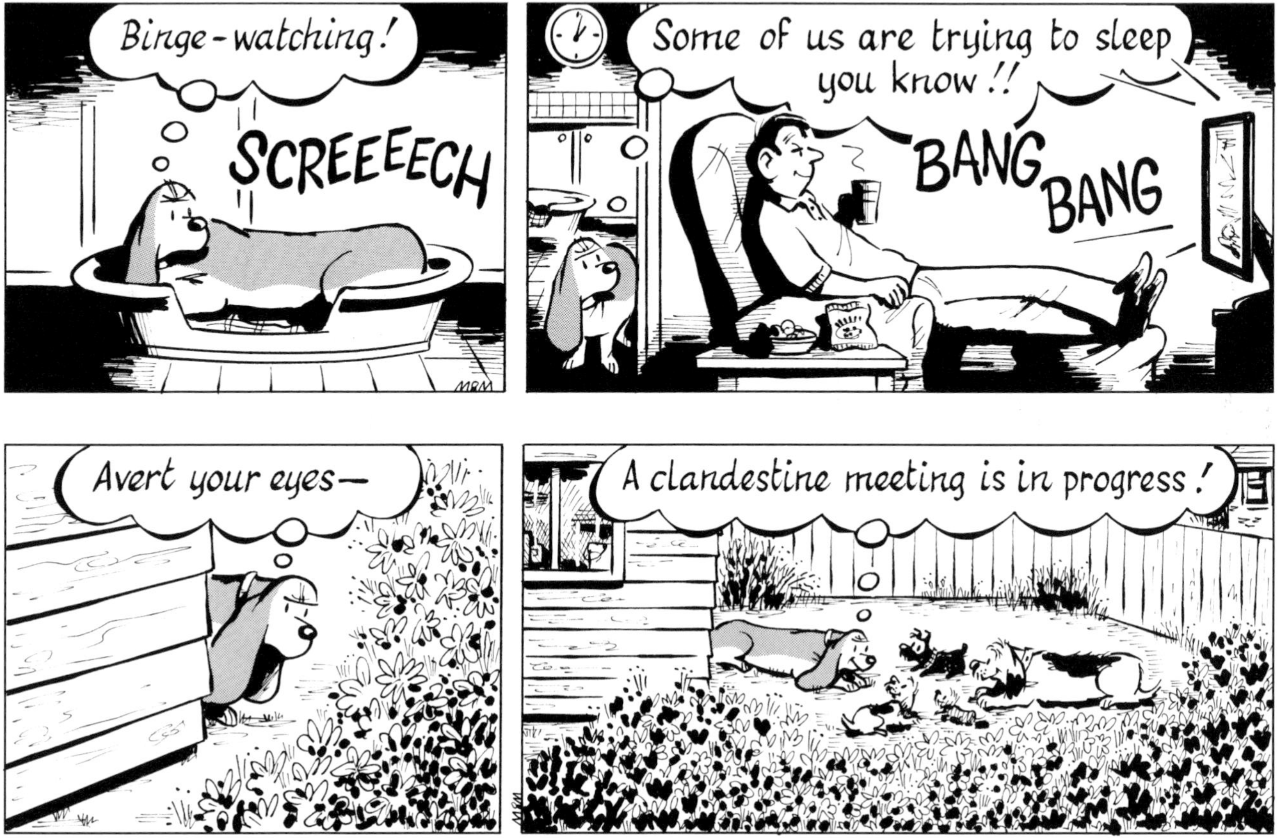
Binge-watching!
SCREEEECH
Some of us are trying to sleep you know!!
BANG BANG
Avert your eyes—
A clandestine meeting is in progress!

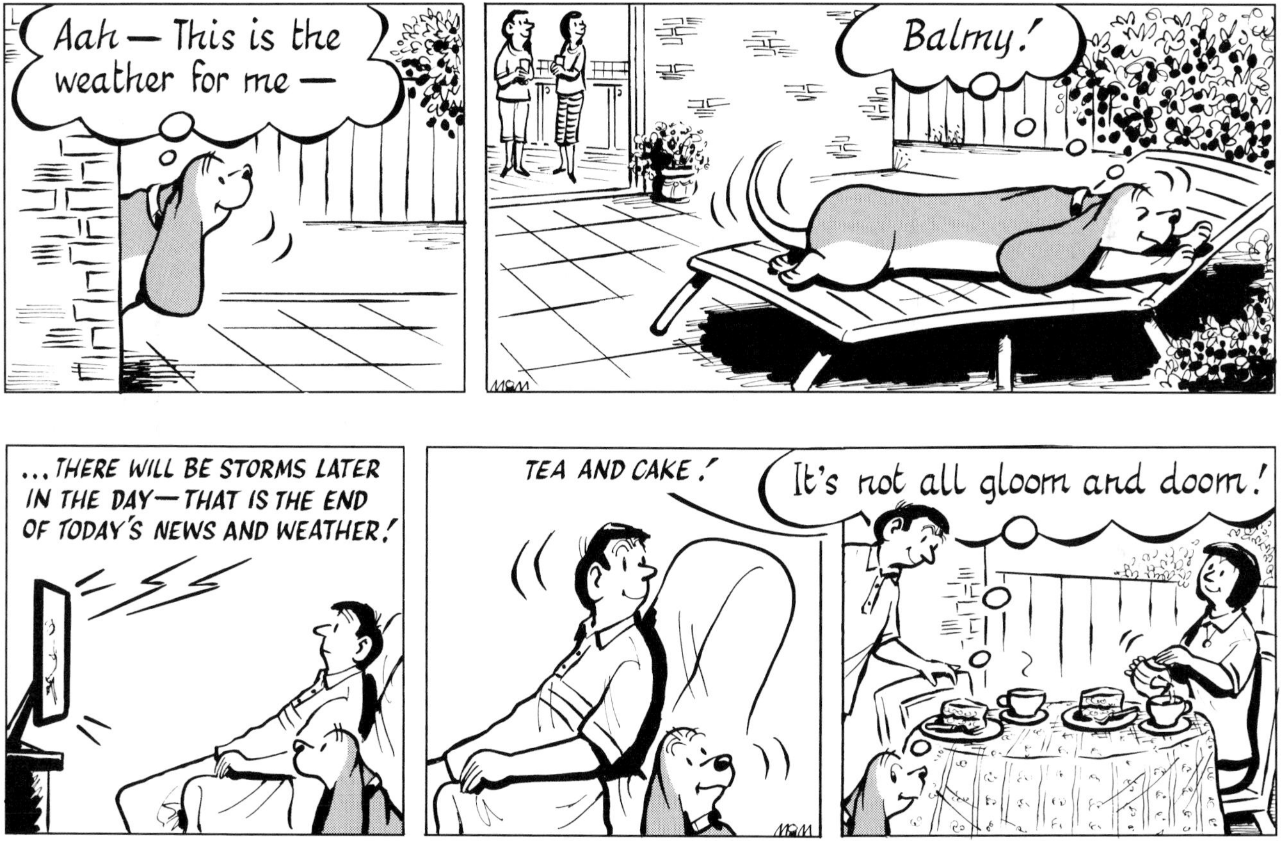
Aah — This is the weather for me —
Balmy!
MOM
...THERE WILL BE STORMS LATER IN THE DAY — THAT IS THE END OF TODAY'S NEWS AND WEATHER!
TEA AND CAKE!
It's not all gloom and doom!
MOM

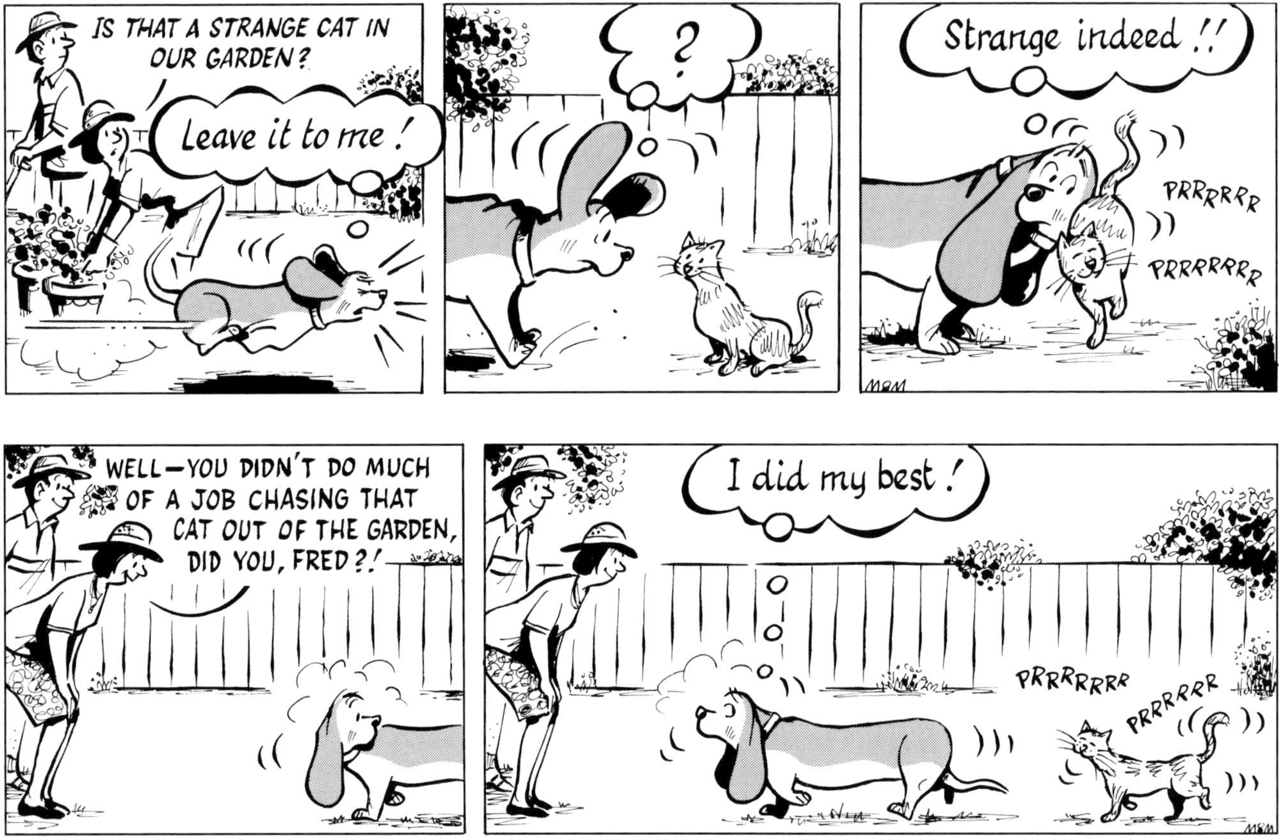
IS THAT A STRANGE CAT IN OUR GARDEN?
Leave it to me!
?
Strange indeed!!
PRRRRRR
PRRRRRRR
M&M
WELL—YOU DIDN'T DO MUCH OF A JOB CHASING THAT CAT OUT OF THE GARDEN, DID YOU, FRED?!
I did my best!
PRRRRRRR
PRRRRRR
M&M

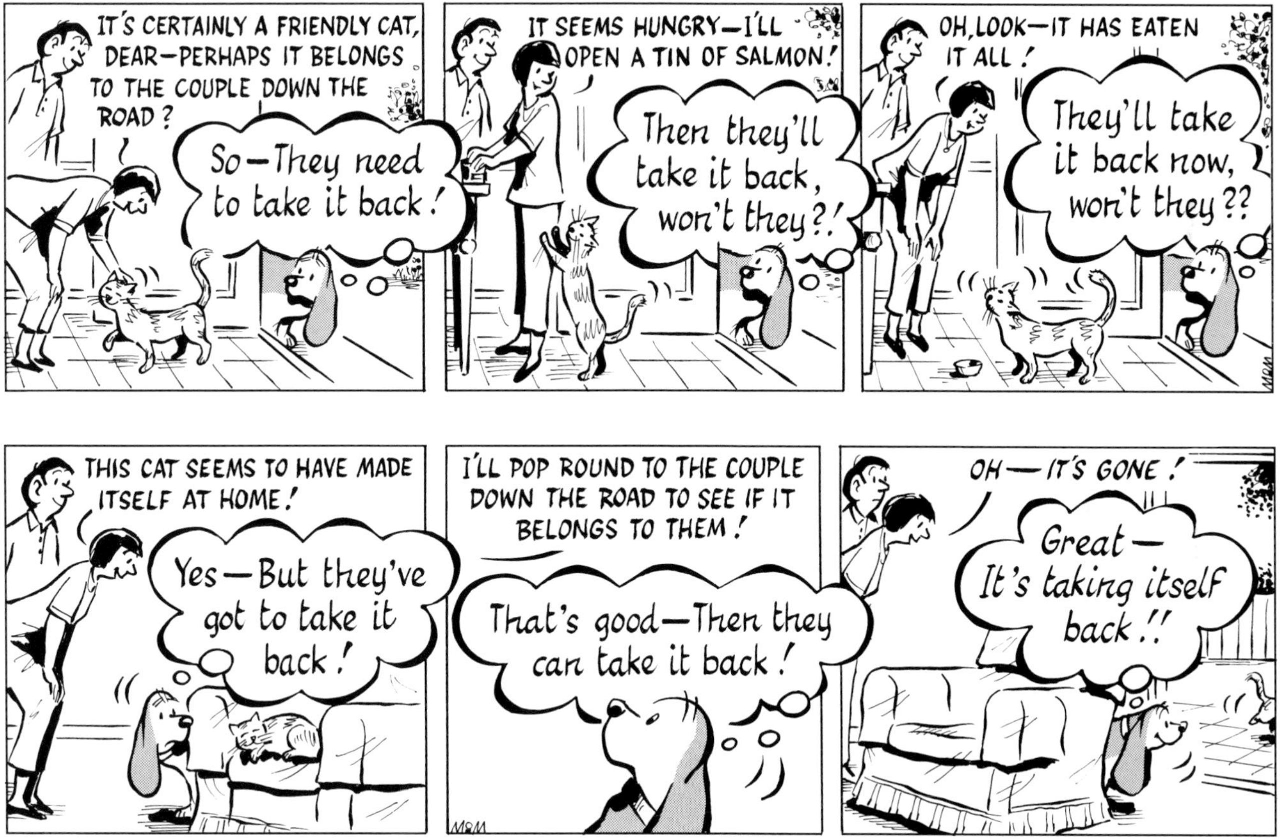
IT'S CERTAINLY A FRIENDLY CAT, DEAR—PERHAPS IT BELONGS TO THE COUPLE DOWN THE ROAD ?
So—They need to take it back!
IT SEEMS HUNGRY—I'LL OPEN A TIN OF SALMON!
Then they'll take it back, won't they?!
OH, LOOK—IT HAS EATEN IT ALL!
They'll take it back now, won't they??
THIS CAT SEEMS TO HAVE MADE ITSELF AT HOME!
Yes—But they've got to take it back!
I'LL POP ROUND TO THE COUPLE DOWN THE ROAD TO SEE IF IT BELONGS TO THEM!
That's good—Then they can take it back!
OH—IT'S GONE!
Great—It's taking itself back!!

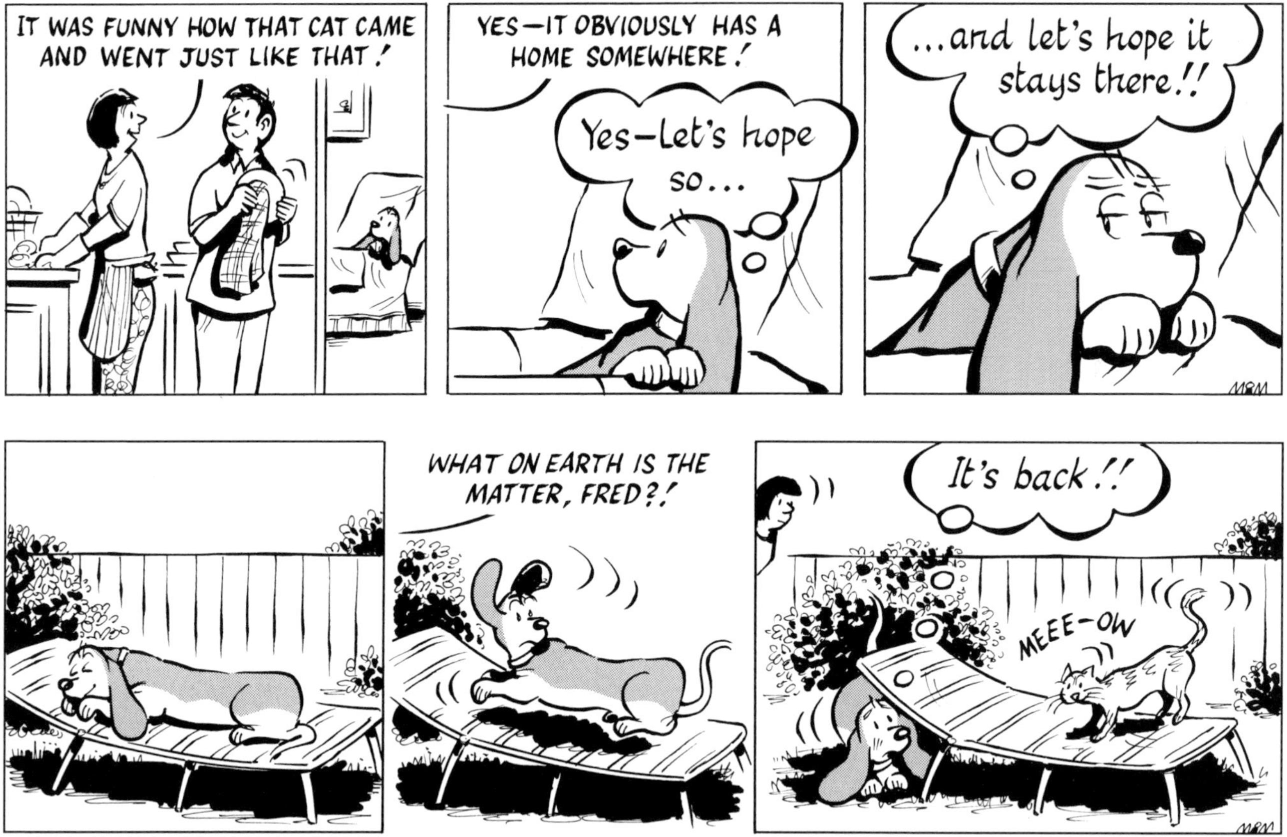
IT WAS FUNNY HOW THAT CAT CAME AND WENT JUST LIKE THAT!
YES—IT OBVIOUSLY HAS A HOME SOMEWHERE!
Yes–let's hope so...
...and let's hope it stays there!!
M&M
WHAT ON EARTH IS THE MATTER, FRED?!
It's back!!
MEEE-OW
M&M

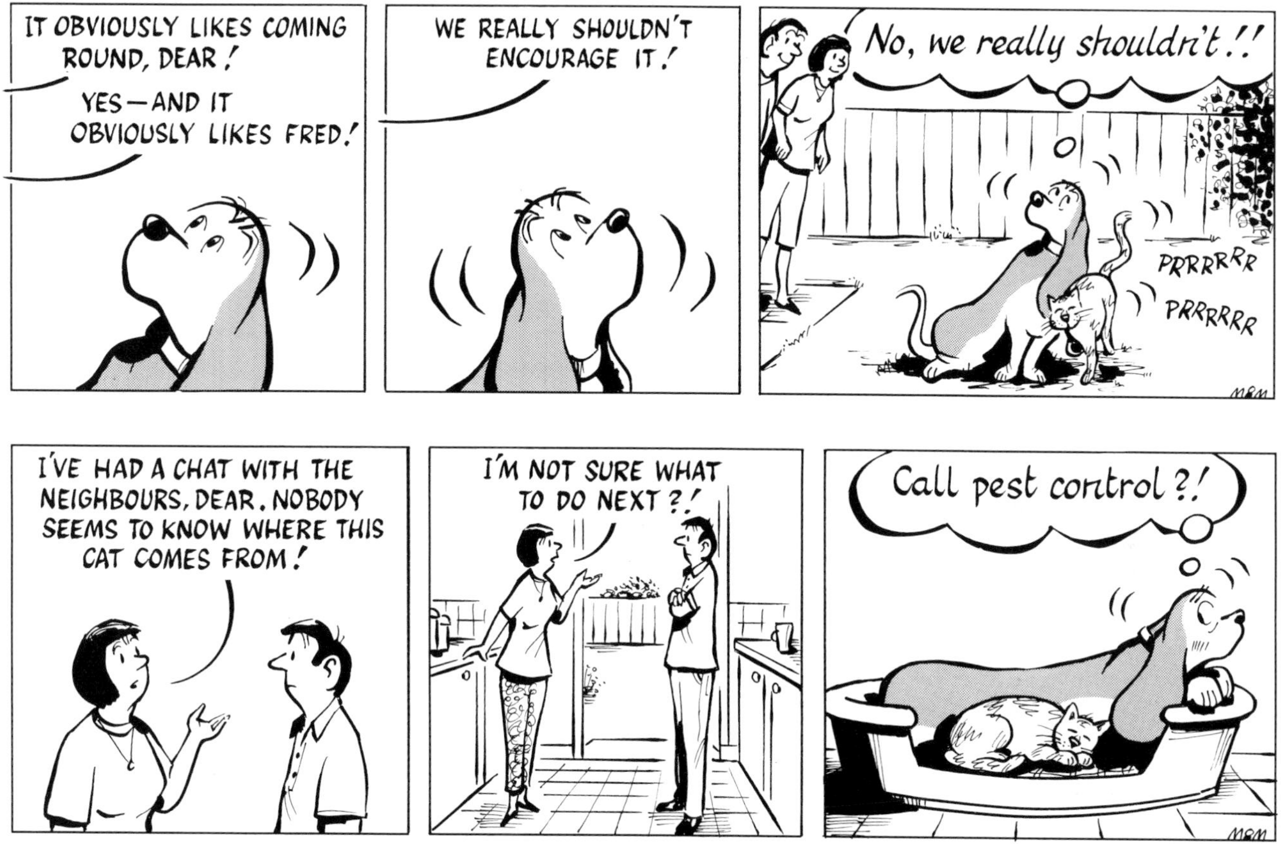
IT OBVIOUSLY LIKES COMING ROUND, DEAR!
YES—AND IT OBVIOUSLY LIKES FRED!
WE REALLY SHOULDN'T ENCOURAGE IT!
No, we really shouldn't!!
PRRRRRR
PRRRRRR
MGM
I'VE HAD A CHAT WITH THE NEIGHBOURS, DEAR. NOBODY SEEMS TO KNOW WHERE THIS CAT COMES FROM!
I'M NOT SURE WHAT TO DO NEXT?!
Call pest control?!
MGM

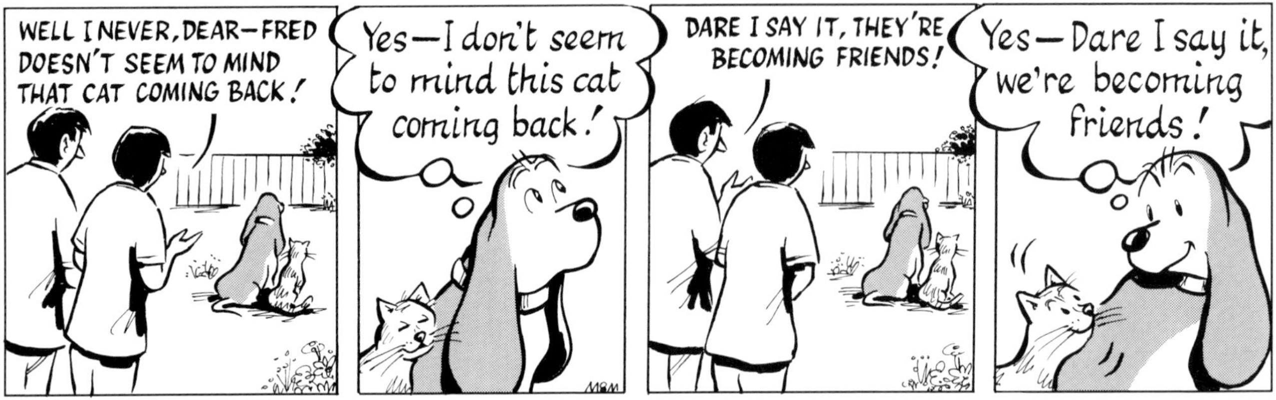
WELL I NEVER, DEAR—FRED DOESN'T SEEM TO MIND THAT CAT COMING BACK!
Yes—I don't seem to mind this cat coming back!
DARE I SAY IT, THEY'RE BECOMING FRIENDS!
Yes—Dare I say it, we're becoming friends!

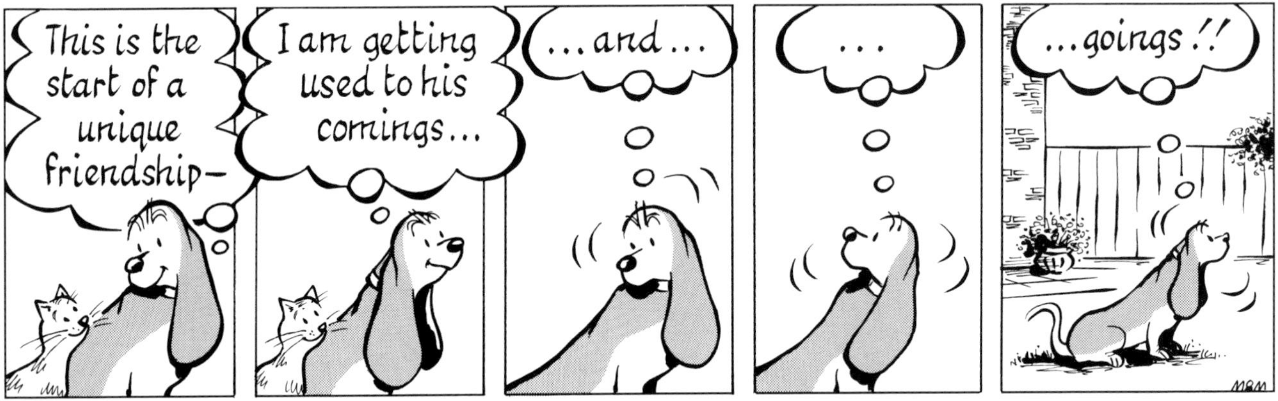
This is the start of a unique friendship—
I am getting used to his comings...
...and...
...
...goings!!

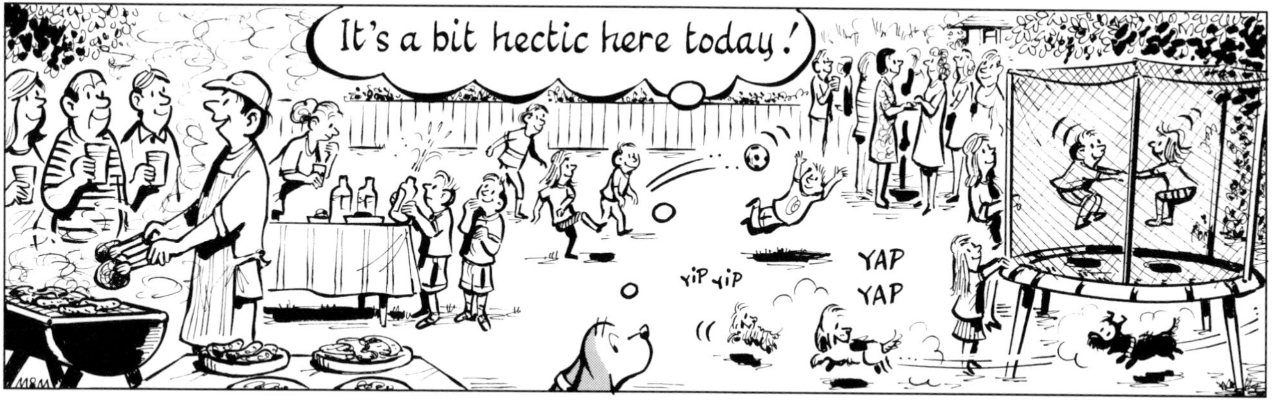
It's a bit hectic here today!
YIP YIP
YAP YAP

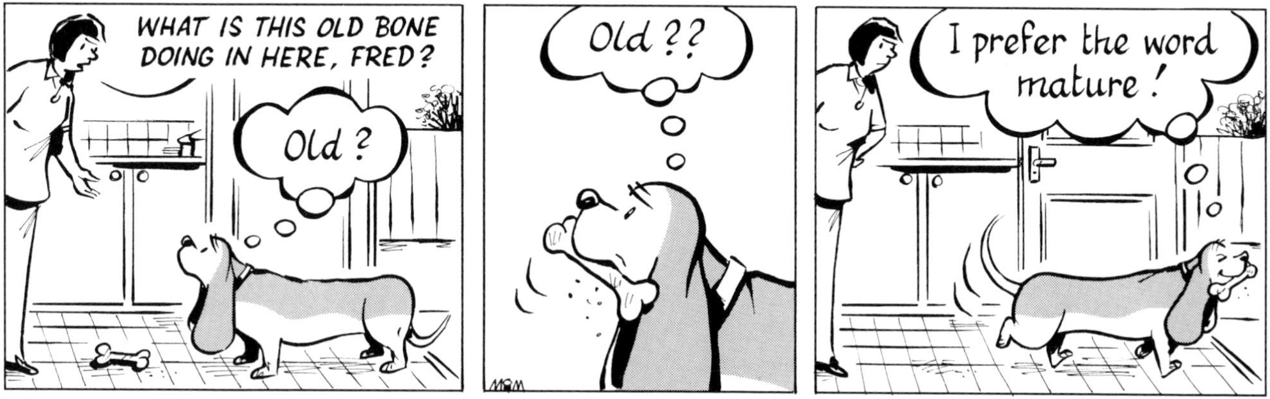
WHAT IS THIS OLD BONE DOING IN HERE, FRED?
Old?
Old??
I prefer the word mature!

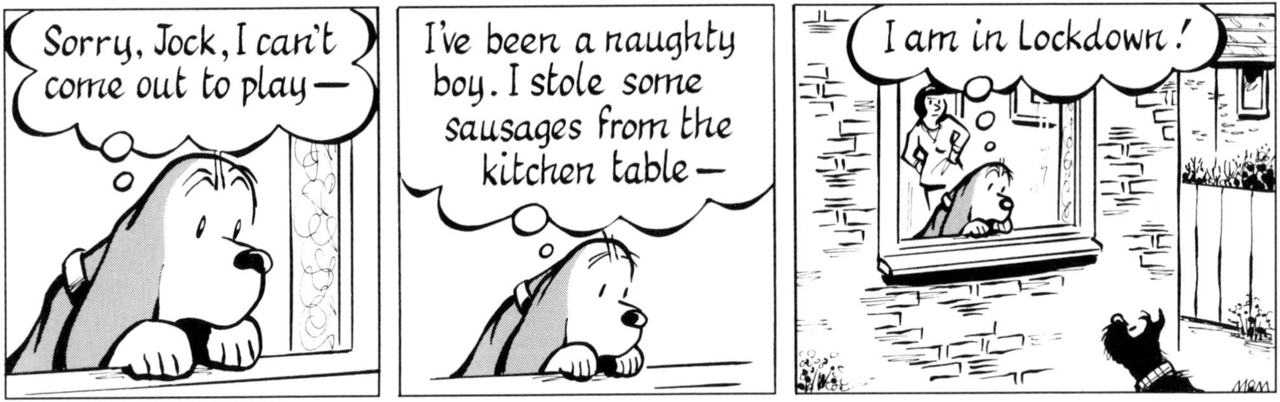
Sorry, Jock, I can't come out to play—
I've been a naughty boy. I stole some sausages from the kitchen table—
I am in Lockdown!
MGM

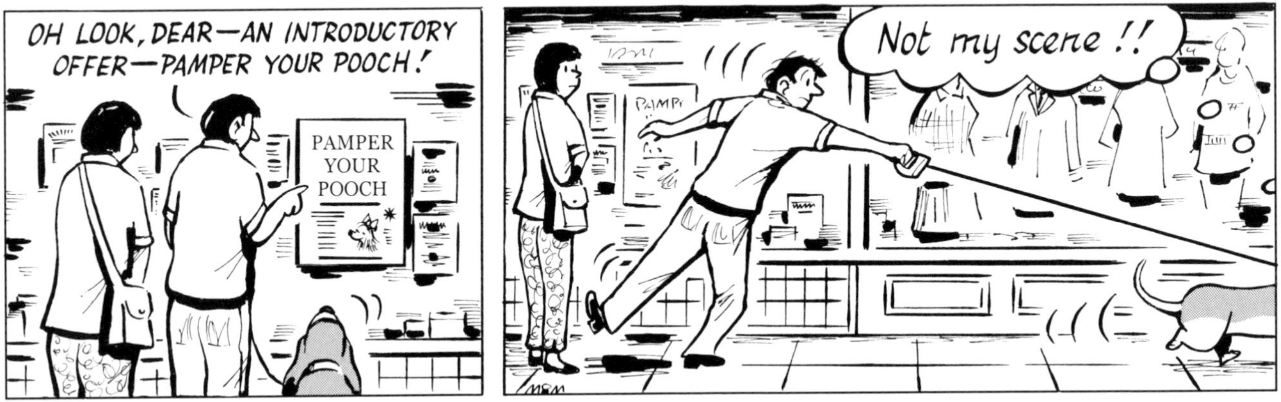
OH LOOK, DEAR—AN INTRODUCTORY OFFER—PAMPER YOUR POOCH!
PAMPER YOUR POOCH
Not my scene!!
MGM

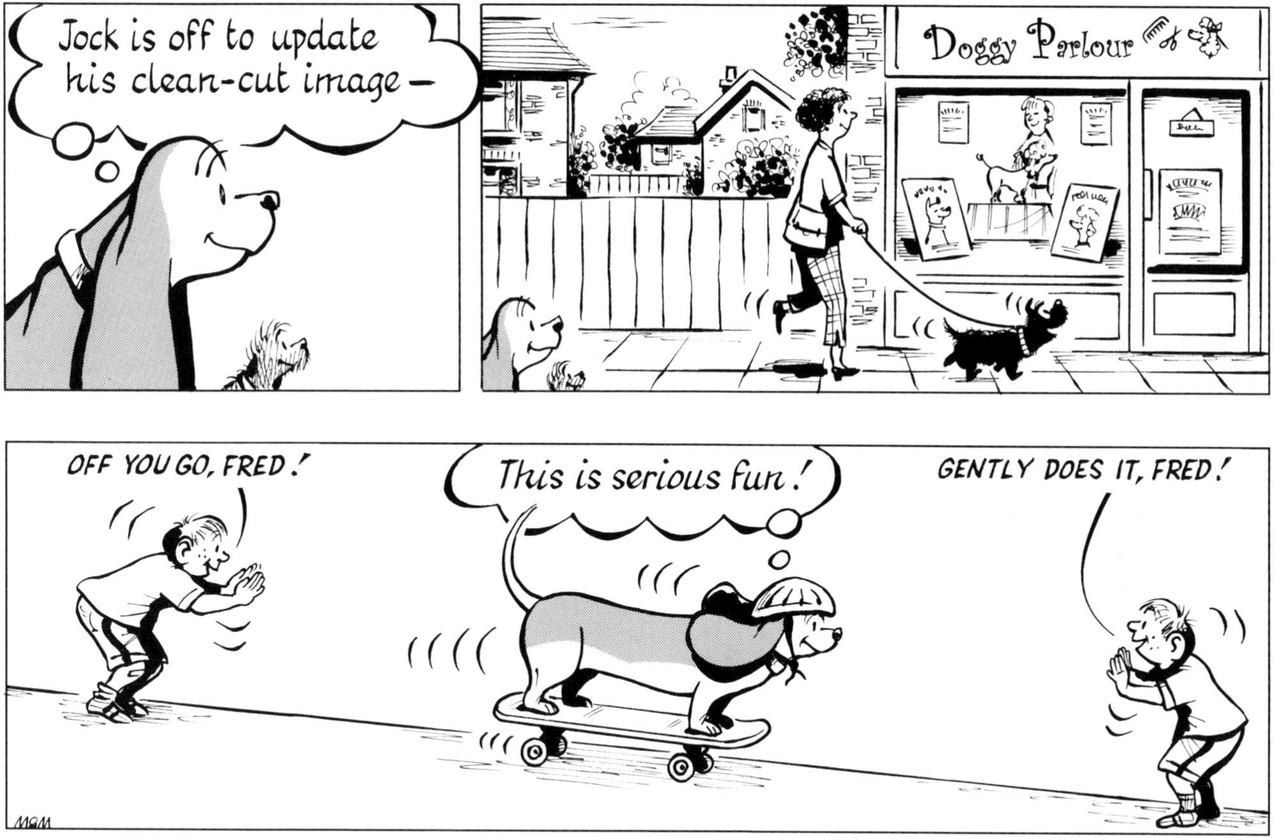
Jock is off to update his clean-cut image –
Doggy Parlour
OFF YOU GO, FRED!
This is serious fun!
GENTLY DOES IT, FRED!

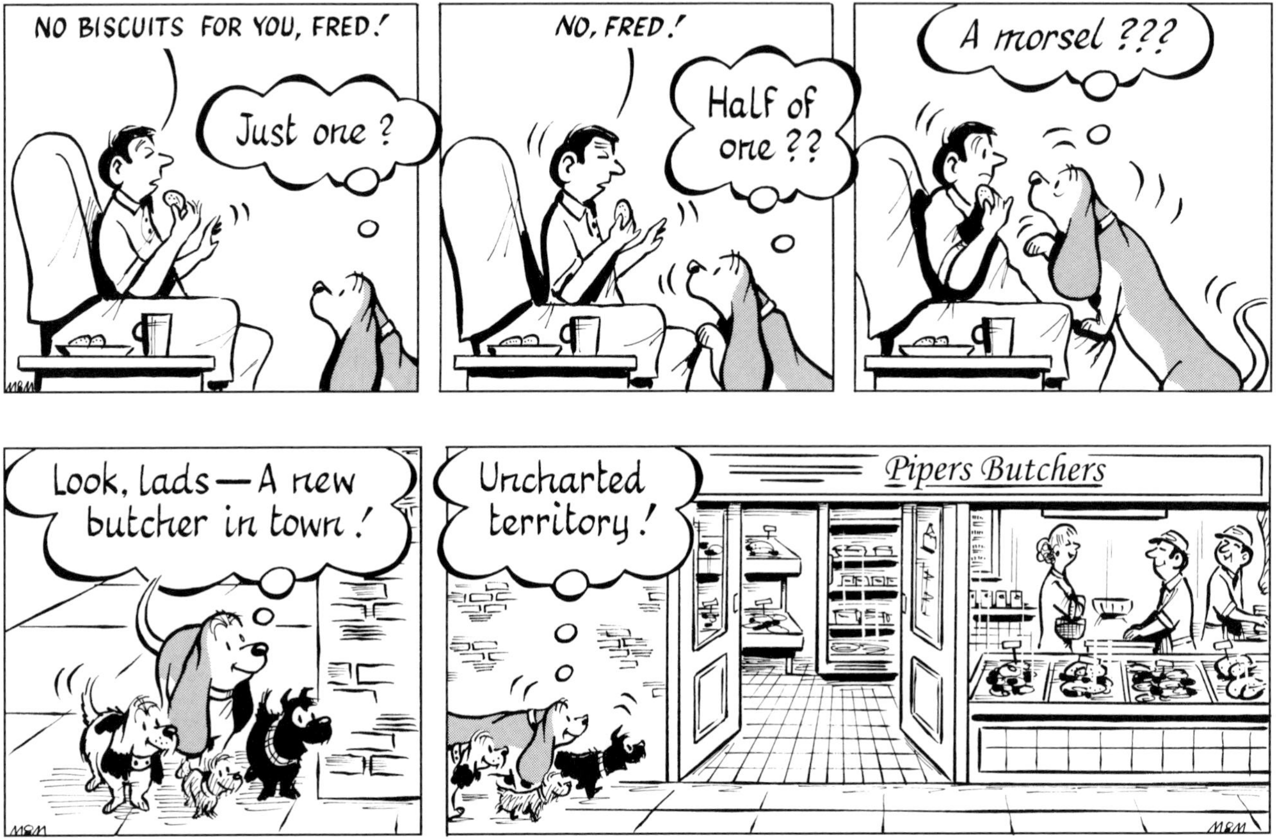
NO BISCUITS FOR YOU, FRED!
Just one ?
NO, FRED!
Half of one ??
A morsel ???
Look, lads—A new butcher in town!
Uncharted territory!
Pipers Butchers

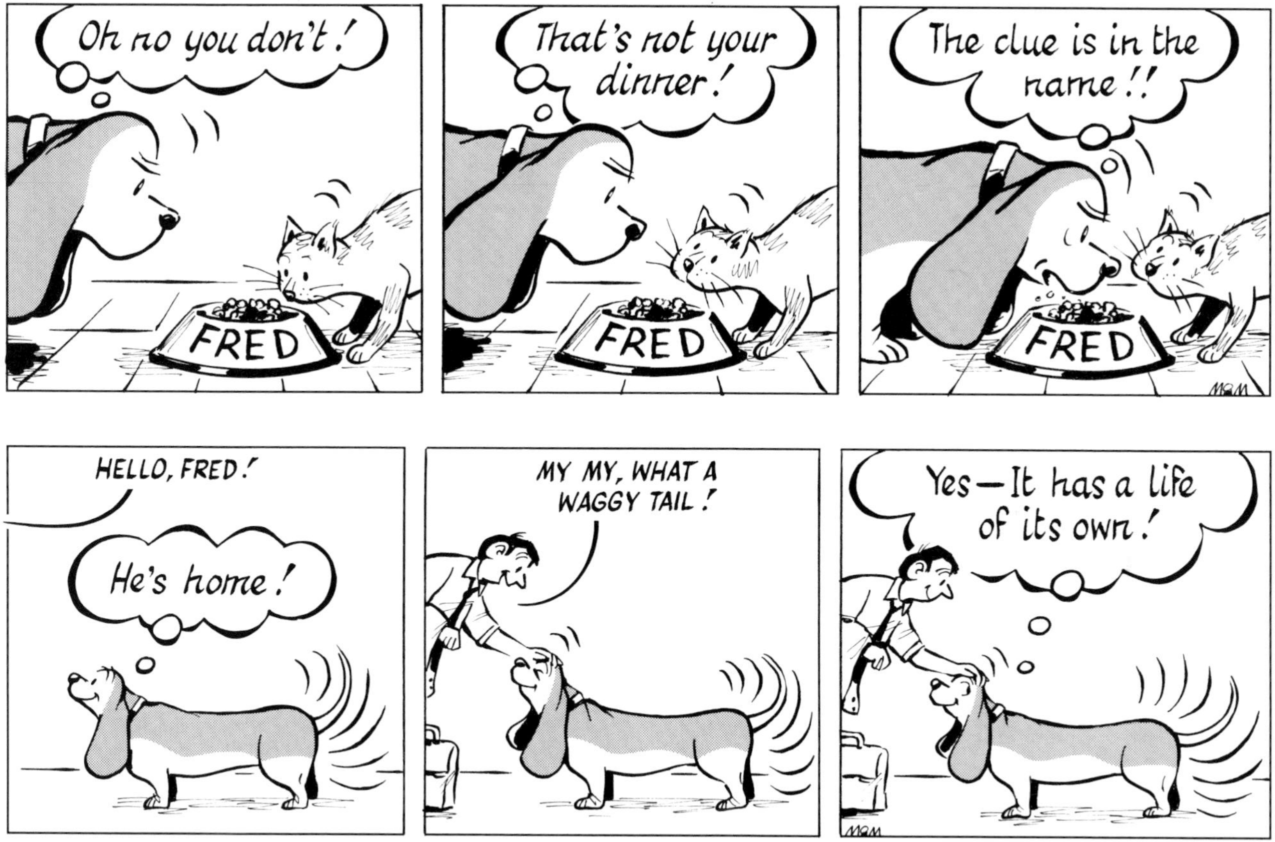
Oh no you don't!
FRED
That's not your dinner!
FRED
The clue is in the name!!
FRED
MGM
HELLO, FRED!
He's home!
MY MY, WHAT A WAGGY TAIL!
Yes—It has a life of its own!
MGM

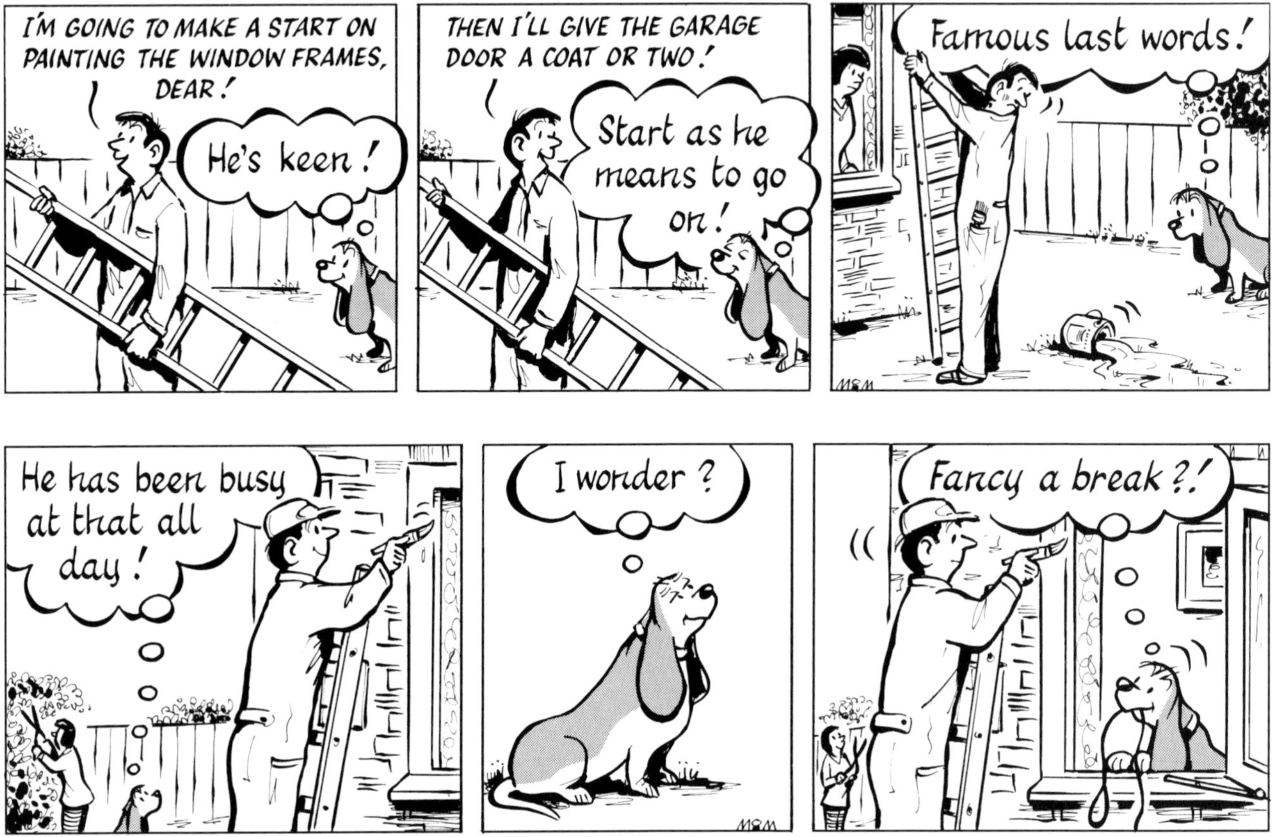
I'M GOING TO MAKE A START ON PAINTING THE WINDOW FRAMES, DEAR!
He's keen!
THEN I'LL GIVE THE GARAGE DOOR A COAT OR TWO!
Start as he means to go on!
Famous last words!
He has been busy at that all day!
I wonder?
Fancy a break?!

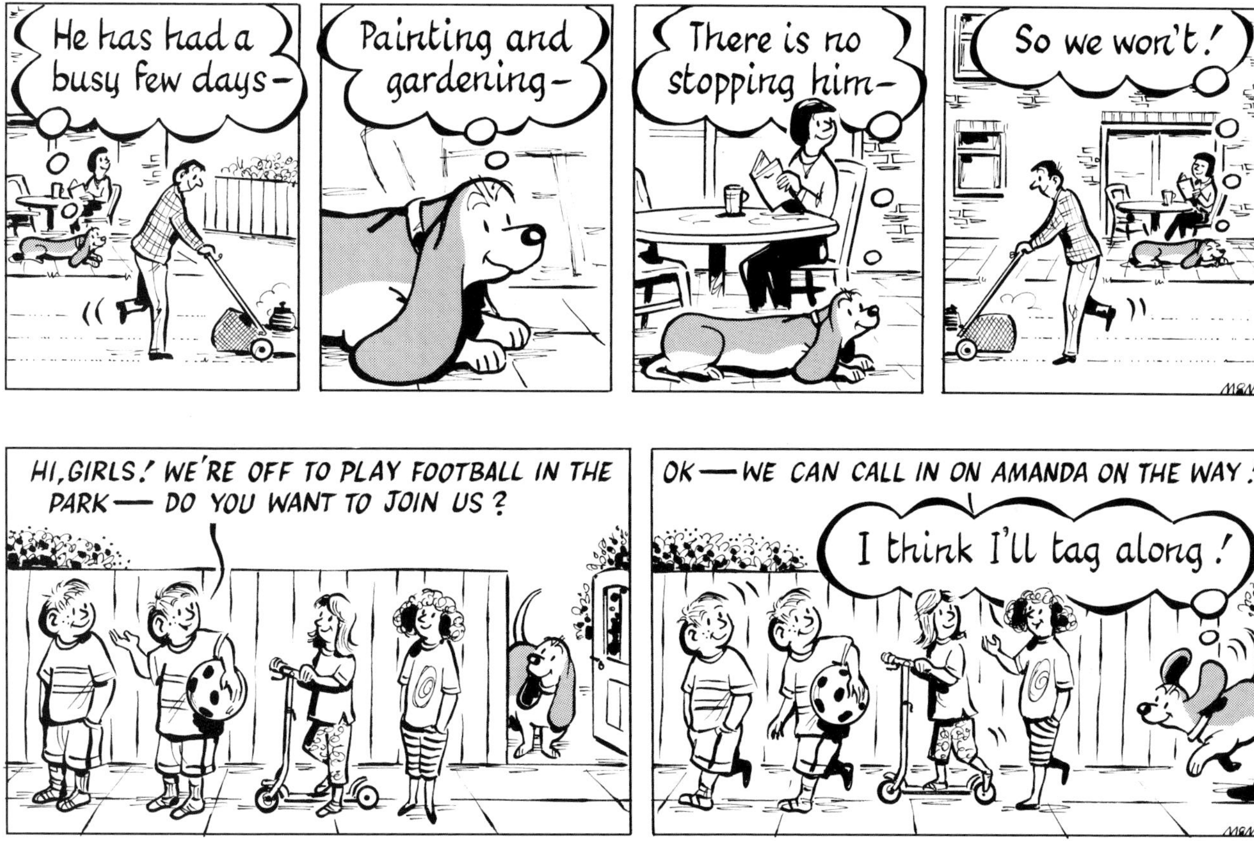
He has had a busy few days-
Painting and gardening-
There is no stopping him-
So we won't!
MGM
HI, GIRLS! WE'RE OFF TO PLAY FOOTBALL IN THE PARK — DO YOU WANT TO JOIN US?
OK — WE CAN CALL IN ON AMANDA ON THE WAY!
I think I'll tag along!
MGM

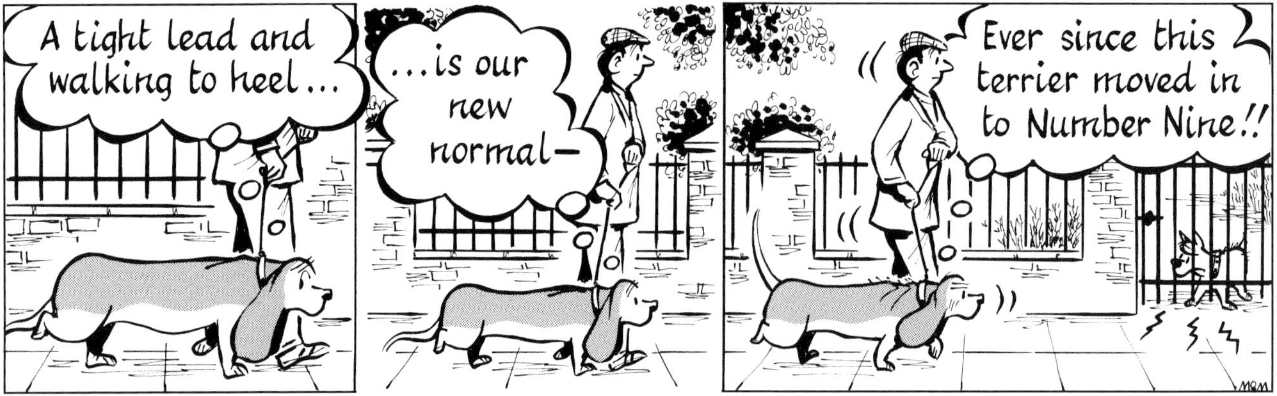
A tight lead and walking to heel...
...is our new normal–
Ever since this terrier moved in to Number Nine!!

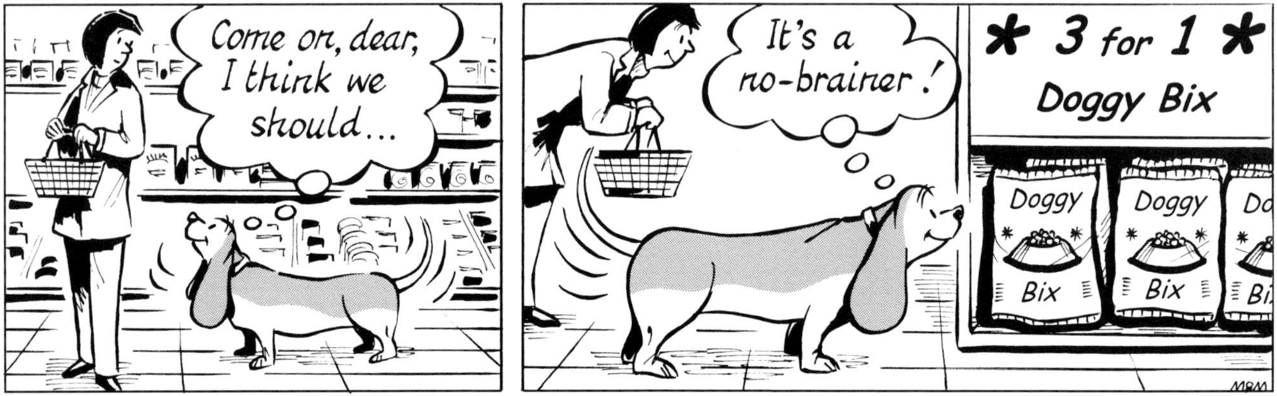
Come on, dear, I think we should...
It's a no-brainer!
* 3 for 1 *
Doggy Bix
Doggy
Bix
Doggy
Bix

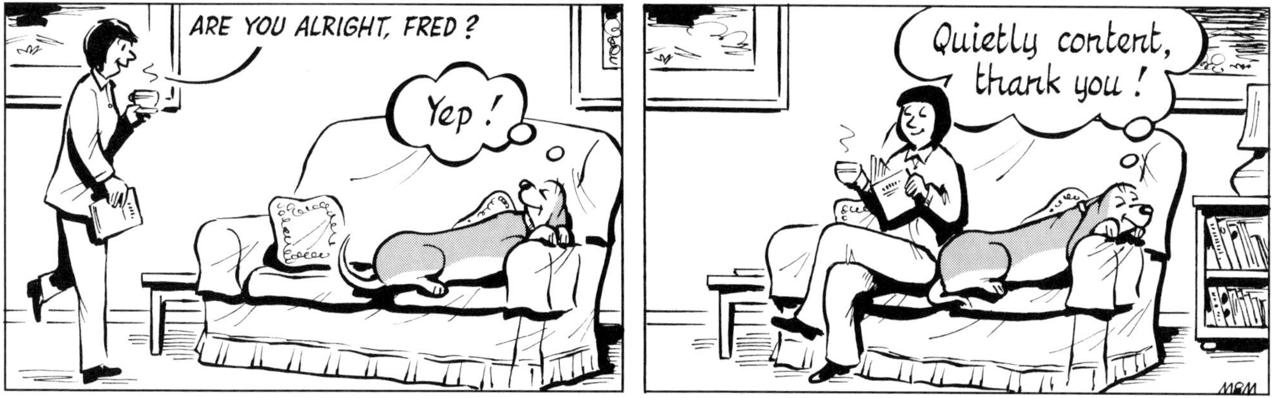
ARE YOU ALRIGHT, FRED?
Yep!
Quietly content, thank you!

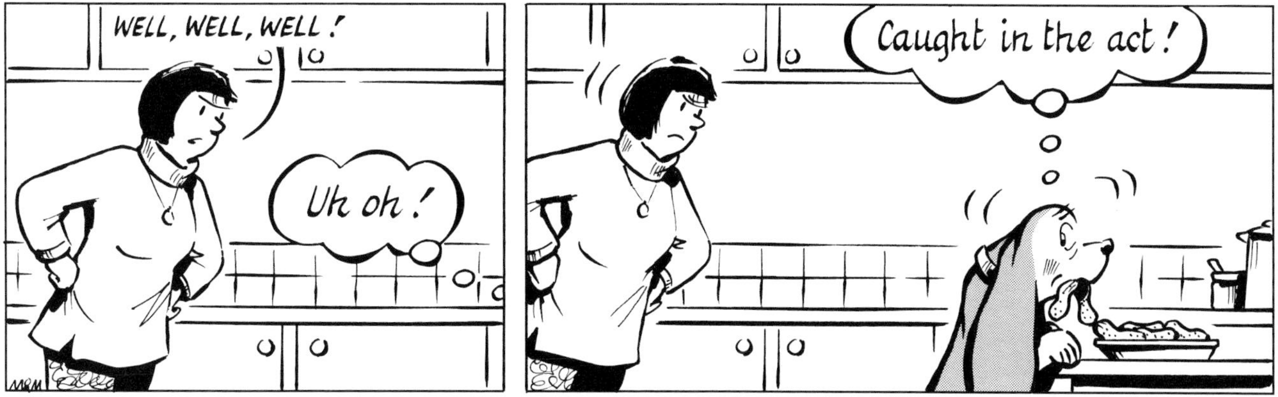
WELL, WELL, WELL!
Uh oh!
Caught in the act!

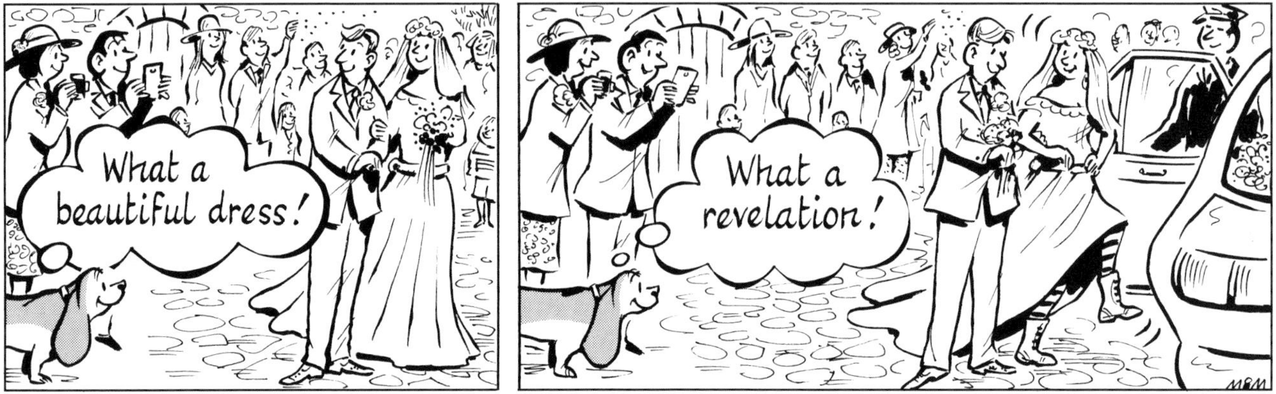
What a beautiful dress!
What a revelation!

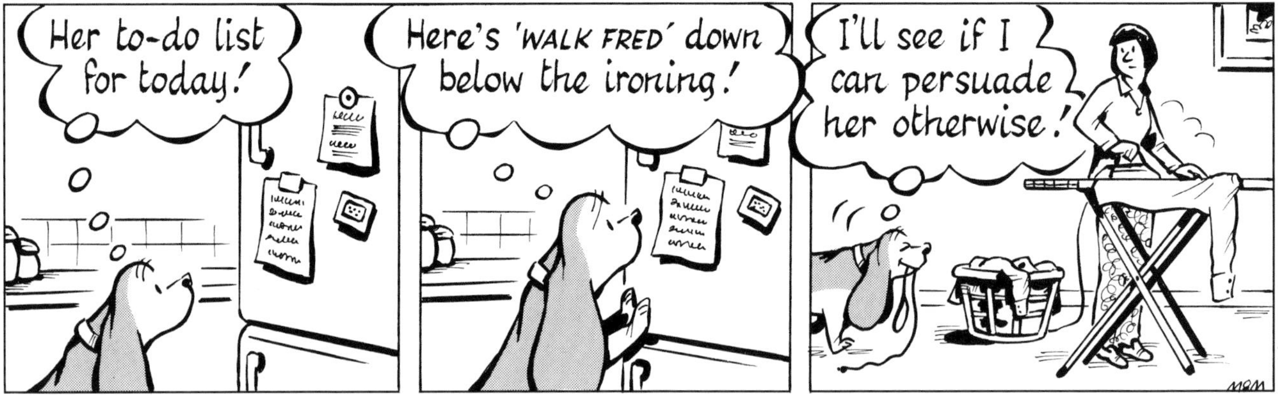
Her to-do list for today!
Here's 'WALK FRED' down below the ironing!
I'll see if I can persuade her otherwise!

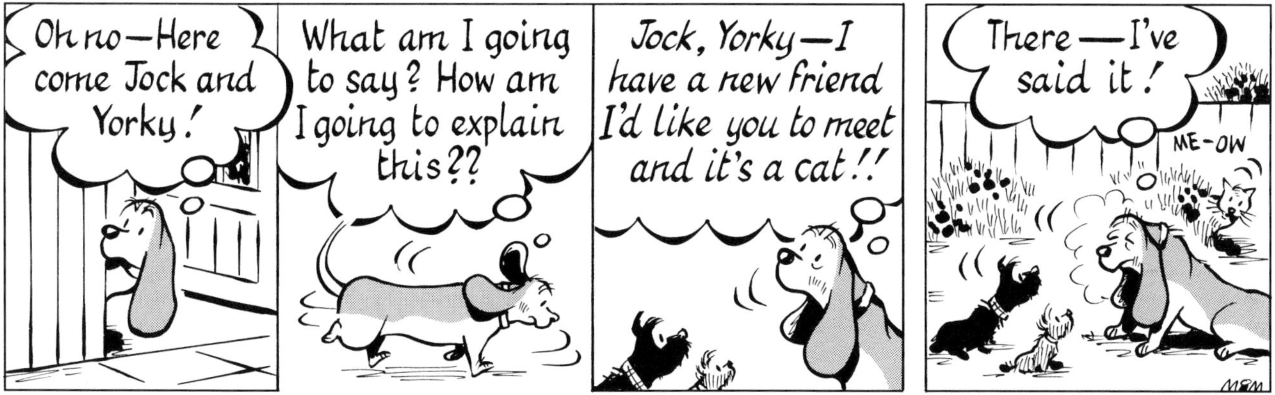
Oh no—Here come Jock and Yorky!
What am I going to say? How am I going to explain this??
Jock, Yorky—I have a new friend I'd like you to meet and it's a cat!!
There—I've said it!
ME-OW
M&M

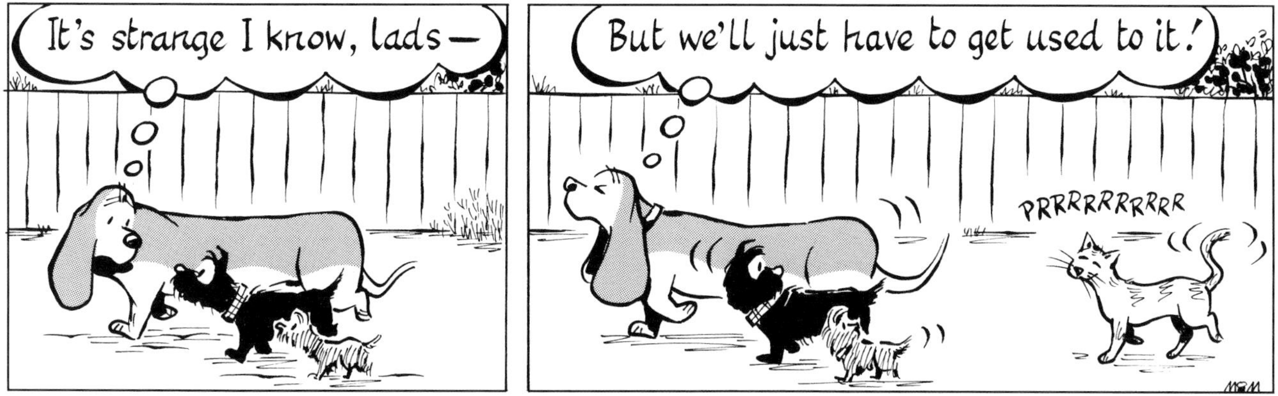
It's strange I know, lads—
But we'll just have to get used to it!
PRRRRRRRRR
M&M

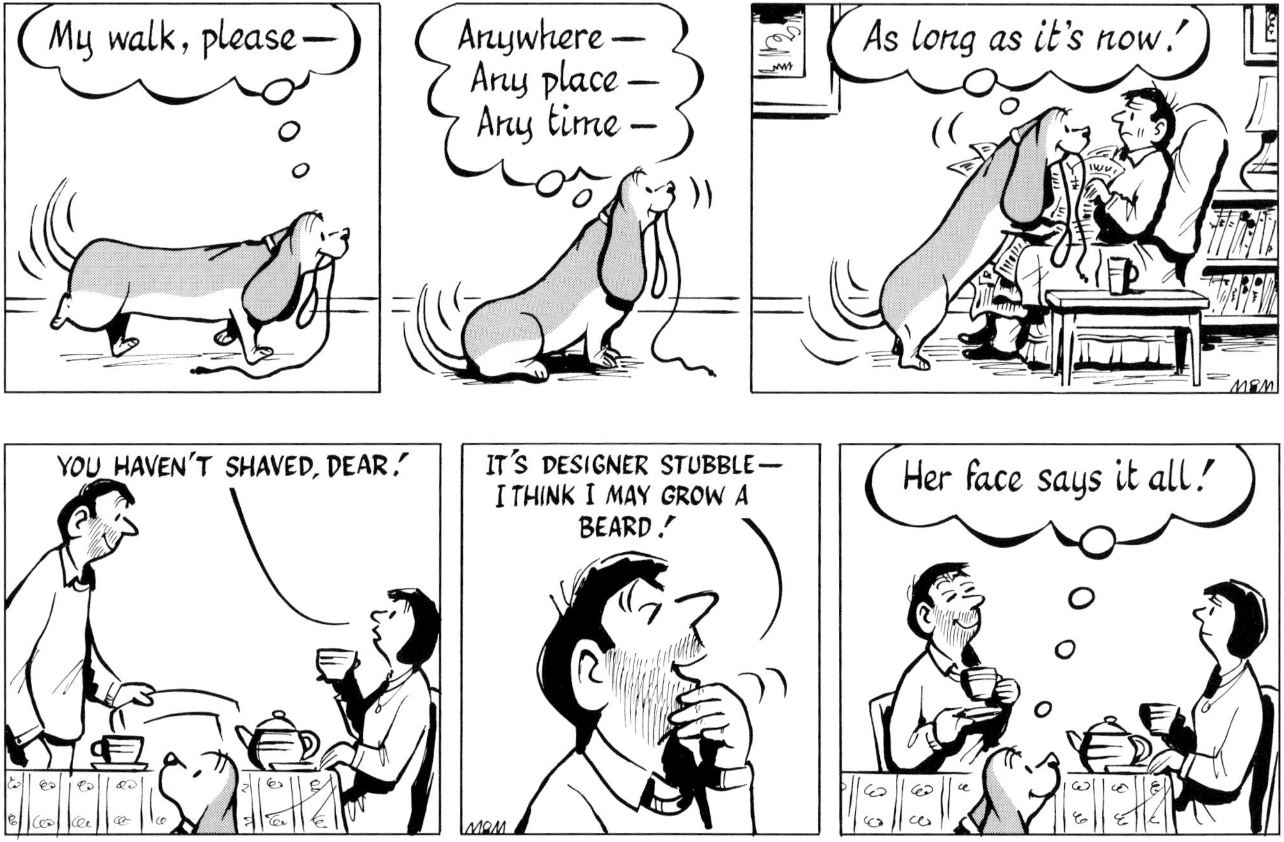
My walk, please—
Anywhere— Any place— Any time—
As long as it's now!
MGM
YOU HAVEN'T SHAVED, DEAR!
IT'S DESIGNER STUBBLE— I THINK I MAY GROW A BEARD!
MGM
Her face says it all!

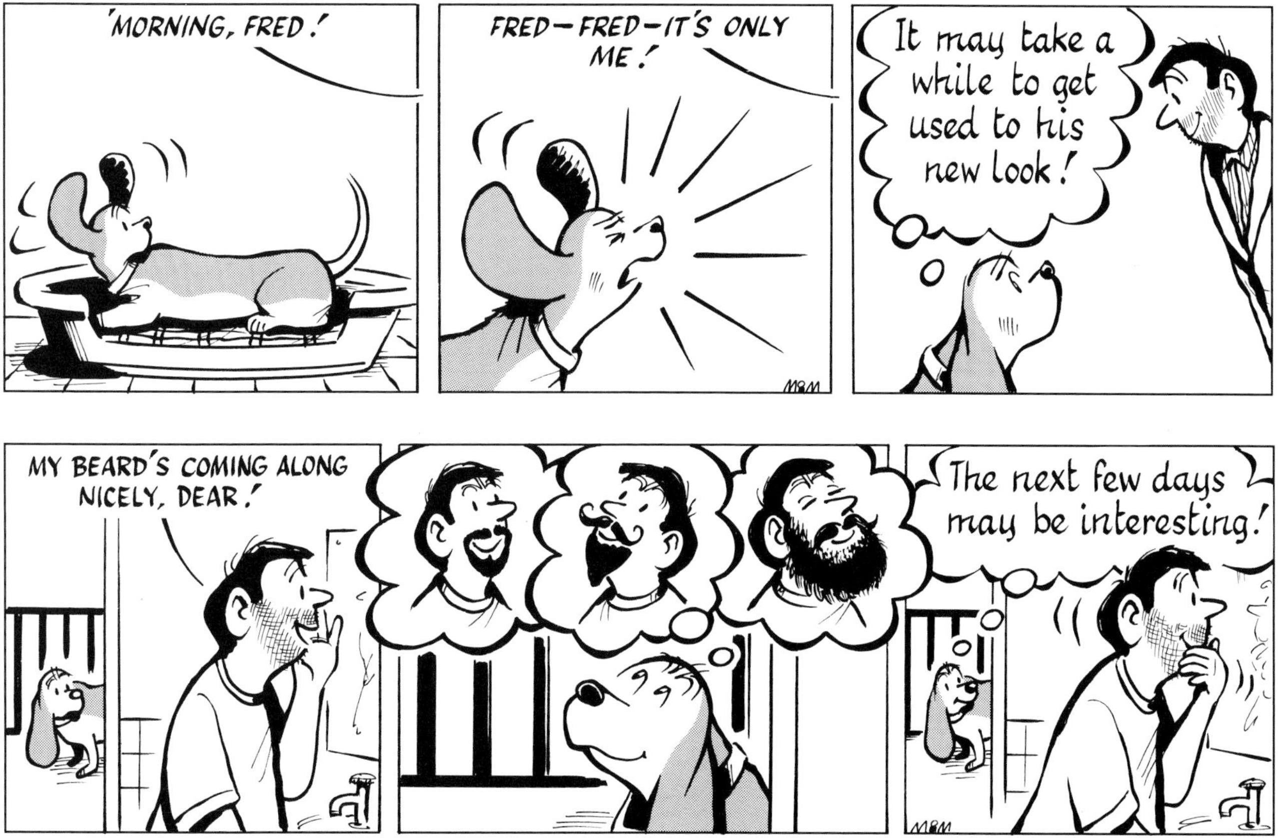
'MORNING, FRED!'
FRED—FRED—IT'S ONLY ME!
It may take a while to get used to his new look!
MY BEARD'S COMING ALONG NICELY, DEAR!
The next few days may be interesting!
M&M
M&M

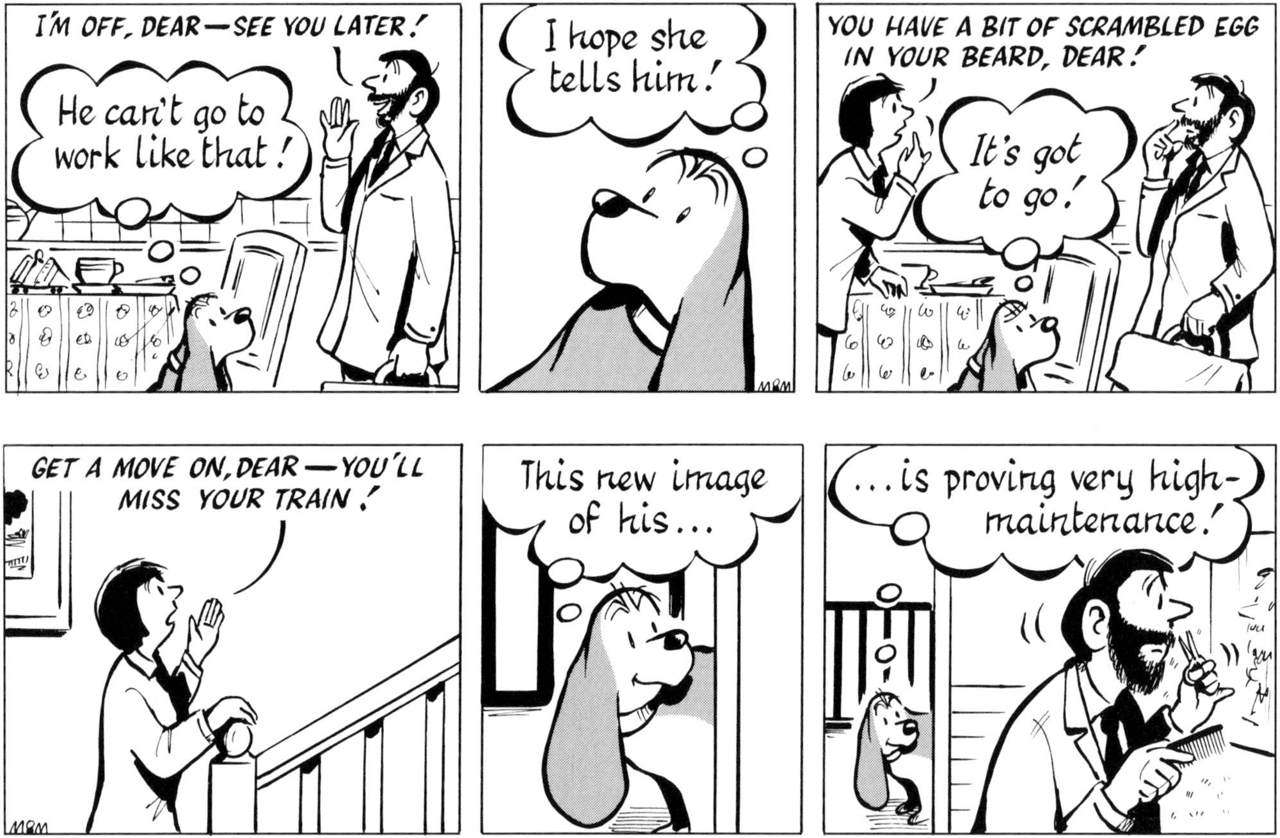
I'M OFF, DEAR—SEE YOU LATER!
He can't go to work like that!
I hope she tells him!
YOU HAVE A BIT OF SCRAMBLED EGG IN YOUR BEARD, DEAR!
It's got to go!
GET A MOVE ON, DEAR—YOU'LL MISS YOUR TRAIN!
This new image of his...
...is proving very high-maintenance!

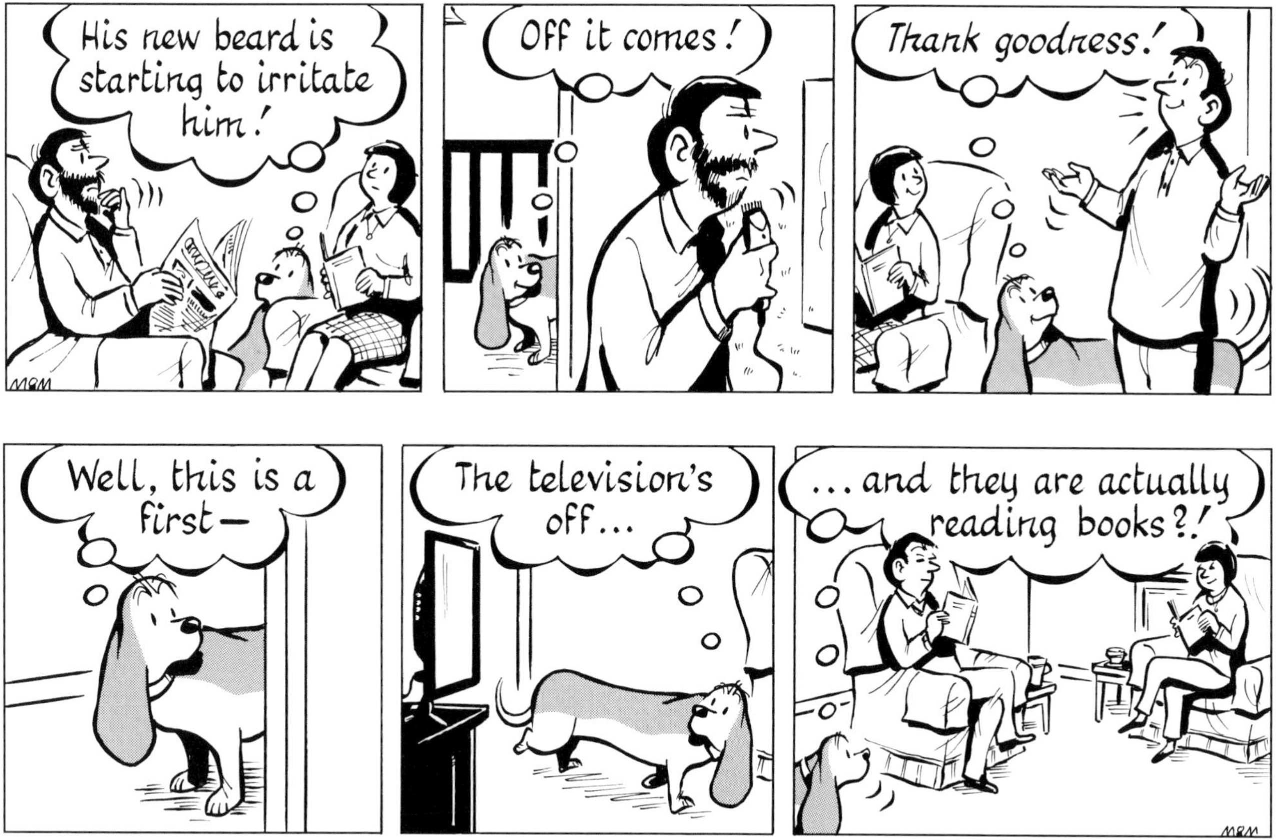
His new beard is starting to irritate him!
Off it comes!
Thank goodness!
Well, this is a first–
The television's off...
...and they are actually reading books?!

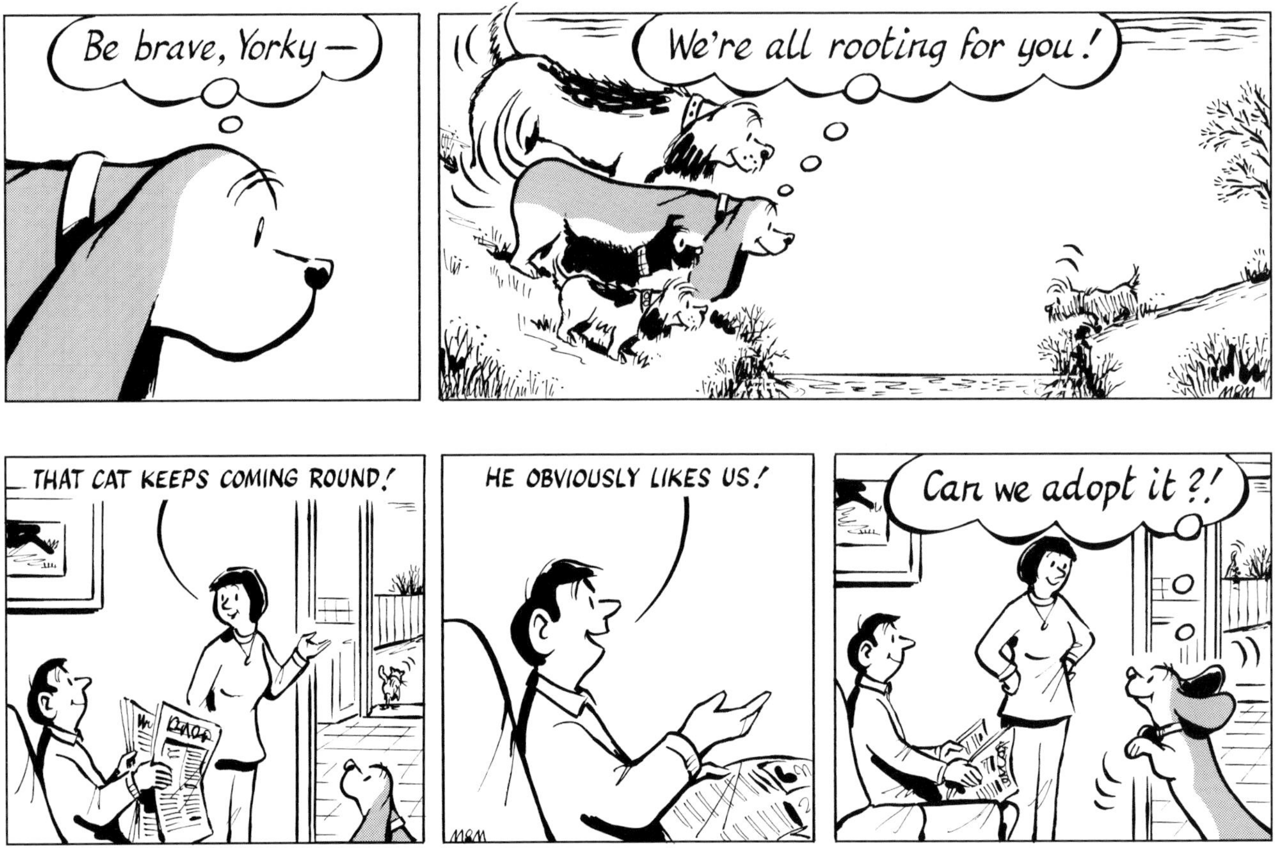
Be brave, Yorky —
We're all rooting for you!
THAT CAT KEEPS COMING ROUND!
HE OBVIOUSLY LIKES US!
Can we adopt it ?!

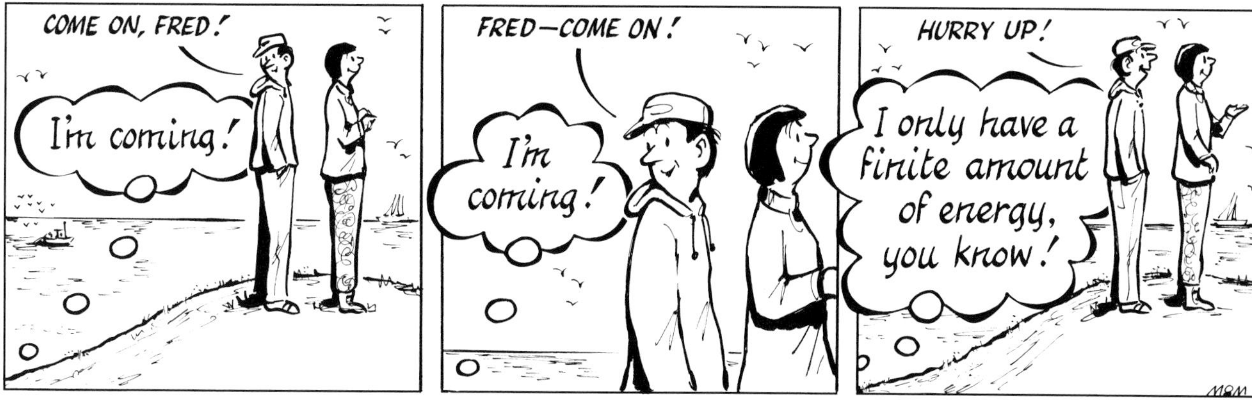
COME ON, FRED!
I'm coming!
FRED—COME ON!
I'm coming!
HURRY UP!
I only have a finite amount of energy, you know!

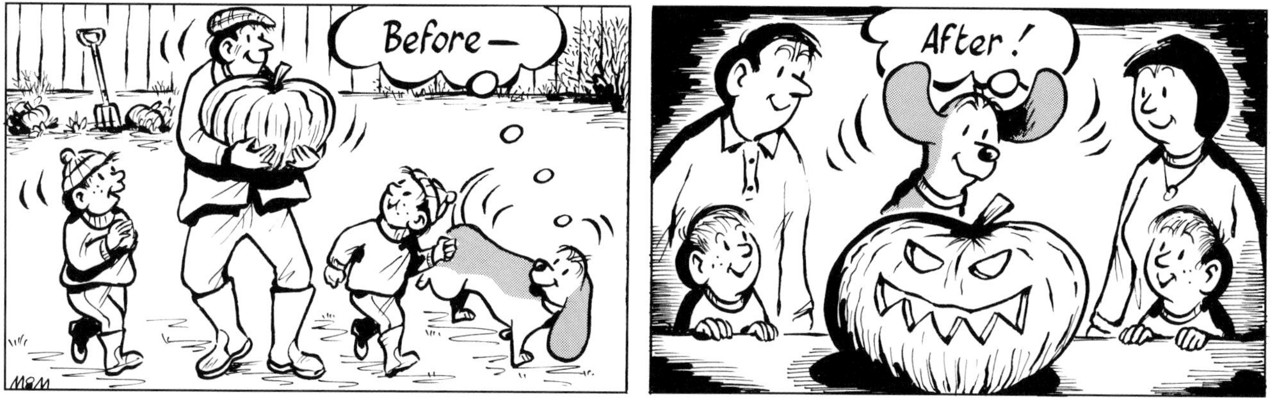
Before—
After!

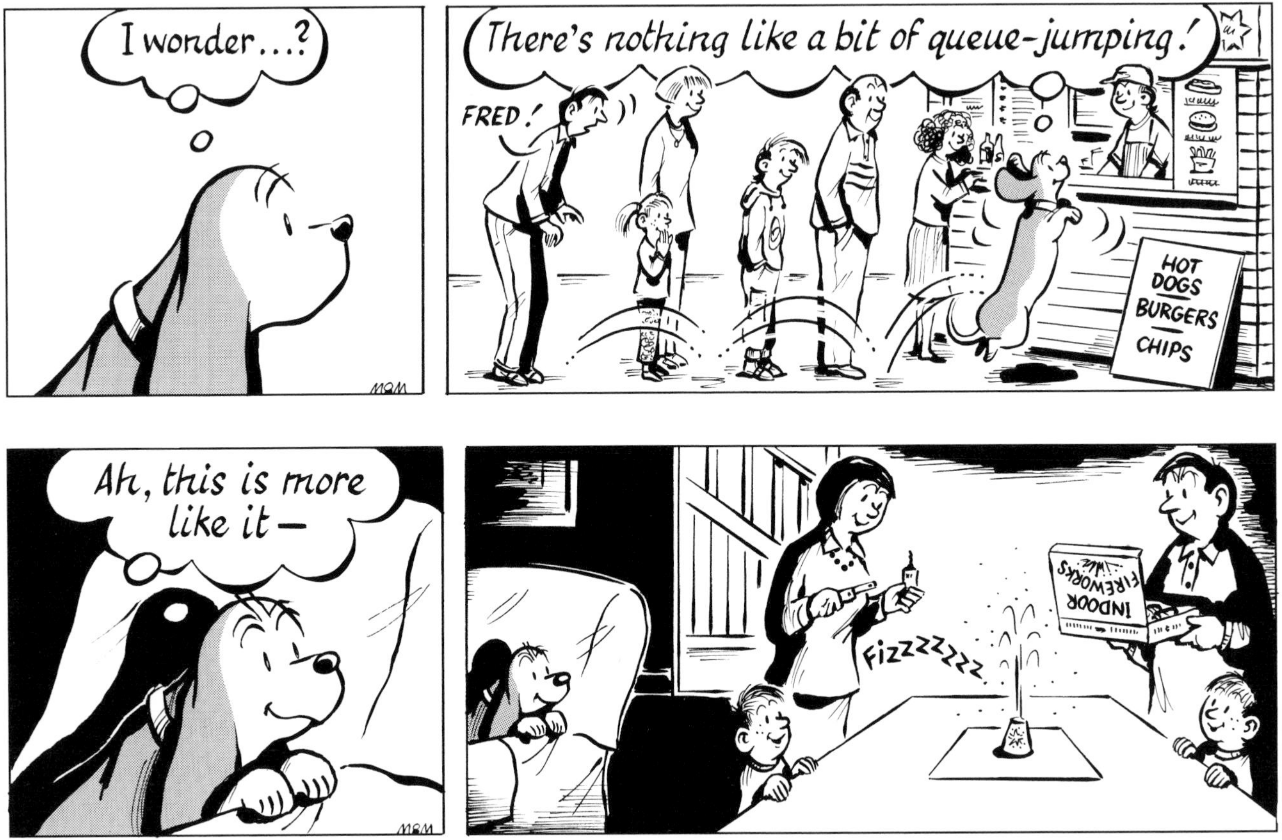
I wonder...?
There's nothing like a bit of queue-jumping!
FRED!
HOT DOGS
BURGERS
CHIPS
Ah, this is more like it –
INDOOR FIREWORKS
Fizzzzzzz

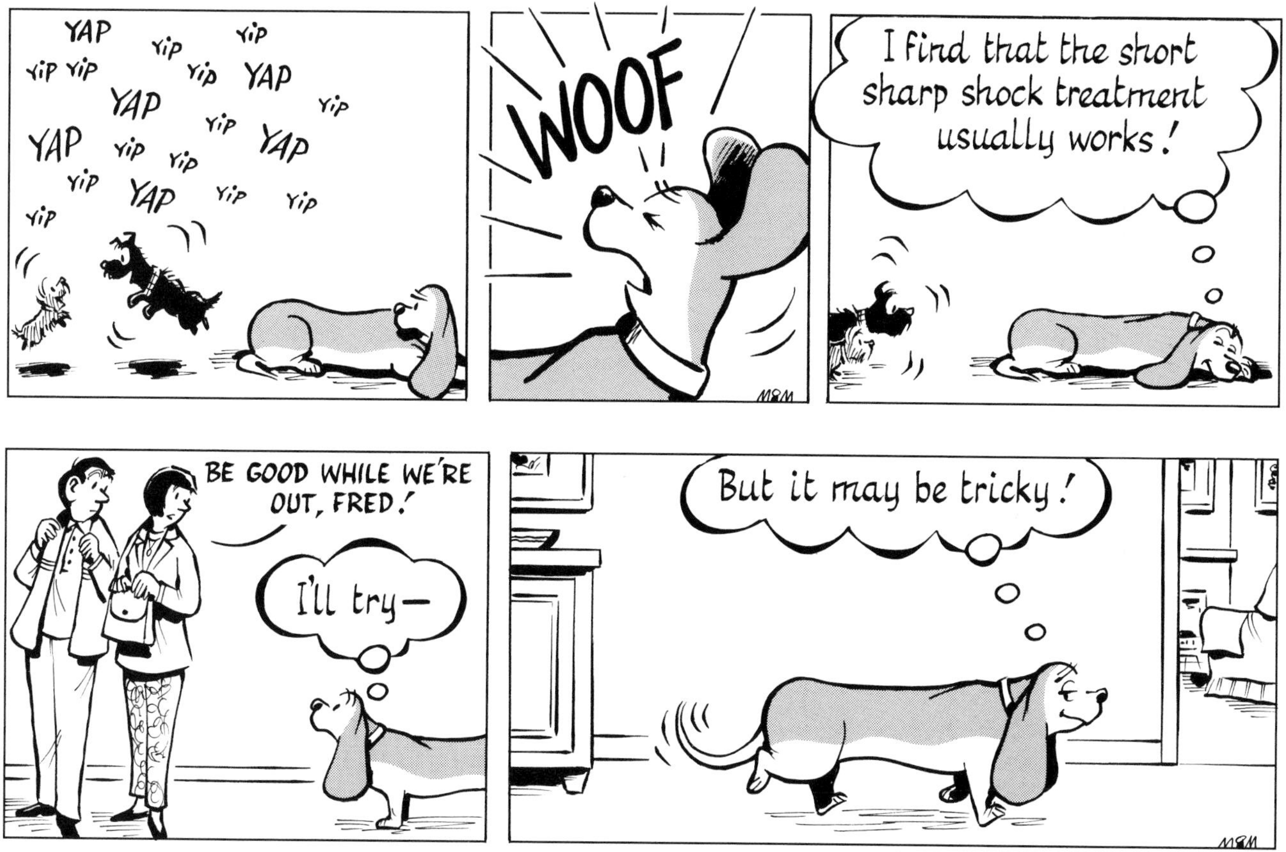
YAP
YIP
YIP
YIP YIP
YIP
YAP
YAP
YIP
YAP
YIP
YIP
YAP
YIP
YIP
YIP
YAP
YIP
YIP
YIP
WOOF
I find that the short sharp shock treatment usually works!
BE GOOD WHILE WE'RE OUT, FRED!
I'll try—
But it may be tricky!

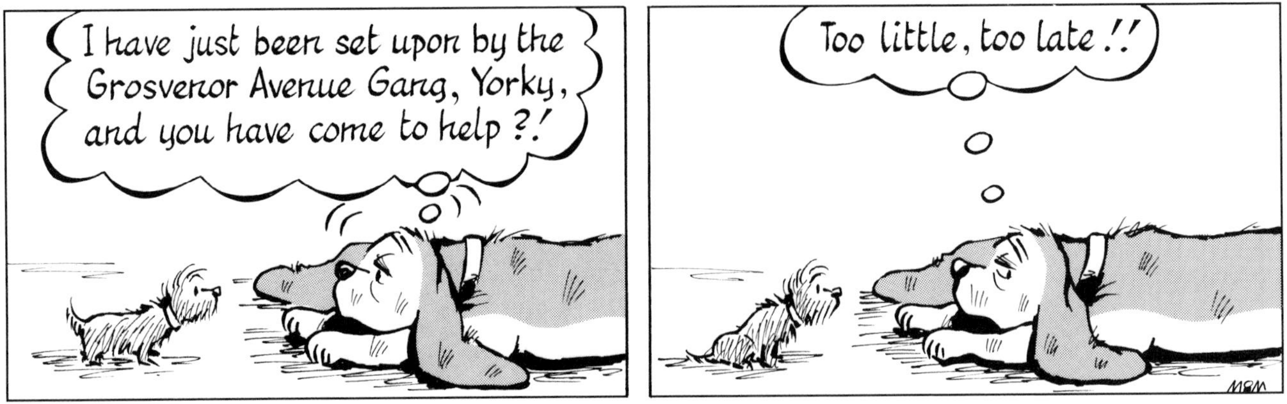

I have just been set upon by the Grosvenor Avenue Gang, Yorky, and you have come to help ?!
Too little, too late !!

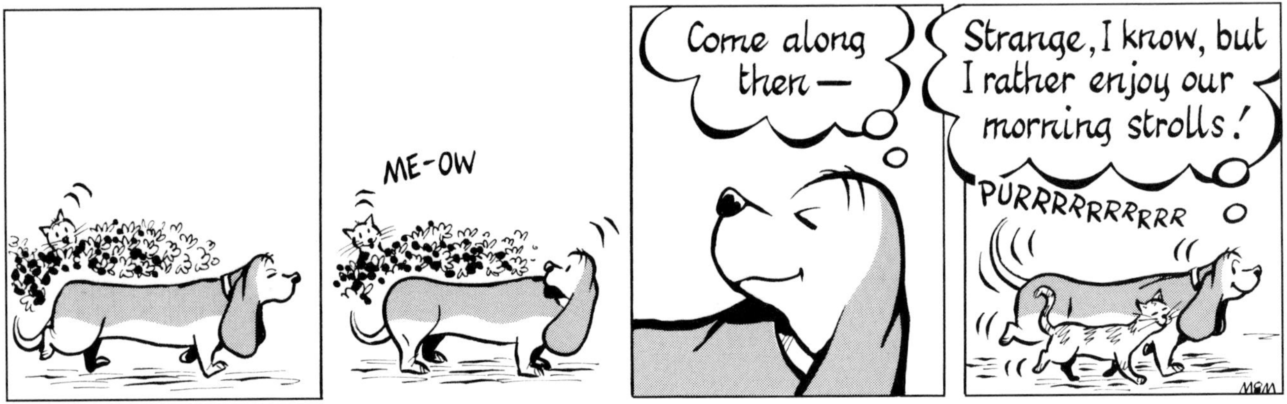

ME-OW
Come along then —
Strange, I know, but I rather enjoy our morning strolls !
PURRRRRRRRRR

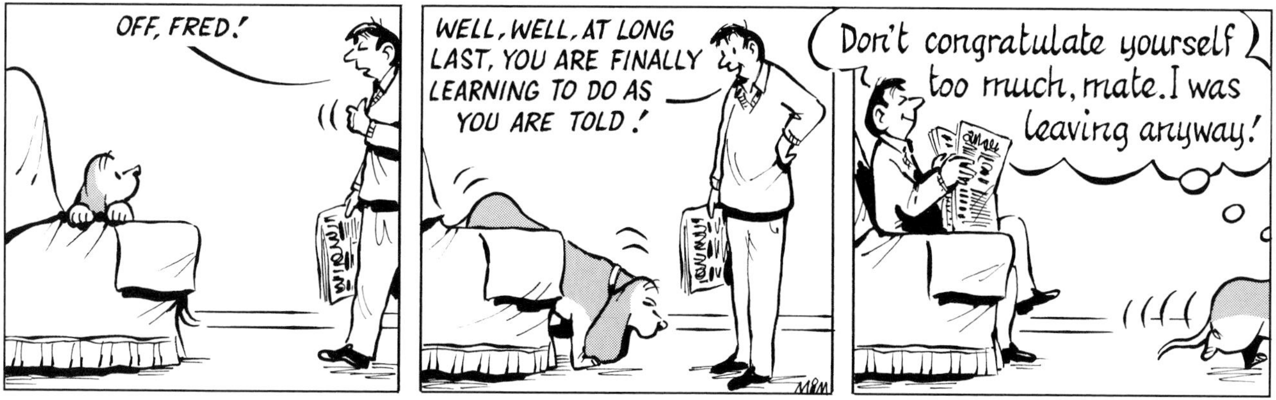
OFF, FRED!
WELL, WELL, AT LONG LAST, YOU ARE FINALLY LEARNING TO DO AS YOU ARE TOLD!
Don't congratulate yourself too much, mate. I was leaving anyway!
M&M

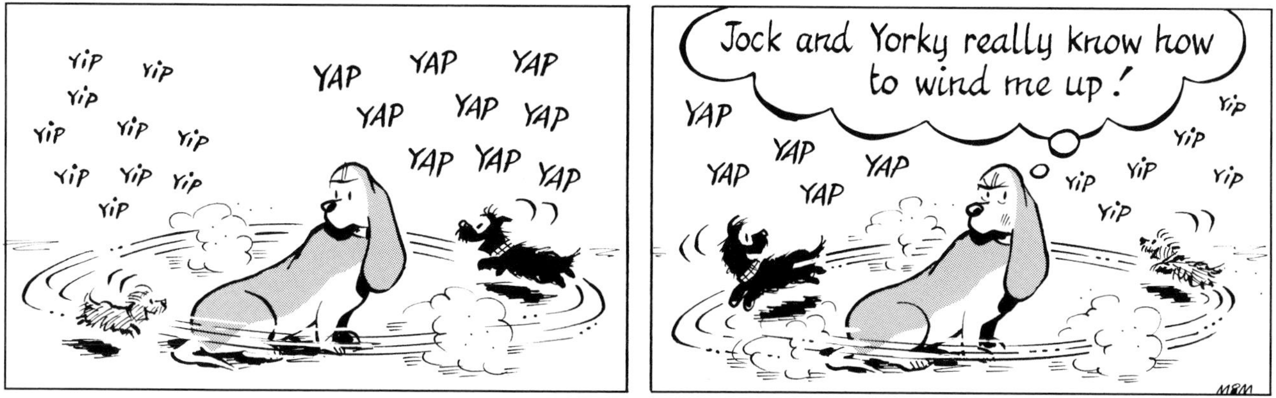
YIP YIP YIP YIP YIP YIP YIP YIP YIP YIP
YAP YAP YAP YAP YAP YAP YAP YAP YAP
Jock and Yorky really know how to wind me up!
YAP YAP YAP YAP YAP
YIP YIP YIP YIP YIP YIP
M&M

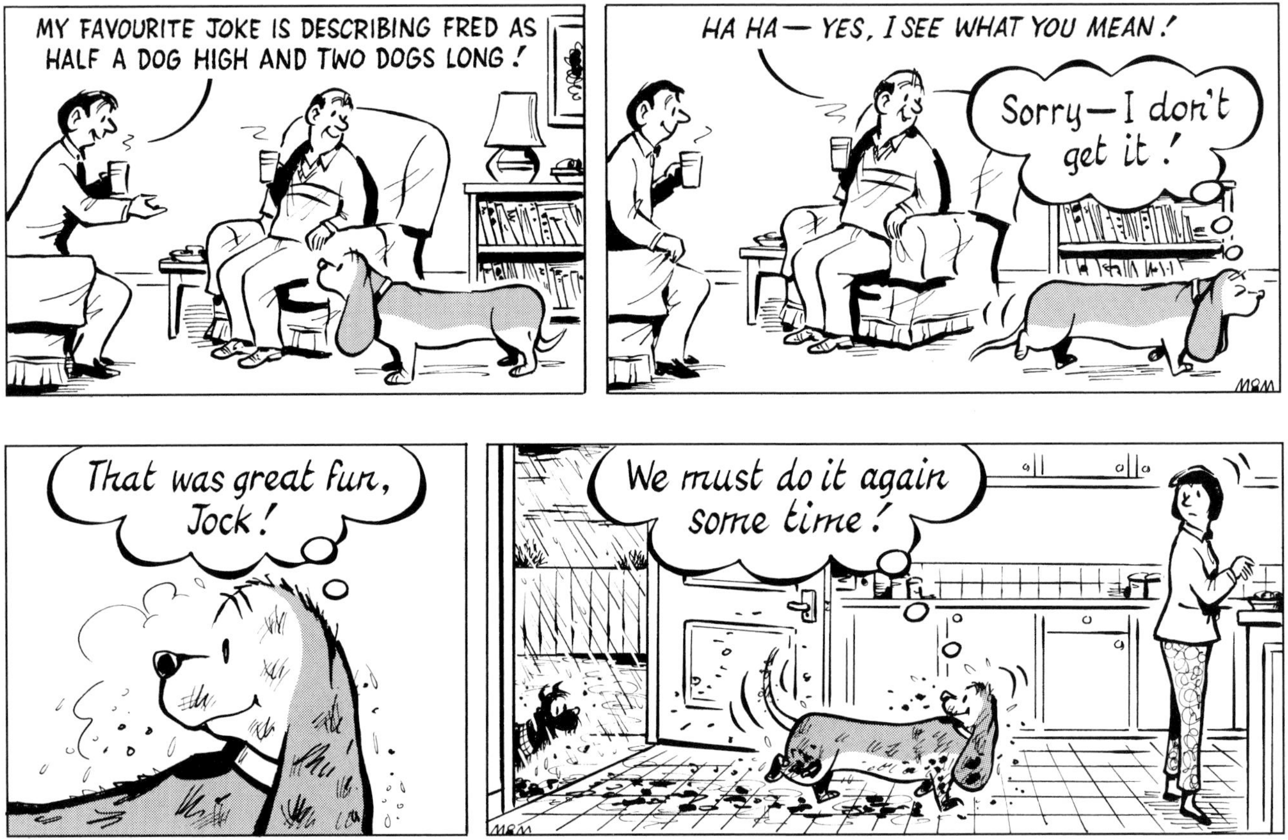
MY FAVOURITE JOKE IS DESCRIBING FRED AS HALF A DOG HIGH AND TWO DOGS LONG!
HA HA — YES, I SEE WHAT YOU MEAN!
Sorry — I don't get it!
That was great fun, Jock!
We must do it again some time!

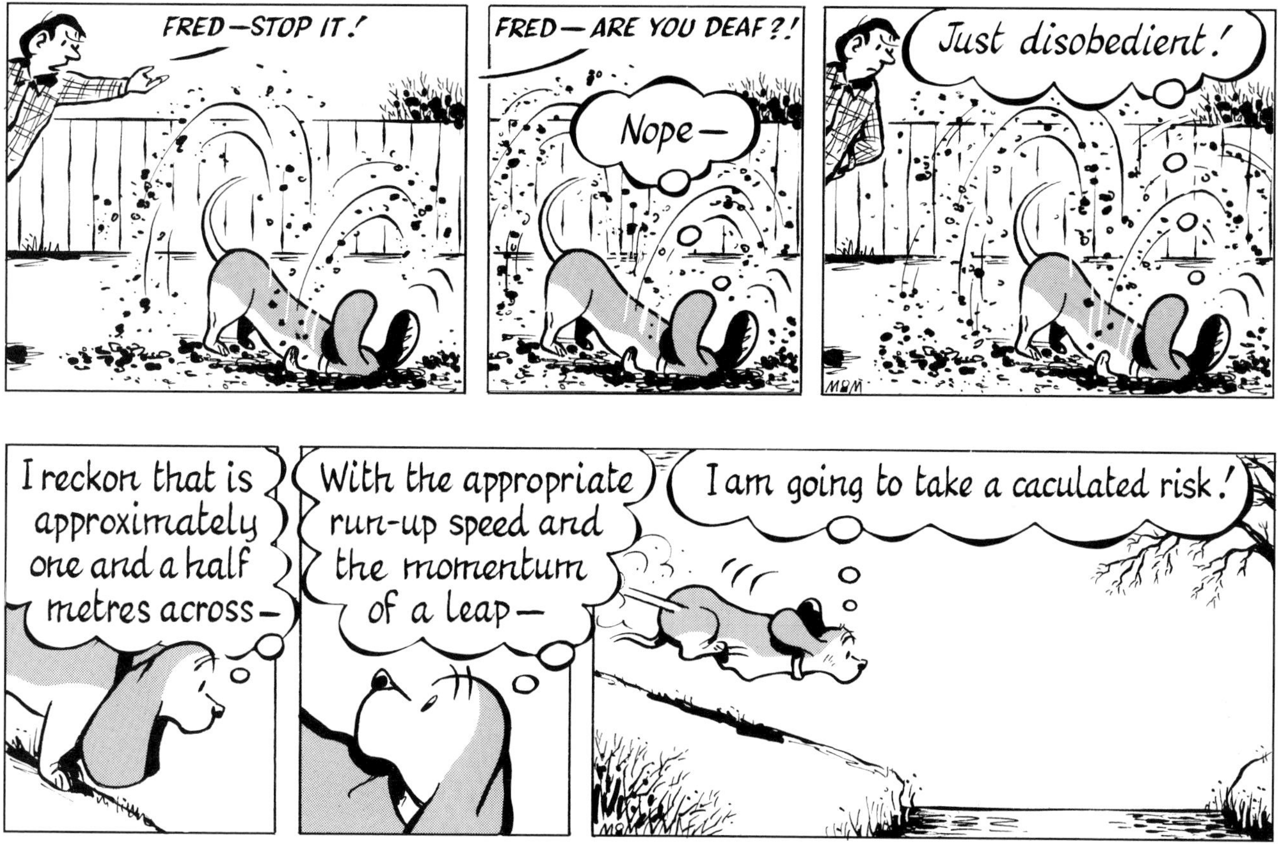
FRED—STOP IT!
FRED—ARE YOU DEAF?!
Nope—
Just disobedient!
MØM
I reckon that is approximately one and a half metres across—
With the appropriate run-up speed and the momentum of a leap—
I am going to take a caculated risk!

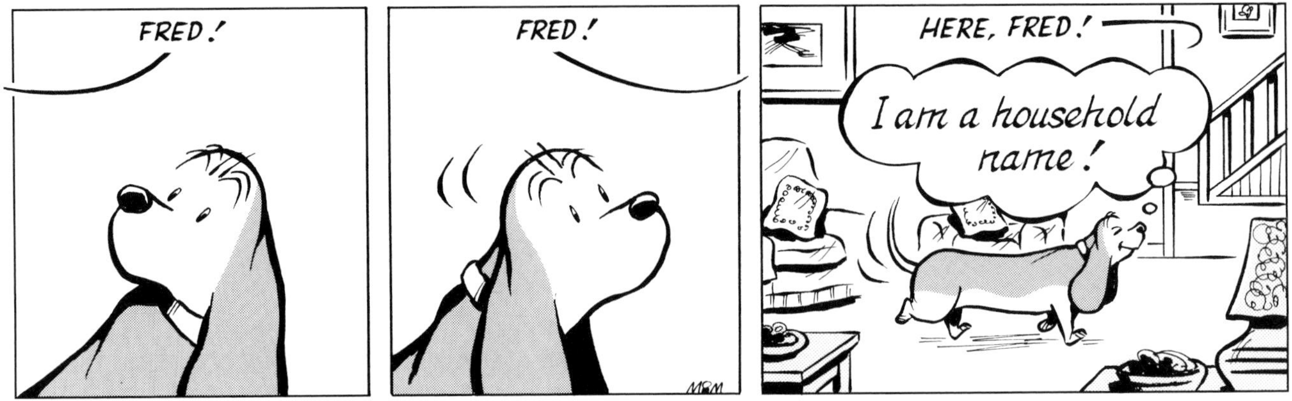
FRED!
FRED!
HERE, FRED!
I am a household name!
M&M

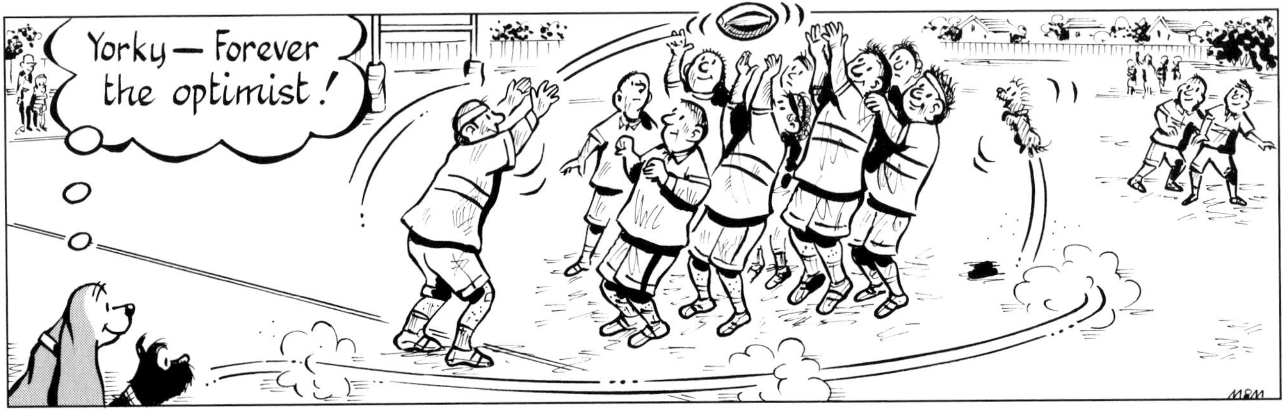
Yorky — Forever the optimist!
M&M

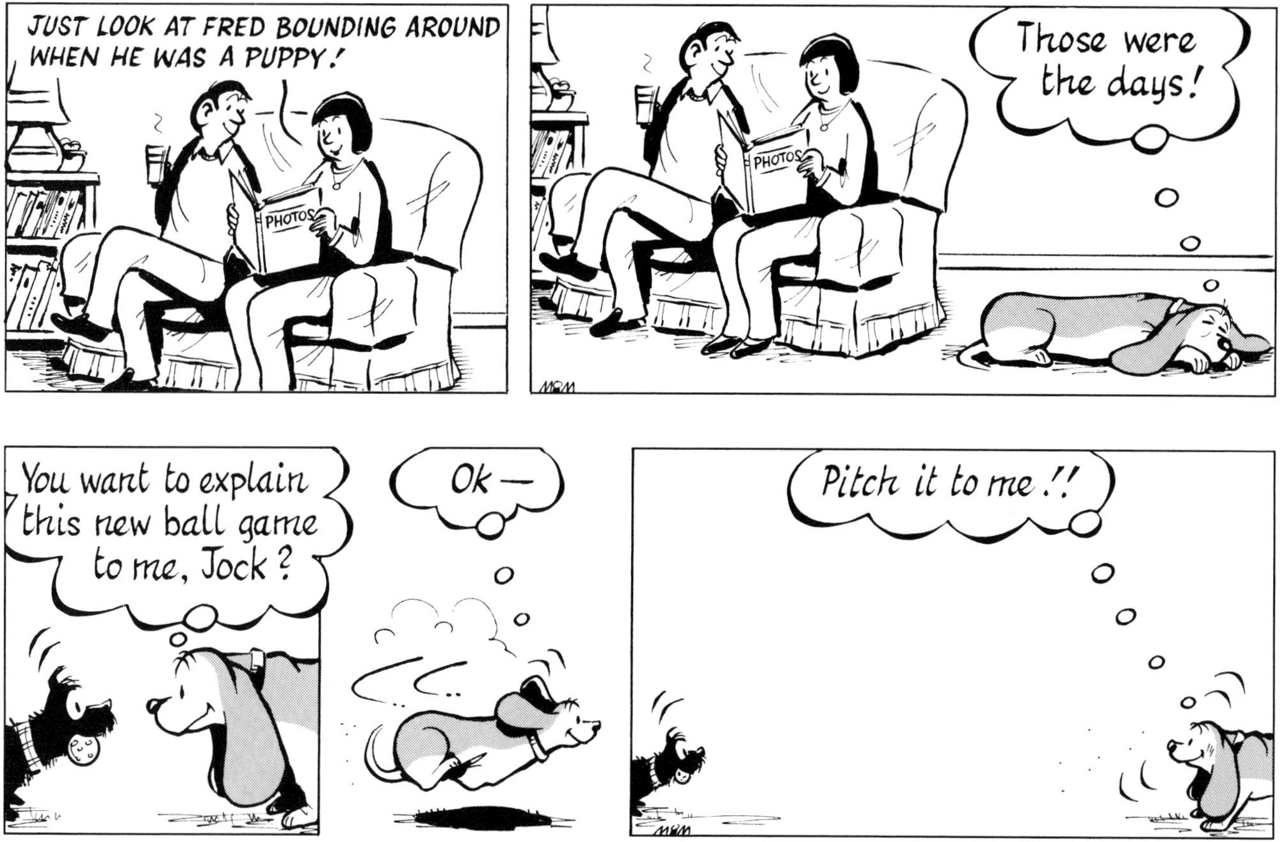
JUST LOOK AT FRED BOUNDING AROUND WHEN HE WAS A PUPPY!
PHOTOS
PHOTOS
Those were the days!
You want to explain this new ball game to me, Jock?
Ok —
Pitch it to me!!

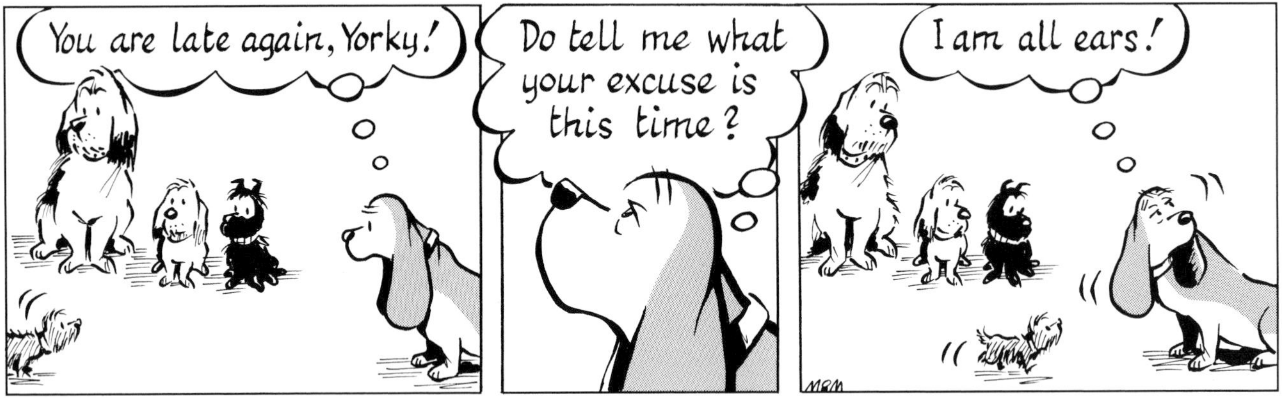
You are late again, Yorky!
Do tell me what your excuse is this time?
I am all ears!

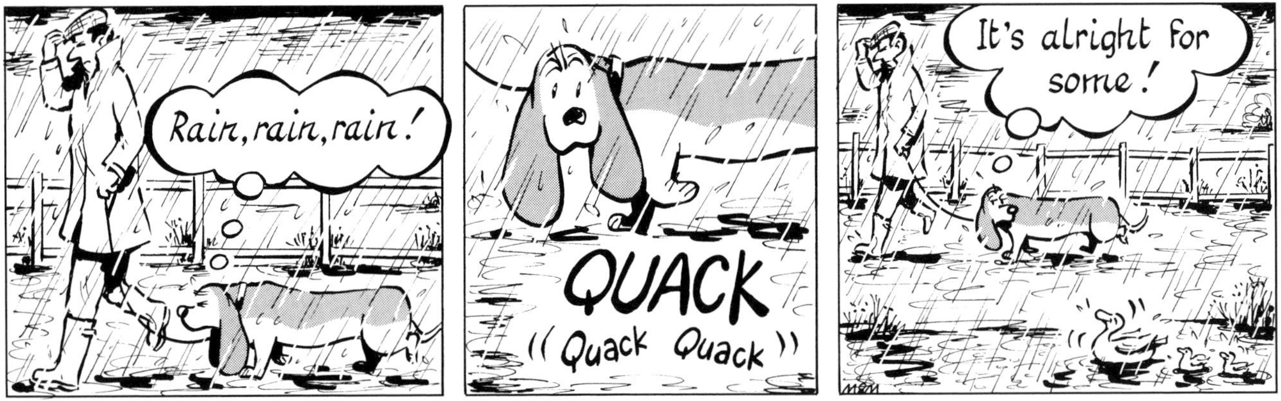
Rain, rain, rain!
QUACK
Quack Quack
It's alright for some!

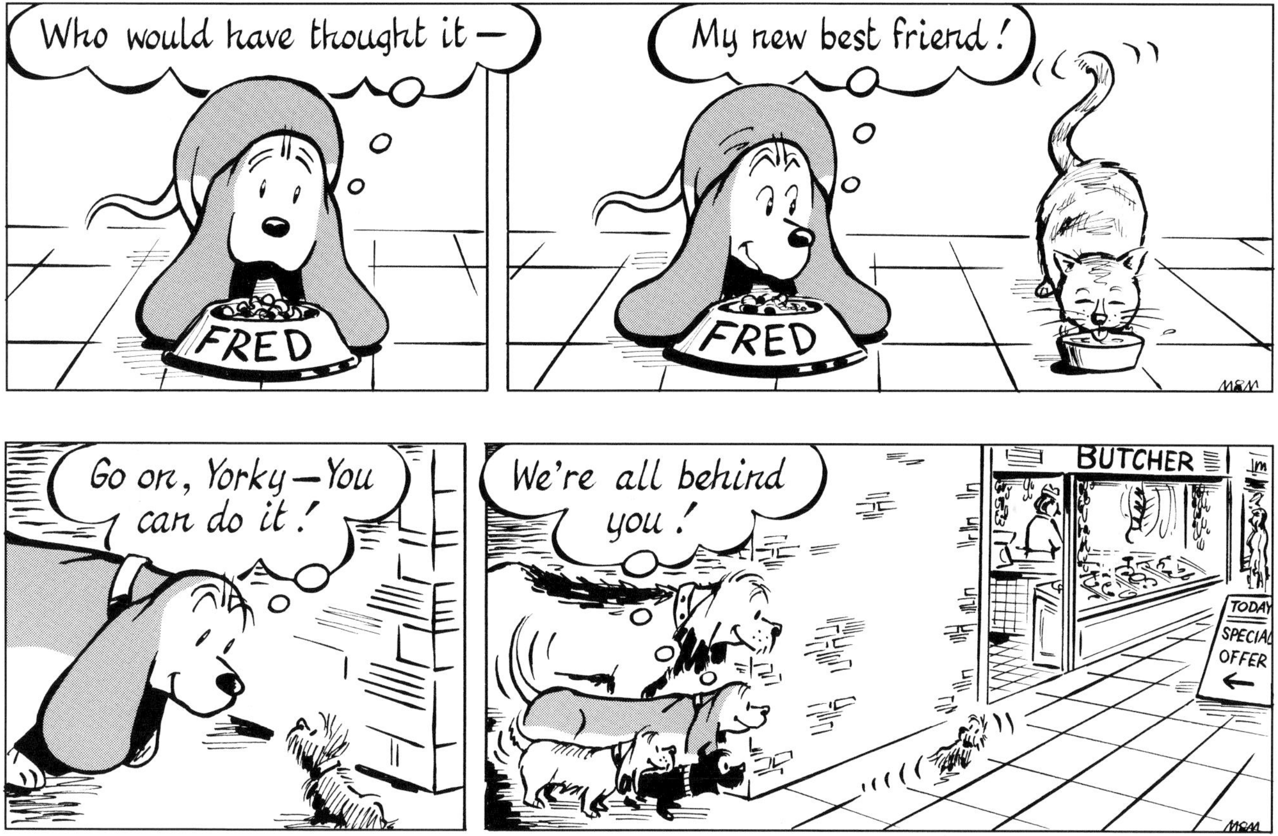
Who would have thought it —
FRED
My new best friend!
FRED
Go on, Yorky — You can do it!
We're all behind you!
BUTCHER
TODAY
SPECIAL
OFFER

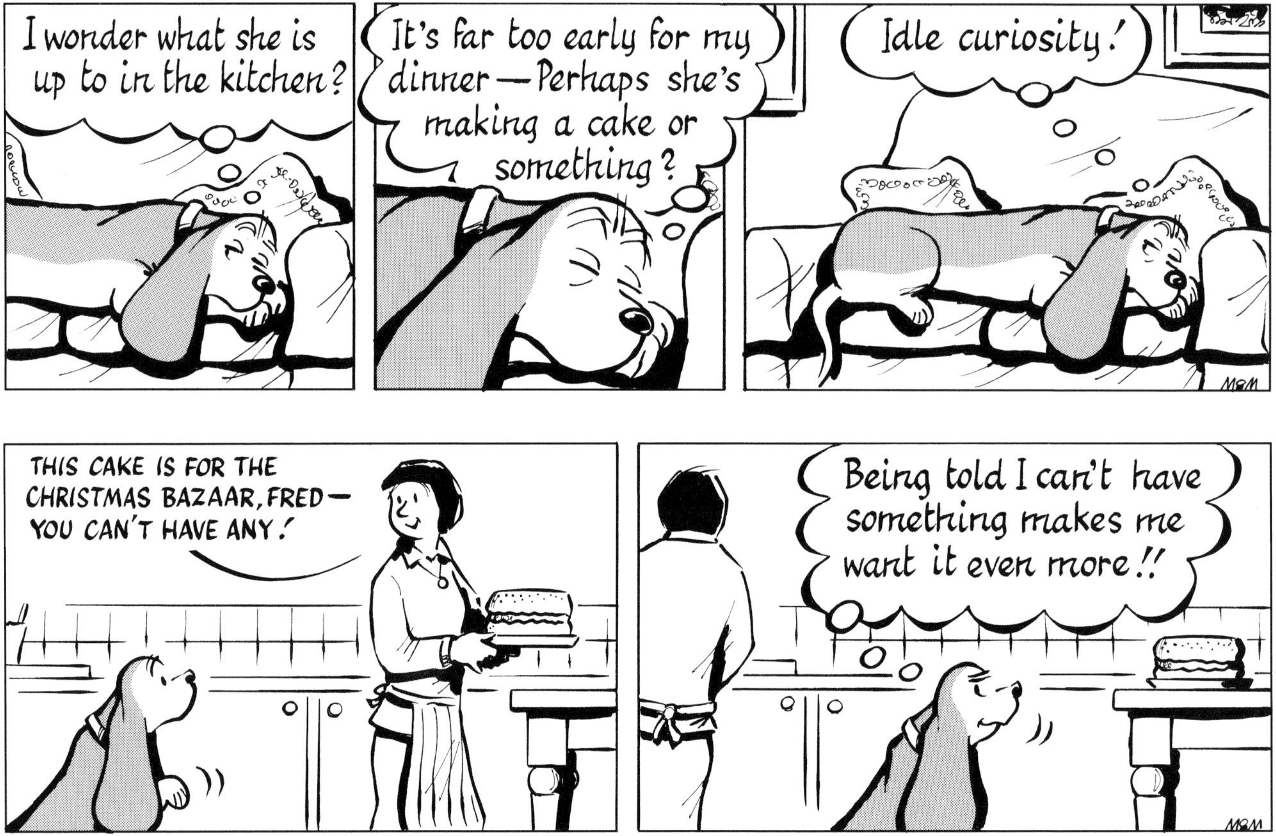
I wonder what she is up to in the kitchen?
It's far too early for my dinner—Perhaps she's making a cake or something?
Idle curiosity!
MSM
THIS CAKE IS FOR THE CHRISTMAS BAZAAR, FRED— YOU CAN'T HAVE ANY!
Being told I can't have something makes me want it even more!!
MSM

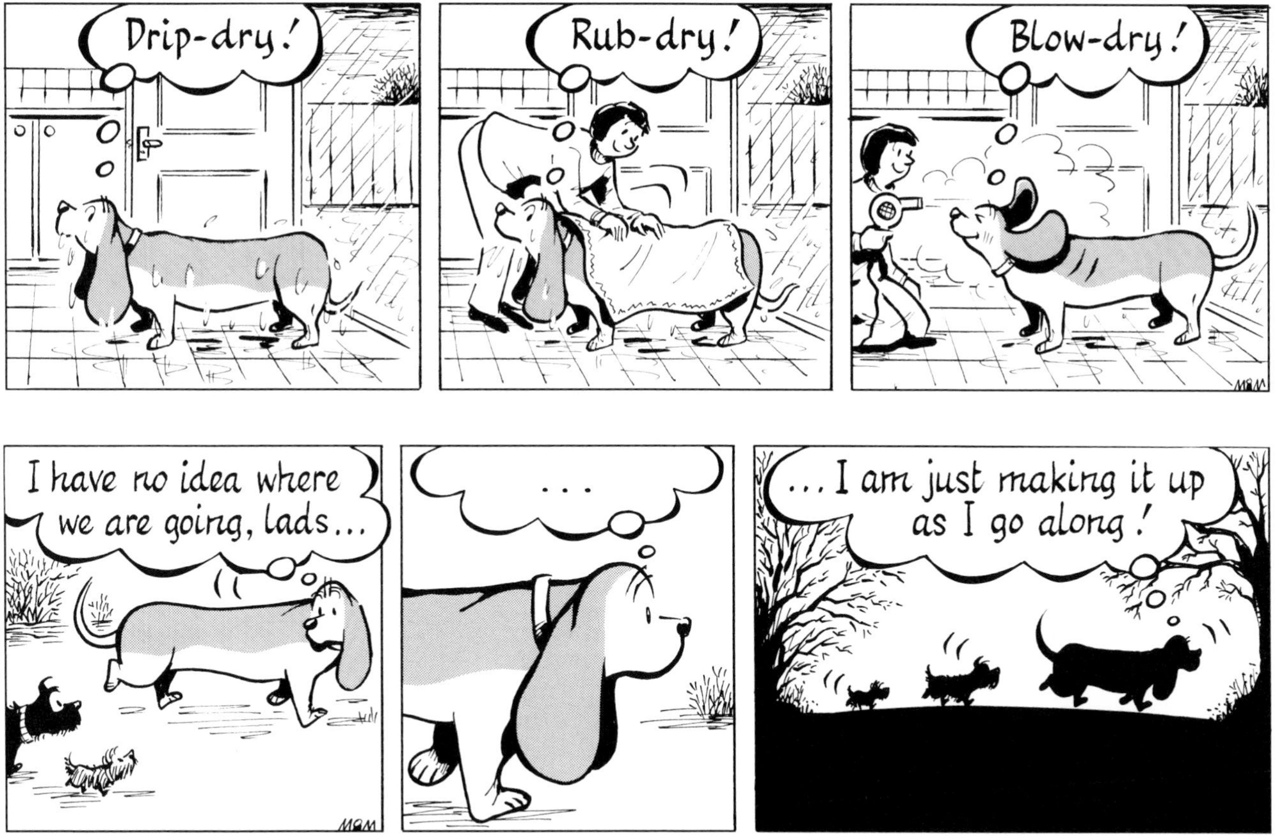
Drip-dry!
Rub-dry!
Blow-dry!
MGM
I have no idea where we are going, lads...
...
...I am just making it up as I go along!
MGM

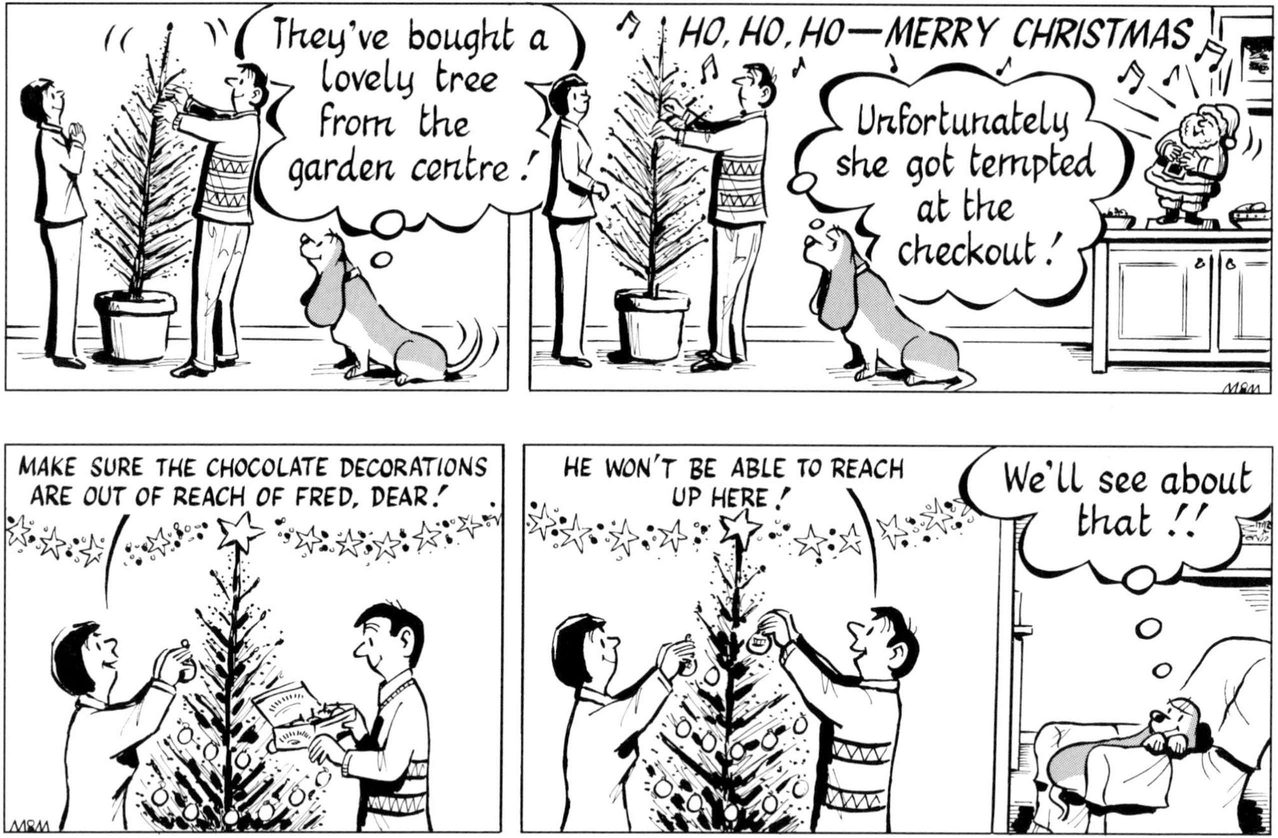

They've bought a lovely tree from the garden centre!
HO, HO, HO—MERRY CHRISTMAS
Unfortunately she got tempted at the checkout!
MAKE SURE THE CHOCOLATE DECORATIONS ARE OUT OF REACH OF FRED, DEAR!
HE WON'T BE ABLE TO REACH UP HERE!
We'll see about that!!

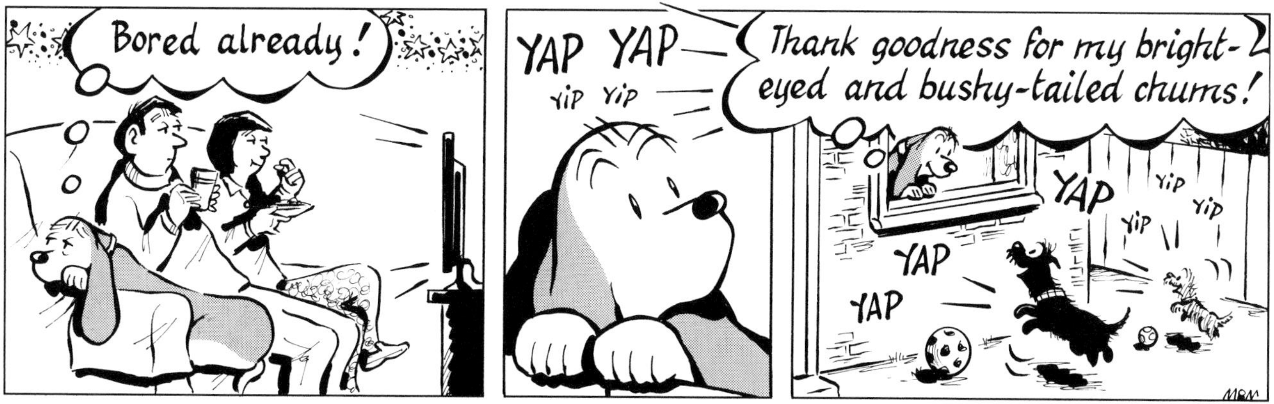
Bored already!
YAP YAP
YIP YIP
Thank goodness for my bright-eyed and bushy-tailed chums!
YAP
YIP
YIP
YIP
YAP
YAP

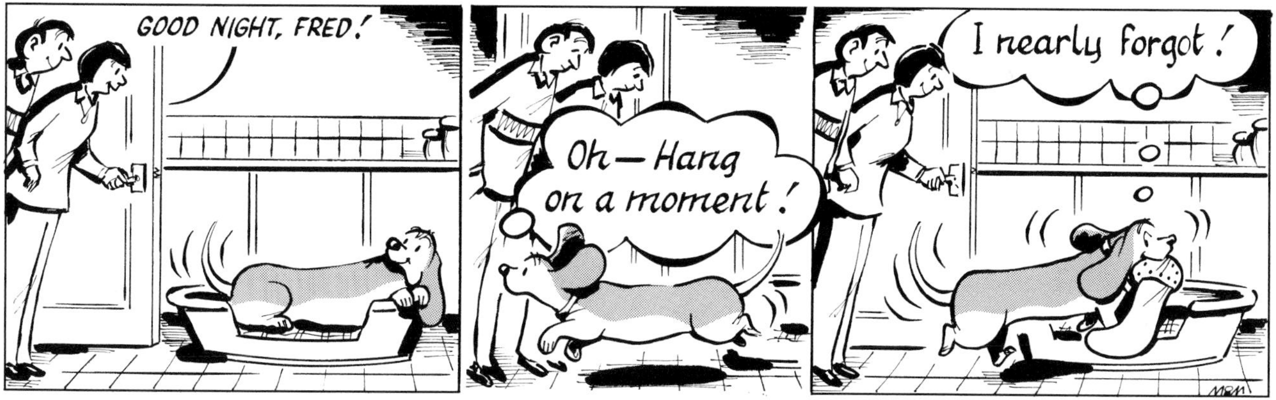
GOOD NIGHT, FRED!
Oh—Hang on a moment!
I nearly forgot!

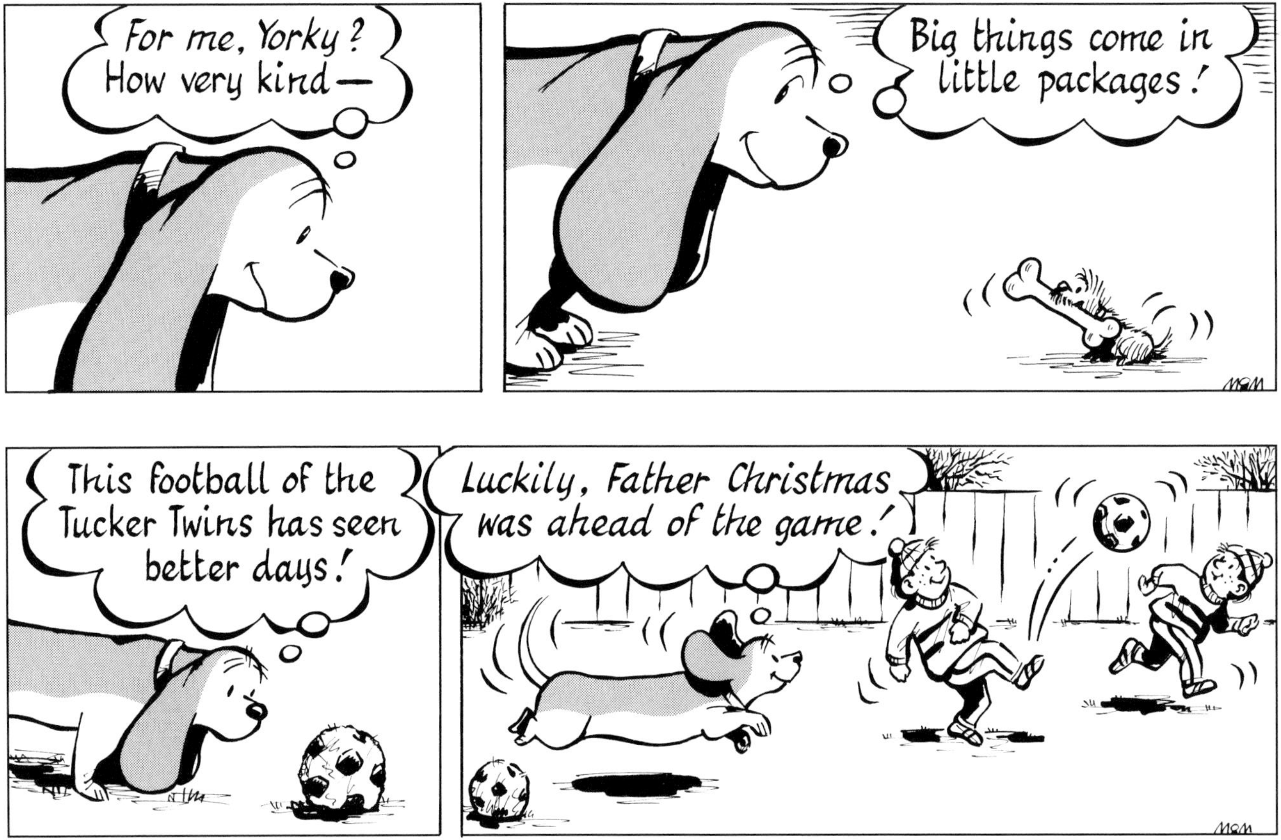
For me, Yorky? How very kind—
Big things come in little packages!
This football of the Tucker Twins has seen better days!
Luckily, Father Christmas was ahead of the game!

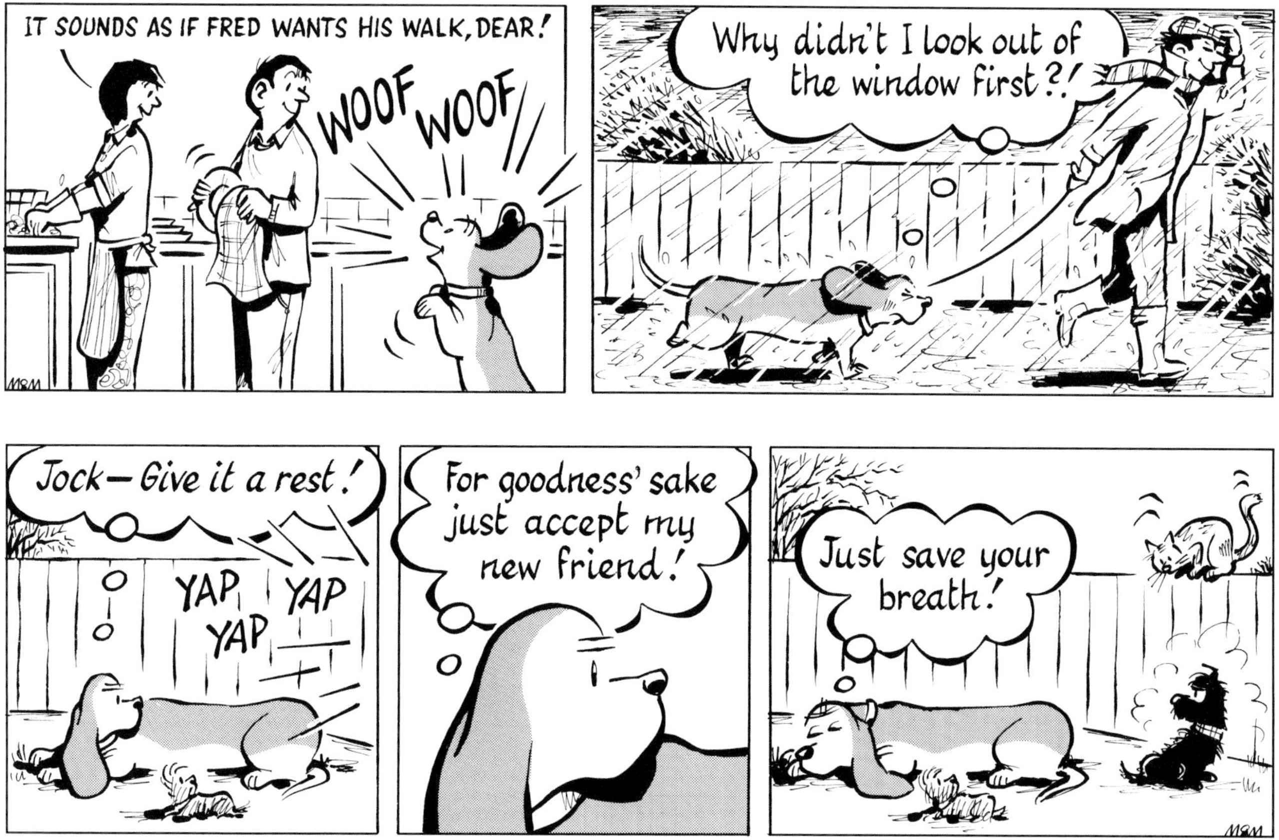
IT SOUNDS AS IF FRED WANTS HIS WALK, DEAR!
WOOF WOOF
Why didn't I look out of the window first?!
Jock— Give it a rest!
YAP YAP YAP
For goodness' sake just accept my new friend!
Just save your breath!

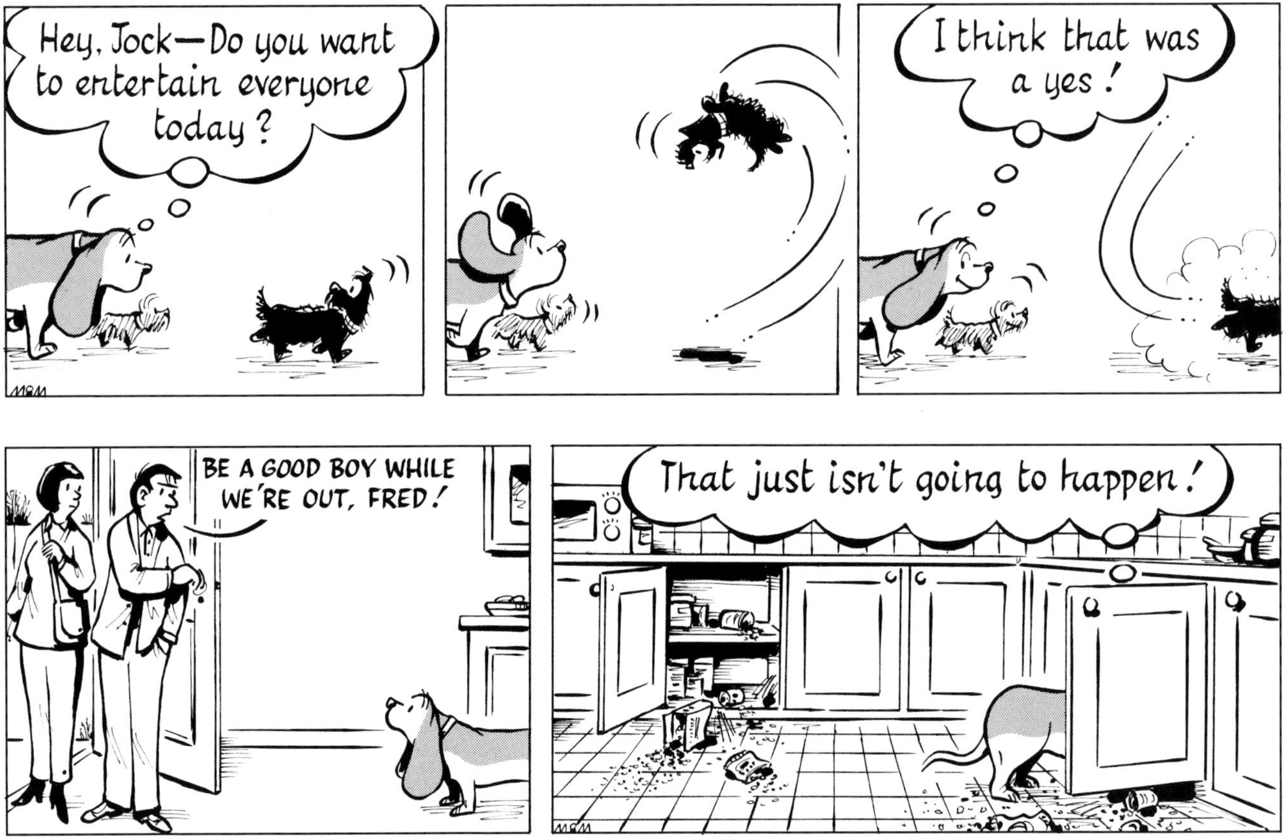
Hey, Jock—Do you want to entertain everyone today?
I think that was a yes!
BE A GOOD BOY WHILE WE'RE OUT, FRED!
That just isn't going to happen!